HETEROLOGY AND THE POSTMODERN

Post-Contemporary Interventions
Series Editors:
Stanley Fish and Fredric Jameson

HETEROLOGY AND THE POSTMODERN

Bataille, Baudrillard, and Lyotard

• • •

Julian Pefanis

DUKE UNIVERSITY PRESS *Durham and London 1991*

© 1991 Duke University Press
All rights reserved
Printed in the United States of America
on acid-free paper ∞
Library of Congress Cataloging-in-Publication Data
appear on the last printed page of this book.

For Mary and Nikolas

CONTENTS

Acknowledgments   ix

Introduction   1

1   W(h)ither History   9

2   The Gift of the Stars   21

3   The Issue of Bataille   39

4   Theories of the Third Order   59

5   Lyotard and the Jouissance of

Practical Reason   83

6   Revenge of the Mirror People   103

Notes   121

Bibliography   155

Index   165

ACKNOWLEDGMENTS

Although writing a book may seem to be, at times, an arduous task, it is salutory to remember that putting up with the author is sometimes equally arduous. So what could my thanks be compared with the patience and efforts of those who generously assisted me, of those who gladly accepted challenges and returned them with good humor and rigorous logic? To these people I offer this work as a mark of my gratitude for their confidence and goodwill. This book began its life as a dissertation at the University of Melbourne, and its genesis would have been impossible without the support of my supervisor, Dr. Fiona Mackie, whose engaged readings and thoughtful interventions, always offered with interest and good humor, enabled me to clarify my arguments; and the support of my head of department, Professor Margaret Manion, whose diplomatic skills and sound advice helped to guide the work through its trickiest passages. Particular thanks are due to David McNeill, Don Miller, and Rocque Reynolds for assisting through readings and to Philippa Bateman and Neale Trowart for assistance with the preparation of the manuscript; to the Centre for General and Comparative Literature at Monash University and the Power Institute of Fine Arts at the University of Sydney for their support; and likewise to friends who shouldered an invisible burden. Special thanks are due to my parents, Kitty and Steve, for their emotional and material support; to my editor at Duke University Press, Reynolds Smith, for his diligence and patience; and last but not at all least to Mary Hoban for her unreserved commitment and love.

INTRODUCTION

It is beyond doubt that one of the consequences of the political transformation in Eastern Europe will be the total reevaluation of the premises of Marxism in the West. Just how far this process will go, and what remains of the vast theoretical edifice after this process has run its course—quite beyond the critiques already undertaken in the past two decades—remains to be seen. At the very least, the evolutionary schema of historical society, in which capitalism is seen as an intermediary form between feudalism and socialism, will have to be rethought. And not simply by rearranging the order or substituting a new final term for the discredited communism—it's an unthinkable prospect. Critical thought is indeed going to have to come to terms with the changed circumstances. It will have to reconstitute itself outside of the givens and certainties of Marxism, and it would do well to seriously reconsider those theories which have radically put into question totalizing historical or social schemas.

Such heretical thought is not in fact new; it has been articulated in different ways both prior to and since Marx's own time and constitutes a line of theoretical development shadowing orthodox theory. This book is, in a sense, a history, or perhaps more precisely a genealogy of this thought; it traces a line of intellectual descent starting with the French appropriation of Hegel. It sets out from a now conventional argument that Alexandre Kojève's reading of Hegel in the 1930s at the Sorbonne constituted a decisive moment for the development of a theoretical countertradition in France. Not only was the significance of Hegel's master/slave dialectic recognized in the psychoanalytic writings of one of Kojève's most famous students, Jacques Lacan, but a history of the philosophical concept of desire would regard Kojève's lectures as an important mediator of this Hegelian concept in the problematics of modern French philosophy. Kojève's lectures were carefully assembled by another famous student, Raymond Queneau, and appear under the title of *Introduction to the Reading of Hegel's Phenomenology of Mind*. In the 1948 edition Kojève added a footnote whose importance belies its lowly status. In speaking of the "disappearance of man" Kojève suggests that the Hegelian/Marxist "End of History" is already *present:*

> One would have to say that the post-historical animals of the species *homo sapiens* (which will live amongst abundance and complete security) will be content as a result of their artistic, erotic and playful behavior . . . the *definitive annihilation* of man properly so-called also means the definitive disappearance of human discourse (*Logos*) in the strict sense.[1]

Kojève goes on to add that the "end of history" was "virtually attained" as "the limit of man's historical evolution" in the Battle of Jena, and that the revolutionary force unleashed by Napoleon/Robespierre was evident in the Russian and Chinese revolutions, "bringing the backward civilisations of the peripheral provinces into line with the most advanced historical positions." In a remarkable aside, which demonstrates Kojève's Marxism as heretical in relation to orthodox traditions, he claims that "One can even say that, from a certain point of view, the United States has attained the final stage of Marxist 'communism.' . . . I was led to conclude that the 'American way of life' was the type of life specific to the post-historical period, the actual presence of the United States in the world prefiguring the 'eternal present' future of all humanity."[2] (He might also agree with Gertrude Stein's proposition that America was the oldest civilization on earth—because it was the first to enter the twentieth century.)

This book argues that the Hegelian thought of Kojève prefigures many of the themes addressed and transgressed in French postmodernism and post-structuralism. The reader familiar with the reception of these fields may have already recognized them: the concept of the "disappearance of man" and the simultaneous disappearance of history as a Hegelian-Marxist project, and thus the disappearance of the project of modernity; the challenge to the philosophical discourse of legitimation represented by the deconstructive enterprise of post-structuralist writing; the reign of frivolity in the Nietzschean return of "artistic, erotic and playful behavior"; and the importance of anthropological thought to the critique of totality. (It could, of course, be argued that it was Heidegger, rather than Kojève, who is central to this tradition; or even that Kojève's understanding of Hegel was indebted to Heidegger. The genealogical character of this study does not necessitate discovering the truth of Kojève any more than it necessitates discovering the truth of Hegel—even if it was possible. We start with Kojève because of the role he plays in the thought of Bataille; but this in no way precludes the existence of other genealogies.)

For in order to counter the universalist tendencies of Hegelian anthropology, and its reiteration in Marxism, several thinkers paradoxically turned to Maussian anthropology, and to the category which Mauss had isolated as the "total social fact" of primitive societies: the gift. While the gift (*don*) should not necessarily be privileged over other theoretical developments, it has to be recognized that it constituted a category or problematic of great significance—capable of being incorporated into linguistic, psychoanalytic, and economic discourses. It is argued that the interpretation of Mauss's gift split on epistemological questions, and that it was this split which formed the basis for the lively opposition between structuralism and its counter-discourse—let's call it post-structuralism or heterology. On one side the structuralist Lévi-Strauss employs the gift-economy as a model for the reciprocating relations in familial, linguistic, and social structures, as well as the structures of mind. While on the other side, Bataille, and later Baudrillard, "read" the gift as precisely an antieconomic principle; for each, in different contexts, reciprocity is bound up with contestation—in radical versions of the Hegelian dialectic of desire. So the texts of Bataille are of great importance here, since they make use of a radical reading of Mauss's gift-economy and the psychoanalytic concept of symbolic exchange in the formulation of the concepts of *dépense, la part maudite* and the general economy. Bataille's writings can be regarded as a conduit for the reflection on these concepts in the thought of the postmodernists, and as an early contribution to that anthropological critique evident in the work of Robert Jaulin, Michel Foucault, and, more recently, in the work of Pierre Clastres and Jean Baudrillard.

A critical moment, in the sense of a crisis, was produced in the "peripatetics of the dialectic" by the texts of Georges Bataille. Bataille was both an ardent exponent and a trenchant critic of dialectical thought, and he was also another famous student of Kojève. The thought of Bataille is regarded, by Foucault, as a milestone on the escape route from Hegelianism. It amounts to a type of anti-project which enlists Nietzsche in the philosophical problematics of "transgression." In terms of the Kojèvian schema, transgression operates as an inverted figure of the dialectic, its end in the sense of an outcome. In Bataille's texts interpretation of transgression has to be linked to the loss of philosophical and authorial sovereignty, and hence the loss of the place which is accorded the human in the human sciences. The issue of Bataille is the projection of a third term, dépense, beyond the conventional dualisms of Western thought. The third term, moreover, has a Nietzschean, rather than a Hegelian, origin.

Bataille's heterodoxical theory of the "general economy" places dépense, a generic term covering sacrificial, erotic, and symbolic practices, in opposition to the system of identities in economic and philosophical thought based on equivalence. The "restricted economy" of capital restricts, in a general tendency, nonproductive expenditure by the delay and deferral of consumption—and the reinvestment of the surplus (*la part maudite*) in the means of production. Thus the general economy, insofar as it might account in a concrete way for the modes of unproductive expenditure, is at a repressed, restricted level in the discourses of equivalence and utility. Bataille's critique of equivalence and utility, parallel in so many ways to the analyses of the Frankfurt school, is inherited and given impetus by the "critique of the political economy of the sign" produced by Jean Baudrillard. The latter's critique of structuralism and Marxism, as the second degree discourses of instrumental and political economic thought, takes Bataille's antieconomism into a new, profoundly antisociological dimension.

The post-structuralists aim at deepening epistemological crises wherever they occur—this is no less true of Derrida's investigations at the interior of philosophy than it is of Baudrillard's and Lyotard's analyses at a social, theoretical level of Marxism, psychoanalysis, and structural linguistics. These traditions of thought are spurned for harboring a hidden agenda: hegemony in the sphere of theory, and a taste for power in capitalizing the desire of revolutionary thought in the political sphere. This is perhaps no more evident than in the case of Althusserianism, as a specific example of structural Marxism which combined, in the worst possible way for these postmodernists, claims of structuralist scientificity with a moral and epistemological Stalinism. In the work of Jean-François Lyotard in particular, we can witness a progressive distancing from the praxis philosophy which had been the basis for the political intervention of the group *Socialisme ou barbarie* (itself countertraditional to the correct-line theory of the *Parti communiste français* [PCF]). Lyotard's and Baudrillard's investigative techniques, descriptive analyses, and their models of writing fictive criticism—implicit in the analytics of "libidinal economy" and "symbolic exchange"—share, with Bataille's heterology, a similar refractory quality, a similar refusal to abide by the rules of the game of scientific, critical discourse. In Bataille's theory of the heterogeneous, science itself represents a limit to experience.

It is possible that Lyotard's incredulity before the "Great Narratives," the so-called "postmodern condition," had already been outlined in the *Economie libidinale*.[3] In the context of that work libidinal refers to the second meaning that Freud attached to the theory of the libido: relations of love, and hence hate, affections and disaffections, affects and disaffects. At this stage Lyotard is indeed more interested in the dysfunctional, perverse aspects of the theory of the libido; in that book the analysis of Marx's text is a type of literary profanation of the body of theory in the name of intensity. In this regard it is understood to stand squarely in the tradition of the transgressive text of Bataille—which Foucault prophesied would form the "calcinated roots" of a new era of thought.

The paradigmatics and pragmatics of the game, the philosophies of erotics, and the privilege accorded the work of art and literature—as players in the critical/theoretical field—have to be related to the question of writing in post-structuralism. Kojève's remarks on the reign of frivolity might well have been alluding to the example of Bataille who, in his struggle with dialectical philosophy as inherited by Kojève, turned to Nietzschean and gnostic traditions of thought; this struggle culminated in the impossible philosophy of "acephality." Writings assessed on the basis of performance and pragmatics, as works of art, escape from the regimes of truth in scientific discourse. Those discourses which consider writing as a theoretical and philosophical entity in its own right discover an exemplar in the works of Bataille, and this modernist category, *écriture*, is championed in the works of the postmodernists—they valorize the works of the critical modernists and celebrate their radical insights. It is argued that postmodern aesthetics, in their positive (Lyotard) and negative (Baudrillard) forms, are manifestations of the *thought of nonidentity* and as such are related to the problematic of the Freudian death drive. They are examples of thought aiming to preserve the difference of otherness, resisting the totalizing and totally compromised tendency of civilization. In this sense their thought shares with other species of postmodern and post-structuralist thought, (Derrida, Foucault, and Clastres), a common ethical perspective which does not rely on the universality of norms, but to the contrary, relies on their relativity, on their situological character.

The problematic which this book addresses might be best explained with reference to two recent texts on the reception of postmodernism. In his essay, "Postmodernism and Consumer Society," Fredric Jameson concentrates on distinguishing postmodernist art as "specific reactions against established forms of high modernism, against this or that dominant high modernism which conquered the university, the museum, the art-gallery network, and the foundations."[4] For Jameson there is a paradox; the features of postmodernism in the arts involve a "restructuration of a certain number of elements already given" in modernism, but minor, marginal, and secondary elements which in postmodernism are transformed into "something new when they become central features of cultural production." By way of examples, Jameson refers to the "idea" of pastiche and to "postmodernist temporality." He concludes that the emergence of postmodernism is closely related to the "emergence of . . . consumer or multinational capitalism . . . its formal features in many ways express the particular logic of that particular social system." The example of this complicity of logic is shown in the theme of the "disappearance of a sense of history, the way in which our entire contemporary social system has little by little begun to lose its capacity to retain its own past, has begun to live in a perpetual present and in a perpetual change that obliterates traditions of the kind which all earlier social formations have had in one way or another to preserve."[5] Leaving aside possible objections to this conclusion (why would Jameson argue against himself on his own evidence of the innovating and subverting characteristics of "high modernisms" committed to the destruction of bourgeois morality, or ignore Marx's testimony on the liquidation of archaic relations by the revolutionary character of capitalism?), Jameson uses it to pose the question: "We have seen that there is a way in which postmodernism replicates or reproduces—reinforces the logic of consumer capitalism; the more significant question is whether there is also a way in which it resists that logic. But that is a question we must leave open."[6]

The second text is by the politically engaged former Lacanian, now nomadic, psychoanalyst Félix Guattari in *Flash Art*, entitled "The Postmodern Dead End." It opens:

> A certain idea of progress and modernity has gone bankrupt, and in its fall it has dragged along all confidence in the notion of emancipation through social action. At the same time social relations have entered an ice age: hierarchy and segregation have solidified, poverty and unemployment tend now to be accepted as

inevitable evils, the workers' unions cling to the last branches of the institutions they still have at their command and limit themselves to the sort of corporate practice that leads them to adopt a conservative position very close to that of reactionary groups. The Communist Left is barricaded in a hopelessly dogmatic sclerosis, whereas the Socialist Parties, in their effort to put up a front as reliable technocrats, have given up any pretence of a renewal of existing structures. So indeed it is not surprising that the ideologies that used to pretend to be guides in an effort toward the reconstruction of a more equitable society have lost all credibility.[7]

Guattari then asks if it is inevitable "that we must remain passive in the face of a rising wave of cruelty and cynicism . . . that would seem to be the deplorable conclusion to which many intellectual and artistic groups have come, especially those who claim the banner of postmodernism." The specific target of Guattari's attack is the thought of Baudrillard and Lyotard—which is condemned for never leaving the "purest tradition, the modernist tradition of structuralism whose influence in the social sciences seems to have been borrowed from the worst aspects of the Anglo-Saxon system." He goes on to say that he believes their "philosophy to be no philosophy at all; it is nothing but a state of mind that happens to be in the air, a 'condition' of public opinion that gets its truth out of the surroundings."[8] Attacking Lyotard's "research into pragmatics" of speech acts, and the "royal place of the linguistic signifier," Guattari calls for new types of semiotization which would cause the downfall of the signifier from its transcendent position and which would permit "the emergence of new practices of subjectivation" and the "subjective autonomization of postmedia operators." If the carrot of resubjectivation fails, the hammer of the apocalypse will follow: "If the future does not follow these paths it is unlikely to endure longer than the end of the present millenium."[9]

A comparison of these two texts reveals two possible critical attitudes toward postmodernism. Despite certain misgivings Jameson refuses to impose a closure on the discussion of the postmodern by leaving open the question of its resistance to the logic of consumer capitalism. In failing to similarly provide this opening, Guattari reveals himself as a reactive critic who, by dint of a wilful or negligent misinterpretation of postmodernism, simply provides a set of protocols for its reception. The question which Guattari poses is no question at all, since it is answered in advance. This book is, therefore, directed toward the theoretical space opened at the end of Jameson's text, rather than toward rejoining Guattari's abstract negativity. In providing the context for an answer to Jameson's question, by referring to a specific moment of theoretical postmodernism, this book might also challenge those interpretations, in this case Guattari's, which have misunderstood or misread the critical significance of postmodernism.

1 W(H)ITHER HISTORY

If those arrangements were to disappear as they appeared, if some event . . .
were to cause them to crumble, as the ground of classical thought did . . . then
one can certainly wager that man would be erased, like a face drawn in the sand
at the edge of the sea.—Michael Foucault, The Order of Things

The great historical machine lurches, groans, and grinds to a halt in the
sands of time. Powerless to conquer this final frontier, to fulfil its
mission of delivering *society* to the colonized regions, the beached
behemoth is a disquieting spectacle. It is a scandal: unable to progress
against the force of its own inertia or to stem the flow of the irritant
medium immobilizing this or that fantastic mechanism, the great machine responds by reprogramming the coordinates of its destination—
henceforth nowhere—and recommitting its subjects to the project of
reproduction and system maintenance: damage control. At the end of
history we are all mechanics tending the autoteleological machine.

Was the great machine ever all it was cracked up to be? The precon-
dition of historical society was the suppression of the archaic, the
very possibility of its existence the suppression of the nonhistorical.
Lyotard's idea of fantastic archeology reveals the nonhistorical in
Bataille's transgressive, Foucault's silent, Deleuze's schizo and Baudrillard's dead (and much else besides). At the end of history the transgressive laughs, the mad walk free, the silent speak and the dead live. . . . A
philosopher once said that as science gets better the problems get
weirder.[1] Lodged in the "baroque orrery" of Louis Althusser's epistemological model is a prescription for 'pataphysics. For it is in his
science that the products of ideology (generality I), the representations
of "imaginary relations to real conditions of existence" form the raw
materials for his theoretical practice.[2] It is a formula, parented in some
perverse fashion, that is remarkably close to Alfred Jarry's recom-

mended 'pataphysics, "the science of imaginary solutions." Let us recall the probable parents that Jarry unleashed on the world: Ubu, "the human blunderbuss who smashed history as he went" and his double, Dr. Faustroll, engaged in a "stupendous effort to create out of the ruins Ubu left behind a new system of values, the world of 'pataphysics" or, as Ubu puts it, "a branch of science which we have invented and for which a crying need is generally experienced."[3] As the "science of laws that rule the exception" 'pataphysics has little truck with rationality. Docteur Sandormir: "Like the apprentice sorcerer we are victims of our knowledge—above all our technical and scientific knowledge. The supreme resort from ourselves is in 'pataphysics. Not that 'pataphysics can change history: this gigantic improvisation of the past is already the last resort of the science of sciences."[4] For the pataphysician Sandormir *there is no history:* whatever the details of institutions, of social and economic structures and individuals at play, it is always the same drama, the smashed fables, the strong occupying the whole scene with their follies and crimes, and to top it off and to add to these calamities produced by man are those lavished by a blind nature. To the pataphysician the play of aesthetic values has replaced religious and divine prestige—and this love of art, which is merely the effect of a prejudice common to an epoque, ensures that all we produce and will produce will end up in the museum.[5] The museum is our answer to Hegel's encyclopedia.

Friedrich Nietzsche wrote in "End and Goal": "Not every end is a goal, but nonetheless, if the melody had not reached its end it would not have reached its goal either. A parable."[6] If we substitute history for melody in this parable, we might get a Hegelian understanding of history.

In French a single term, *histoire,* on the one hand serves to designate "history" properly speaking, as the succession of events, the play of forces in the unfolding of the idealist schema, a designation warranted by the quasi-juridical form of evidence, fact, and the dialectic. On the other hand histoire also refers to the story, fiction, fable, or myth bound by a narrative structure. The bivalence of the term permits a double articulation of fictional elements within the unfolding of history, and a factual basis in the fiction of the fable. It is precisely this articulation, of the narrative within the philosophy of the dialectic of history, that has led to the latter's demise in the face of instrumental knowledge. Thus the crisis of the "meta-narratives"—"the dialectics of Spirit, the hermeneutics of meaning, the emancipation of the rational or working subject, or the creation of wealth" occurs, according to Jean-François Lyotard in *The Postmodern Condition*,[7] when knowledge ceases to be authorized in the name of one of these meta-narratives, because they themselves have come to be viewed with incredulity. What is put into question in the passage from modernist to postmodernist science and knowledge is both the philosophy of history and the whole of meta-physics. What disappears for Lyotard is knowledge authorized by these narratives, warranted by narrative authority where the content of the narration is never exposed to argument or proof because the subject of this content is both the narrator and the listener (the future narrator). To lament the loss of meaning in postmodernism, writes Lyotard, apropos Baudrillard one supposes, consists of regretting that knowl-edge is no longer principally narrative; but neither is it ruled simply by performance. The idea that function itself is a paradigm of knowledge is also on the way out:

> Postmodern science—by concerning itself with such things as un-decidables, the limits of precision control . . . "*fracta*," catastro-phes and pragmatic paradoxes—is theorizing its own evolution as as discontinuous, catastrophic, non-rectifiable, and paradoxical. It is changing the meaning of the word *knowledge*. . . . It is produc-ing not the known, but the unknown. And it suggests a model of legitimation that has nothing to to with better performance, but has as its basis difference understood as parology.[8]

Of all the philosophical narratives one of the greatest is Hegel's dialectical schema of history, or more precisely in our present context, the mythic formulations of Alexandre Kojève's readings of Hegel's *The Phenomenology of Mind* delivered as lectures at the Sorbonne in the 1930s to an audience composed of a future generation of French theory: Sartre, Merleau-Ponty, Lacan, Bataille, Queneau, and a host of existentialists, Catholics, Communists, and surrealists who eagerly awaited the event of Hegel's epiphany.[9] It is ironic, therefore, in the face of this mass initiation to the mysteries of the dialectic, that Foucault later claims that "our age, whether through logic or epistemology, whether through Marx or through Nietzsche, is attempting to flee Hegel."[10] In admitting that the price of this escape might cost us dearly, Foucault also speculates that perhaps Hegel has one last trick to play: "We have to determine the exact extent to which our anti-Hegelianism is possibly one of his tricks directed against us, at the end of which he stands, motionless, waiting for us."[11]   ·

Long praised for its elegance and simplicity, Kojève's reading of Hegel is also suspected, reluctantly, of being a selective and distorted account of the peripatetics of the dialectic because it privileges, where Hegel had not, the "dialectic of recognition," giving it a materialist and anthropological gloss.[12] In Kojève's Hegel the relationship of consciousness to the self is established by a negating desire—not the desire for a thing—but the desire for another's desire and recognition.[13] The narrative that is extracted from the *Phenomenology* has all the exemplary qualities of a *grand récit,* the tale of brothers fighting a battle according to the rules of a historical destiny, a fight marking the consciousness of the master from that of the slave by the former's willingness to risk life for prestige in his opposition to the latter's submissive consciousness and servility. This is the "myth of origin" of the dialectic of recognition in the genealogy and phenomenology of the spirit, and the mythic end of this process is grounded in the perception that the domain of history and the process of history belongs to the slave, and it is the slave's work—the negating action of transforming nature via technique—that reveals in the end the ideal of the autonomous consciousness of self, which is thus the truth of history.[14] In the historical process it is likewise the work of the slave which is the basis of science and art: "laborious slavery is the source of all human, social, historical progress. History is the history of the working slave."[15] The end and goal of all this, the truth of the absolute "consciousness of self," is achieved when the ladder of philosophical ideologies has been scaled and surpassed.[16] The end of history is the culmination of this process, its realization and negation. The dialectic of history is summed up by Kojève:

> Man is Desire directed towards another Desire—that is, Desire for Recognition—that is Negating action performed for the sake of satisfying this Desire for Recognition—that is, bloody Fighting for prestige—that is, the relationship between the Master and Slave— that is, Work—that is, historical evolution which finally comes to the universal and homogeneous State and to the absolute knowledge that reveals complete Man realized in and by this State.[17]

And so it is that at the end of history a wise man (who was named Hegel) was able to appreciate the disappearance of man, the dialectic, philosophy, and logos.[18]

Under the sign of Hegel's dialectic Kojève absolves us of all historical responsibility; for him the World Wars and wars of revolution are but the effect of bringing the world's peripheral regions into line with the "most advanced historical positions." For him the revolutionary force of the Russian Soviets and the Chinese Collectives were the equivalent to an earlier effect produced by Napoleon (universal man of action) and Robespierre (simulation of the risk of death) which rid Europe of various anachronisms. For Kojève the United States, from a certain point of view, has attained the final state of Marxist communism and the Russians and Chinese are but poor Americans, but getting richer quickly. For Kojève the American way of life prefigures a life at the end of history, and so does that of the Japanese who have lived life at the end of history for a couple of centuries according to purely formalized values, empty of human content "in the historical sense."[19] "As the threshold of post-history is crossed, humanity disappears while at the same time the reign of frivolity begins, the reign of play, of derision (for henceforth nothing that might be done would have the slightest meaning)."[20] So, everywhere at the end of history are the signs of work, the signs of Hegel's universal citizens; but beyond and beneath the warm reflecting glow of the furnaces in the faces of the worker-citizens a different type of enlightenment is occurring. From the depth of Plato's cave and the mysteries of representation the slaves drag themselves into the light of Bentham's panopticon and the mysteries of naked power. Can we speak of a genealogy of the nonhistorical subject? History, for Michel Foucault, is linked to the necessity of madness—characterized by him as the "absence of work"[21] (because work is the condition of citizenry). At the heart of the culture an identity is formed, a "we" of the collectivity that equilibrates itself on the basis of an exclusion in the great split of "reason and unreason."[22] Living beyond the logic of operationality, of functionality, of speech as a coherent discourse, the mad have to be confined to the limits of the city, to be rendered silent and invisible. Here it can be argued that Jean Baudrillard makes a contribution to this genealogy of discrimination by his insistence, in *L'Echange symbolique et la mort*[23] that the model of social exclusion is that of "death and the dead." It is the dead who are first put at the periphery of the city in order to ensure the operationality of the living, of the human. Thus the quintessence of normality:

> At the limit all "categories" are excluded, segregated and prescribed; in a society that is finally universal, the universal will be confused under the sign of the human. . . . (I)f the cemetery no longer exists it's because modern cities have assumed their func-

tion: they are dead cities and cities of the dead. And if the great metropolis is the accomplished form of all culture, then simply ours is a dead culture.[24]

Baudrillard muses "To be dead is to be abnormal today—this is new." Paul Virilio muses in his turn "is there life before death?" [graffiti].[25]

Finally, it is only the question of death that remains; perhaps this too is the legacy of Kojève's reading of Hegel. For it is death that is the "genuine motor" of the dialectical movement of history. Man "attains human self-consciousness, conceptual and discursive consciousness in general, by the risk of life accepted without any necessity, by the fact that he goes to his death without being forced to it."[26] Death and freedom are, therefore, but two phenomenological aspects of the same thing. To say "mortal" is to say "free" and suicide is the most obvious manifestation of this negativity and freedom.[27] But to say that it is only death that remains is not to invoke either biological or private death, guilty, mournful, or heroic death, but the death of the Other, of the sovereignty, even of the collectivity. As it was necessary for the Greeks to polish off their gods, it is now necessary to sacrifice the Greeks in the forms of logos, chief among the pantheon of mythos. This would seem to be the strategy of much contemporary theory, linking Deleuze and Guattari's murder of Oedipus[28] with Derrida's deadly duplicity in his double science,[29] or Baudrillard pushing the system to its limit in his theoretical terrorism[30] with Lyotard advocating the course of active nihilism.[31] Much of this murderous activity is performed with a more or less explicit relationship to the thought of Georges Bataille[32] whose project was to grant excess and the science devoted to its description and analysis a place in discourse, practicing a mode of writing (*écriture*) in which the linguistic "I" is surpassed in laughter, death, and ecstasy.[33]

In the mine shafts and subterranean spaces beneath the city we discover a heterogeneous and transgressive zone, a circuitry of catacombs, rivers of effluent, of treasures too precious to see the light of day. It is the circuit of Bataille's signifying chain which specifies a psychic relationship between death, shit, and gold.[34] This circuit passes through the territory of the "sovereign" text, which is that of the dead, dying, and soon-to-be-dead, the condition of the mortal author. Immune to the incandescent enlightenment and beyond the shadows cast by the light of the "white mythology"—this is the zone where Bataille's sovereignty rules. Here the sun of knowledge (like Plato's) is too withering for the returned look; here the odor of death (mixed with whiffs of

the erotic) is all-pervasive, giving rise to frenzy and the work of purifi-
cation—to literature and art. For the latter are, to Bataille, the sole
inheritors of a transgressive zone that mediates the "sacred and the
profane."[35] Jacques Derrida has asserted that all of Bataille's concepts
"immobilised outside of their context" are Hegelian[36] (peals of laughter from Bataille).[37] Here the study needs to refer to transgression,
sovereignty, heterogeneity, and *dépense*. These concepts form both a
continuous signifying chain and signposts for a massive work of interpretation that, over the past twenty years, has attempted to track these
feral species back to their lair.[38]

Before these concepts are examined (chapter 3), recourse should be
made to a historical perspective which informs the general critique of
reason underpinning much of this theory. In the great era of colonial
expansion, co-temporaneous with the development of the human sciences—those discourses, in Foucault's sense, connected to the three
great positivities: life, labor, and language[39]—the entry of "anthropological man," the anthropos, into the philosophical discourse, constituted a critical moment in the legitimation of these sciences. The
anthropos can be understood as the subject around whom the philosophical discourse (Kant, Hegel, and Marx) constructed a meta-
narrative of legitimation—as formulated by Lyotard in *The Postmodern Condition*—as the story of man. It may be added that the "incredulity," to which Lyotard refers, finds expression in the work of Foucault
and, according to a tautological definition, Foucault's theses may be
considered postmodern. The discovery of the "primitive" other, which
was the inevitable result of the centrifugal force of Western expansion,
provided the ground for the constitution of the empirical, as opposed to
the philosophical, analysis of man: anthropology.[40] For Foucault a
combination of the empirical and philosophical species of anthropology answered the question posed by Kant, who addended a fourth
question to his traditional trilogy: What can I know? What must I do?
What am I permitted to hope?—and the fourth: *Was ist der Mensch?*
(What is Man?).[41] Now the discourses of the anthropological human—
whose essence is discovered in the man of nature (psychology), labor
(political economy), and language (linguistics)—constitute for Foucault the anthropological "quadrilateral," the "fold" in which the transcendental function (of the species-being) "is doubled over so that it
covers with its dominating network the inert, grey space of empiricity."
It is Foucault who speaks of the "anthropological sleep" to which
philosophy succumbs "in the hollow of this fold," a sleep "so deep that

thought experiences it paradoxically as vigilance."[42] It is at this point that Foucault rearticulates the project of Bataille by demanding the destruction of this quadrilateral at its very foundations. And for Foucault, as for Bataille, it is in Nietzscheanism that the first attempt at the "uprooting of anthropology" can be observed; and more, it is through the rejection of all species of anthropology—psychologism and historicism, and all the "concrete forms of anthropological prejudice"—that we may "attempt to question afresh the limits of thought, and to *renew contact in this way with the project for a general critique of reason.*"[43] But what could be a critique of reason that did not claim at the same time to be more reasonable than that reason found insufficient? Surely this would be to trap thought in a critical mirror? The notion of a project of this critique resonates with Bataille's struggle to free himself of Hegelianism in the *expérience intérieure,* having concluded that philosophically it was Hegel rather than Nietzsche who was the philosopher of fascism.[44] Hegel's trick had been to ensnare thought in a speculative metaphysic; what trapped Bataille was a residual faith in a science of the heterogeneous, a science that would at one and the same time be a general theory that might explain the third term (dépense, la part maudite), while speaking the mute discourse of unreason and *nonsavoir.* Foucault's debt to Bataille is thus in terms of this critique of reason from the standpoint of "unreason." To grasp this project it is necessary to recognize the privilege that Bataille grants the irrational— as delivered in both the Hegelian/Nietzschean philosophical discourse and the most advanced or radical anthropological positions. It must be recognized too that Foucault himself leaves the possibility open that to surpass the obstacle of anthropology involves "tearing ourselves free from it with the help of what it expresses, and rediscovering a purified ontology or a radical thought of being." Anthropology must be denounced for the "forgetfulness of the opening that made it possible."[45]

The significance of Bataille's thought, in terms of the general argument, is this "condensation" of the anthropological and philosophical discourses. This condensation is palpably physical in his writings—in which discourse volatizes, condenses, and drops in a vertiginous fall. A movement follows this pattern; the stable, homogeneous *subject* of philosophical humanism is annihilated in the sacrificial decapitation of acephality; consciousness is completed at the point of death and measured in the space between the head and the base toward which it plunges. And all of this is myth, a myth which Hegel granted the French by offering them self-consciousness in the form of the understanding of the historical consequences of Robespierre's blade, a consciousness of death. (What is more, a consciousness which has haunted the French as their true end, as it is said.)

In Foucault's terms anthropology (and psychology in another context) projected a region toward which the human advanced, inexorably converting the "different" (the other) into the "same" in the name of humanism, in the universalizing progress of Western expansion. Prior to the turn of the twentieth century, the general perspective which dominated anthropological discourse (very crudely) tended to regard its object—primitive society—as either the inhuman or a type of static undeveloped version of the West. This perspective prevailed, according to Claude Lévi-Strauss, until Marcel Mauss challenged the subject/object dichotomy in his recognition that so-called primitive thought had a claim equal to that of enlightened rationality to the study of man.[46] In some eluctable way the product of Mauss's research and contact with primitive thought—the analyses of the Melanesian *kula* and the Chinook *potlatch*[47]—have insinuated themselves into the system of prestations and exchanges in the charmed circles (or are they spirals?) of French theory. The discovery of a principle of exchange that appeared to defy and deny the logic of political economy, to be founded on the irrational principles of prestige and rank in the "destruction of wealth," represented by the potlatch, formed the basis of Bataille's notion of dépense and the all-embracing category of the "general economy."

> The question of a general economy is located at the same level as that of political economy, but the science designated by the latter refers only to a *restricted* economy (to market values). The general economy deals with the essential problem of the use of wealth. It underlines the fact that an excess is produced that, by definition, cannot be employed in a utilitarian manner. Excess energy can only be lost, without the least concern for a goal or objective, and, therefore, without any meaning.[48]

Thus the mode of dépense, the fashion of dealing with the excess, is what determines the nature of political economy for Bataille. And what is more, a mode that defines the "sovereign moment" in the economy of writing: the mode of consumption. In its extreme versions wealth is either destroyed in ritual and collective display, in feasts or human sacrifice—or else it is committed to the development of the machinery of production, it is put to work. For Bataille, and Baudrillard in his turn, modern consumption bears little resemblance to sovereign dépense, and the paradox of the consumer society is that it defers consumption via work and investment, substituting the society of the spectacle for that of the festival.[49] So the distinction is one between those societies that know how to destroy their surplus and those that do not, and which are thus in danger of being destroyed by the hubris of accumulation. It follows in all this that the difference between the capitalist and the socialist versions of industrial society matters little to Bataille, except in the sense that the Soviet state had reduced the West to a paralysis of inertia, impotent before the avatar of the universal state.[50] In the end they are both examples of the restricted economy, "where the automatic reinvestment of surplus into the forces of production eliminates expenditure that is not ultimately acquisitive."[51] And though the general economy would suggest an all-encompassing category, it is not so. What is lost or repressed in the restricted economy (and in nonsovereign writing) is the potential sovereignty of the surplus—a will to pure sacrifice of la part maudite in the economy, and a will to self-erasure in writing. Derrida has written:

> Sovereignty transgresses the entirety of the history of meaning and the entirety of the meaning of history, and the project that has always obscurely welded these two together. Unknowledge is then super-historical, but only because it takes its responsibilities from the conception of history and the closure of absolute knowledge, having first taken them seriously and having then betrayed them by exceeding them or simulating them in play.[52]

The entire reserve put aside for self-consciousness in the master/slave relation is opposed and eclipsed in the equation of the moment of erotic ecstasy with consciousness at the "height of death." But, if a Hegelian reserve is annihilated, there is still plenty left over; something for everyone in Bataille: a useless and sacrificial residue that denies all utilitarian knowledge. From the outset, the critique of utility in Bataille's texts is a given—whether from the standpoint of political economy in the work on dépense, or philosophically in the critique of the phenomenology of mind as a discourse of the restricted economy where the economic restriction is readable in the figure of the *Aufhebung,* that privileged and untranslatable term which, in putting consciousness at stake, conserves, invests, and amortizes its proposition via a determinate negation. For Derrida, the Aufhebung works in the production of meaning, a work which renders it into a term of value; just as for

Bataille, the Aufhebung belongs "in all its parts" to the "world of work"—and this world of work is essentially defined by prohibitions. The Aufhebung "is the form of the passage from one prohibition to another, the *circulation* of prohibitions, history as the truth of the prohibition."[53] The operation of Bataille's sovereignty and Hegel's lordship should not be confused, since mastery in the dialectic of mind "maintains and suppresses" the negated term, while the operation of sovereignty renounces the reserve of consciousness put aside, then sacrifices this sacred portion of consciousness in play, rapture, laughter, and death. Sovereignty is, therefore, dedicated to pure loss, it involves the dissolution, rather than the absolution of value and meaning. The sovereign operation (a term which Bataille finds loathsome—"comic operation would be less deceptive") is thus related to a theory of writing and to the "writing of sovereignty" or the transgressive text. In this regard Derrida's comments on Bataille and writing, which focus on the trace and erasure, are extremely significant in terms of his deconstructive practice. He certainly enlists Bataille in his struggle against classical logic and logocentrism. In speaking of the "erasure of discourse" he writes:

> it multiplies words . . . in an endless and baseless substitution whose only rule is the sovereign affirmation of the play outside meaning. Not a reserve or withdrawal, the infinite murmur of a blank speech erasing the traces of classical discourse, but a kind of potlatch of signs that burns, consumes and wastes words in the gay affirmation of death: a sacrifice and a challenge.[54]

The reference to the potlatch reminds us that, in his engagement with Hegelianism, and later with Marxism—the issue of which is clouded with doubt and ambiguity, as both Foucault and Derrida suggest[55]—Bataille availed himself of what Baudrillard has referred to as a "cosmogenetic" principle of loss,[56] a principle which is formulated in the context of a meditation and alteration of Maussian ethnology.[57] Now this reference to Mauss, which will later have a significant role to play in the work of Baudrillard, is too important to pass over in silence. As the mediator and vehicle of the Maussian gift, Bataille's work is indeed of some moment in the problematic which is constituted in postmodern philosophy around the critique of ethnocentrism in the philosophies and theories of totality. It also suggests a type of "anthropology of anthropology." In Mauss's version of the gift-economy he identifies two phenomena (or perhaps two forms of the same one) that, as he said, "contain all the threads of which the social fabric is formed: religious, legal, moral, economic . . . aesthetic"[58]—the kula, potlatch, the "total social fact." Societies of the gift-economy are governed by the obligation to return the gift (*don*)/potlatch/prestation with interest. In the potlatch societies there is a continual overbidding, of putting more and more at stake: "The total event is remarkable for the rivalry involved . . . nor does one stop at the purely sumptuous destruction of accumulated wealth." In order to eclipse a rival chief, all of the members of the tribe and all of their things may be involved. It is called "killing wealth."[59] It might be said that there is something of all this in the ahistorical sphere of French theory; the sense that there is also a continual overbidding in the return of Mauss's gift (on loan from the Indians). There is a thread that links chapter 4 of the *Phenomenology* to Mauss's *Gift*, to Bataille's *part maudite* and Baudrillard's *L'Echange symbolique*, a thread that draws these thinkers to risk everything up to the point of death (metaphorically and textually), in defiance and challenge to risk the entire treasury of language and signs in the sacrifice of everything in the service of a principle—"turning and turning in the widening gyre." At the heart of the enormous spiral of thought is the problematic of the gift, not simply understood in its anthropological context, but, analogously to the centrifugal movement of the primitive world, as a dispersed and motivated category with profound phenomenological and linguisitic significance.[60]

2 THE GIFT OF THE STARS

Symbols in fact envelop the life of man in a network so total that they join together, before he comes into the world, those who are going to engender him "par l'os et par la chair" [by bone and flesh]; so total that they bring to his birth, along with the gift of the stars, *if not with the gifts of the fairy spirits, the design of his destiny; so total that they give the words which will make him faithful or renegade, the law of the acts which will follow him right to the very place where he* is *not yet and beyond his death itself; and so total that through them his end finds its meaning in the last judgment where the* verbe *absolves his being or condemns it—except he attain the subjective bringing to realization of being-for-death.—Jacques Lacan,* The Language of the Self *(emphasis added)*

This passage from Lacan testifies to the debt owed by both the psycho-analyst and the structural anthropologist (whose presence is marked by the binary pair, flesh and bone) to Maussian ethnology: the gift of words. Not only was the gift a crucial category in the development of structuralist theory, but also to the formulation of other theories, some clearly antithetical to structuralism. As we have already noted, it plays a key part in Bataille's thought—where it evolved specifically in relation to his reception of Hegel and Nietzsche—set against the wholesale appropriation of the German tradition by French thinkers.

As a problematic, the gift is imbricated in a wide range of disciplinary fields. Lacan's "symbolic order" shares many affinities with Lévi-Strauss's theory of the don as a sort of pre-given linguistic and social firmament of signification[1] because it defines indebtedness as a structure of reciprocating relations in linguistic, marriage, and power phenomena. Posing the analogy between the structure of language and kinship systems, continuing the work of Freud in *Totem and Taboo,*[2] Lacan and Lévi-Strauss in a way ramify the psychological depth of linguistics, associating the relationships involved in naming with those of a psycho-linguistic "code" (the so-called symbolic code of the father); and to a level of prohibitions characterized, though often confusingly, by the permutations of the Oedipal myth.

It is also possible, however, to locate a major split in the interpretation of the Maussian gift. On one side the structuralists have inferred a reciprocating, perhaps ultimately economic, structure in the relations of the gift exchange. Given the influence of structuralism itself, this interpretation has become something of a paradigm. But on the other side of the split there is another, more radical and certainly more marginal, interpretation of the phenomena identified by Mauss. If the kula represents the model of the reciprocating exchange of symbols, then the potlatch is a model motivated by the unreturnable, unilateral gift, the gift of excess; a principle of agonism and the ritual *transgression* of prohibitions. It forms not only the basis for Bataille's anthropological vision, but his entire disposition at the level of writing. Subsequently it is used by Jean Baudrillard in his reinterpretation of the structuralist/psychoanalytic symbolic exchange according to the principles of the counter-gift (contre-don) and reversibility. In the alternative reading of Mauss—which perhaps amounts to little more than a nuance, but a momentous one—a different model of reciprocity is put into play, one that argues that it is not so much the prohibition that is decisive, but the category for which the prohibition acts as a raison d'être: transgression.

It has to be acknowledged that what is being described here is a vast field of interrelated concepts. Rhizomatic in a Deleuzian sense. One is in danger of grasping a concept which, when pulled, is connected to a mass of tangled ideas, uprooted, as it were, from the epistemological field.[3] Among the other flowers: an archaic moment in the Situationists when they echo Bataille's call for the return of sacrifice;[4] Derrida's work on the "pharmakon" which plays on the ambivalent relationship of the gift and poison,[5] and his examination of the question of style in Nietzsche.[6] In recognition of the complexity of the problematic— which is not without its detractors[7]—our current purpose is to indicate the scope of influence of the emblematic concept of the gift. Grounding the concept in Maussian ethnology, it will be argued that its significance derives from its implicitly critical stance in regard to dominant forms of economic rationalism, and by extension to those superstructural discourses attendant on such rationalism. And which, needless to say, have been assailed under many different colors in post-structuralist theory; such as in deconstruction, nomadology, micrologics, narratology, and heterology.[8] What is surprising, perhaps, is to discover that

Marxist and Maussian critiques of economic rationalism are not as fundamentally opposed as might be supposed, for they both decry the destruction of symbolic relations in capital.

This is a significant point of agreement, since it permits us to regard Maussian ethnology within the critical movement for which Marxism forms the cornerstone, it also permits us to argue that a theorist such as Baudrillard, who clearly owes much to Mauss, is—in his early works at least—more of a Marxist than many of his Marxist critics might have him. But finally, it allows us to pose a fruitful homology concerning the alterity of the other. For it is a phenomenon which is both internal and external to the consciousness of the West, one that challenges Marxism in its programmatic forms with being complicit with capital in its global expansion.

We might take the work of Pierre Clastres as an exemplary case of this homology when he illuminates what seems to be a generic characteristic of Western culture, the will and capacity to render the culturally different into the culturally same. In "On Ethnocide," Clastres argues that the colonizing vocation of the West (composed of genocidal and ethnocidal moments) was not without precedent before it was practiced on the rest. Both forms of this mind—to terminate cultural unities in the name of a greater unity—had already been rehearsed at the interior of the colonizing cultures. Thus in France, for example, the territory and the linguistic unity of the French was not the result of some vague impulse of culture and civilization, but the result of a distinct historical reality of the suppression of regional boundaries, customs, and rights by the "pale lords from Franchimanie" in the Loire region whose expanded realm established the territorial limits of the modern hexagon of France, which was later to be perfected administratively and culturally in the Napoleonic era.[9]

So what is it then, asks Clastres, that marks the state societies of the West "as infinitely more ethnocidal than all other forms of society," that is, more ethnocidal than the so-called barbarous empires (Incas, Pharoahs, or Oriental Despots)? For Clastres the answer is quite clear:

It is its *system of economic production,* which is precisely a space of the unlimited, a space without places since it is in constant retreat from limits, an infinite space in permanent forward flight. What differentiates the West is capitalism, as much in the impossibility of it remaining on this side of a frontier as in its need to pass beyond every frontier; it is capitalism, that system of production for which nothing is impossible, except the impossibility of it not being, for itself, its own end: be it liberal and private capitalism as in Western Europe or planned State capitalism as in Eastern Europe. Industrial society, the most formidable productive machine is, for that very reason the most terrifying destructive machine. Races, societies, individuals; space, nature, seas, forests and subsoil: everything is useful, everything must be utilized, everything must be productive, have a productivity driven to its maximum rate of intensity.[10]

Not only does Clastres identify capitalism as a global ethnocidal venture but, in so doing, forces an identification of its liberal and socialist faces in the common "system of economic production." This is not to deny the pertinence of a Marxist class-based analysis of industrial society, but is rather to locate a more fundamental split than that between classes: the split between societies with, and those without, systems and modes of economic production. (It is a similar perception to Kojève's analysis of the state in which the Russians and the Chinese are but "poor Americans" who through their revolutions are coming into line "with the most advanced historical positions"—that is in Kojève's terms, undertaking the centralization of political and administrative functions essential for commanding the economy from the center.) Now for Clastres, it is precisely in the existence of the state (as inherited in its modern administrative and bureaucratic form from Napoleon and the Jacobins) that both the split and the profound spirituality (*pace* Hegel) of ethnocide must be located. But Clastres, perhaps unlike Bataille, by no means speaks as an apologist for the so-called barbarous states. For example, the Inca empire, like any conquering state, extracted tributes and oaths of allegiance from the colonized regions, forcing their populations to "celebrate the cult of the conquerors." Yet Clastres claims that the violence exerted by the Incas over the captured tribes "never attained the violence of the maniacal zeal with which the Spanish later annihilated indigenous idolatry."[11] Like every state organization the Incas responded with great brutality when their authority was called into question: "The frequent uprisings against the central authority in Cuzco, pitilessly put down at first, were later punished by massive deportations of the conquered peoples to regions far from the native territory, which were marked by networks of cultural places (streams, hills and caves, etc.): deracination, deterritorialisation, ethnocide."[12] The difference in the ethnocidal capacity of state machines is measurable to the extent to which they permit the risk of opposition as against brute suppression: violence is a measure of weakness rather than strength, and this was why the Incas "tolerated the relative autonomy of the Andean communities as long as they recognized the political and religious authority of the Emperor."[13]

For the West, no; the imperatives of economic expansion combined with the profound ethic of humanism forbade the colonizers from "granting any respite to societies who abandoned the world to its original tranquil unproductivity." This was why the "waste, represented by immense unexploited resources, was intolerable in the eyes of the West." The choice offered to these societies was (and still is): "either cede to production or disappear, either ethnocide or genocide."[14] The process is almost at an end, and will be if the global order of capital has its way—"when there is nothing left to change." The violence, for the most part, is scenodramatic: entire continents become the backdrops, its peoples the stage-extras, their languages so many "backward patois" and their customs a folkloric spectacle designed for a touristic interlude in the last scenes in the history of man. Dragged into the vortices of East and West the societies at the peripheries have little choice; does it matter that the neocolonial masters are called, after an illusory countermovement of nationalism which only ensnares them further, either democrat or socialist, president or secretary? The result in either case is the same—deracination and deterritorialization of the indigenous culture. If it is possible to imagine, in a limited analogy, the dialectical poles of the order of production, labor and capital, as separated by a division similar to the tribal moiety across which the universe is organized in significant dualisms, then this Western imaginary constitutes a single cultural unity whose forms (tending toward one of the poles, invisibly linked by dialectical threads) are the equivalent of the cult of the emperor to which the conquered peoples must submit.[15]

The point of this discussion on Clastres's meditation "On Ethnocide" is the extent to which he clarifies the stakes which are involved in misreading the ethnological reality of the spread of Western culture. He does this in three ways: by identifying the ethnocidal (and at worst the genocidal) consequences of European ethnocentrism,[16] linking this phenomenon with the order of production, which is to say with a certain idea of *modernity*,[17] thus challenging the implicitly evolutionist vision of human society that nourishes Western ethnocentrism;[18] and demonstrating that Western culture (in its mutation as nation-state) is capable of being ethnocidal to other cultures because it has already been ethnocidal to itself. Clastres thus seeks to confirm, in a political way, Foucault's thesis on the emergence of "man and his doubles" in modern thought—the mirroring relations of interiority ("unconscious" alterity) with relations of exteriority ("primitive" alterity).[19]

Now it is possible to tax such theories as extreme cultural relativism which says that the alterity of the Other, primitive or unconscious, is beyond reproach or argument, and that such theories lead to a political philosophy of passivism, to the pluralism of anything goes, be it the murderous rites of the Incas or the tyrannical obsession of the schizophrenic, as long as they are the authentic expression of the speech of the Other. To invite such otherness is to invite a conservatism, and at worst to invite the conditions which would encourage a return of fascism. Surely this is a problem? Well, yes it is. But the problem posed is not one in which alterity is a threat to the social fabric; rather it is one in which alterity itself is subject to a double exclusion from a structure which permits no irruption on its surface save that which dissuades by simulation.[20] Let us put this in another way, in terms of the problematic under examination; the gift-economy, insofar as it posits a mode of economic behavior which is not part of the economic base and posits a rationality of exchange which has no part of economic rationality, stands opposed to the entire realm of political economy in both its dominant (capitalist) and critical (Marxist) modes. On one thing they agree: the primitive archaic relations of the gift-economy have no place in the order of production.

Let us now, after this long digression, move on to an account of the problematic of the gift and to an exploration of its ramifications in theoretical discourse. E. E. Evans-Pritchard, in his introduction to Mauss's *The Gift: Forms and Functions of Exchange in Archaic Societies*,[21] writes that the latter's thought was in the tradition of enlightenment philosophy, a tradition stretching from Turgot, Condorcet, Saint-Simon; to Comte and later Durkheim. Evans-Pritchard characterizes this tradition as one in which "conclusions were reached by analysis of concepts rather than of facts, the facts being used as illustrations of formulations reached by other than inductive methods," and that in spite of this tradition (and we should recall here Mauss's collaboration with Durkheim)[22] Mauss "turns first to concrete facts and examines them in their entirety and to their last detail."[23] A trained linguist (who could read not only the classics but also Hebrew, Sanskrit, Celtic, and the modern European languages as well), Mauss is generally regarded as being the founder of modern French anthropology and, with Durkheim, of modern (French) sociology.[24] Indeed the mark of Durkheimian sociology is firmly impressed in the work of

Mauss, perhaps most particularly in the concept of the "total social fact."[25] Now what constitutes "concrete facts" for Evans-Pritchard is the evidence found in a mass of ethnographic literature culled from the field research of a large number of anthropologists, and an equally large quantity of linguistic material relating not only to primitive, but also archaic (Roman, Germanic, and Indo-European) societies. Whatever else may be said about concrete facts observed secondhand in this way, one thing is clear: Mauss was able to reflect on the observation of several lifetimes of anthropologists, and in a synthesizing holistic analysis arrive at conclusions that remained opaque to the individual fieldworker. So, for example, using Malinowski's research in Melanesia (*Argonauts of the Western Pacific*)[26] Mauss arrived at conclusions opposed to the latter's functionalist interpretations; using linguistic and ethnographic material derived from other sources Mauss could place Malinowski's work against the tableau of a comparative cultural analysis.[27] Working (in the peace and seclusion of an apartment in Paris) on this vast quantity of material (and incidentally providing the role model for the distant ethnographer) Mauss hatched up the *form* of the gift (don as opposed to cadeau) as the key institution of exchange in primitive society, proposed its survival in archaic society, and observed its virtual disappearance in modern society.

Without wishing to overblow the comparison, we might say that Mauss isolated the gift as the generalized form in these societies analogously to the way that Marx isolated the commodity as the generalized form in capitalist society and indeed, analogously to the way in which Jean Baudrillard isolates the sign as the generalized *form* for our own, postindustrial, postcapitalist/socialist, societies. In each case the forms are conceived as total phenomena, each with similarly extensive ramifications for sociological and epistemological perspectives. In the opening passages of *L'Echange symbolique et la mort*, Baudrillard addresses this relationship of Marx to Mauss, foregrounding the figures of Mauss and de Saussure in the concept of symbolic exchange. In speaking of its apparition as the phantasm of a social relation founded on the "extermination of value," haunting modern social formations as "their true death," Baudrillard writes:

> there are other theoretical events which assume a capital importance: the anagrams of Saussure and the exchange/gift (*don*) of Mauss—these hypotheses are more radical in the long run than those of Marx and Freud—perspectives that are precisely cen-

sured by Marxist and Freudian interpretations. However, the anagram and the exchange/gift are not curious episodes confined to the disciplines of anthropology and linguistics, subordinate modalities in relation to the great machines of the unconscious and the revolution.[28]

Here is a strong claim. Is it simply an absurd proposition to imagine that these two figures, one whose renown relied on a single volume of lecture notes carefully amassed by prescient students and the other who wrote one book—a long essay—can be marshaled against the volumes of Marx and Freud; two moments before the weight of history and the unconscious? The idea even achieves a symmetry, these great machines immobilized by a reversible and destructive moment when the word transcends all consciousness and the gift defies all production. Yet it must be admitted that the figures of Mauss and de Saussure have cast long shadows over the sociological-linguistic field.[29] In the case of Mauss there are two effects; a diffuse and refractory influence for which the general concerns of anthropology, *for* anthropology as social anthropology—and the advanced humanism which this implies—would be the evidence. But then there is a more complex and yet more direct line of intellectual descent in the form of a methodological continuity: in a manner similar to the way that Mauss drew conclusions from Malinowski's research *not* drawn by Malinowski himself, Mauss is himself *read against himself.* All in the nature of a dialectical critique where Mauss (of the gift) is transcended and maintained in a textual exchange. This is a question of privileging a moment in Mauss. In Lévi-Strauss, for example, the exchange of the gift forms a model of communication at all levels; for Bataille the principle of dépense (that consumes the part maudite in the potlatch)[30] forms the cornerstone of his general economy; for Lacan the kula, the exchange of prestations, represents the inter-subjective circulation of signs that forms a model for his symbolic realm; for Baudrillard the existence of the counter-gift (contre-don) imbues the Maussian gift with its ambivalent effects, and for Baudrillard a Mauss of the counter-gift has to be read against all these other manifestations and even against the anthropological Mauss of ethnographic classification and more:

> It is necessary to set the principle of reversion (the counter-gift) against all the economistic, psychological or structuralist interpretation for which Mauss opened the way. It is necessary to set the Saussure of the *Anagrammes* against the linguistic Saussure,

even against his own restricted hypothesis on the anagrams. It is necessary to set the Freud of the death-drive against the whole anterior edifice of psychoanalysis, even against the Freudian version of the death-drive. . . . Reversibility of the gift in the counter-gift, reversibility of exchange in sacrifice, of production in destruction, of life in death, the reversibility of each term of value in language in the anagram: a single great form the same in all domains, of reversibility, of cyclical reversion and nullification— above all whatever puts a stop to the linearity of time and language, of economic exchanges, accumulation and power. Everywhere it takes for us the form of extermination and death. It is the form itself of the symbolic. Neither mystical nor structural: ineluctible.[31]

Like Bataille, Baudrillard privileges the destructive consumption of the potlatch against the homeostatic kula—whilst rejecting the former's inclination to turn its negating potential into a positive economic principle; refusing not only the distinction between the general/restricted economies as theorized by Bataille, but also any discussion of the economic at all. In another context it is as though Baudrillard takes Lévi-Strauss and his propositions on language beyond their limits. In a famous passage in his introduction to Mauss's *Sociologie et anthropologie*, Lévi-Strauss reflects on the origins of language—when, in an inspired moment, the entire universe becomes significative (*significatif*), when in an instant the two great reserves were simultaneously created: the body of signifiers, the possible words, and the reserve of meaning and reference of the signifieds, producing the condition of a superfluity of the signifier, leading to the "zero symbolic value" of the floating signifier; *mana, truc,* and gadget.[32] In this scenario language antecedes positive knowledge—which is produced cumulatively as a result of a relationship between the body of language and its reserve of meaning. But in the case where positive knowledge eclipses symbolic thought (which is characterized by a complementarity of available signifiers to the reserve) in a sort of unrestricted economy of signification, then for Lévi-Strauss there is a loss of an originary paradise, of a universe in which words and things and people circulate incessantly—a paradise of reciprocity, mutuality, rights, and obligations—all features of the model of the gift-economy as developed by Mauss.[33] For Baudrillard there is something altogether economistic in this reading of the Maussian symbolic, too idealistic in its resolution and compensation of contradictions between the *real* and the ideal. On the contrary, meaning for Baudrillard is produced in the extermination of signs: in Lévi-Strauss "the symbolic is simply reduced to the imaginary."[34]

A reading of the work in question[35] quickly dispels the idea that the institution of the don has much to do with our (banal) institution of the present except in a remote way; Mauss's gift is phenomenological—notwithstanding the structuralist gloss it has received—a mediator of inter-human relationships governed by a (Hegelian) desire for recognition, negation, and mastery; the phenomenology of the gift is indeed akin to certain propositions in Hegel. Whilst there is no specific reference to Hegel in Mauss, Lyotard claims that there is a "condensation" of the phenomenological Mauss and the structuralist Lacan in the concept of symbolic exchange as employed by Baudrillard, and that this condensation can be traced back to a common source, chapter 4 of Hegel's *The Phenomenology of Mind*.[36] The mediator here is surely Georges Bataille in his reading of Kojève's Hegel, even as Lacan himself condensed Hegel and Freud in his early psychoanalytic studies.[37] Lyotard extrapolates Baudrillard's phenomenological debt. As a "total form" Mauss's gift is phenomenological; it is the form of things charged with personality, of persons as possessions, an intersection of levels (economic, legal, moral, and aesthetic) and irreducible to the epiphenomenology of some more intrinsic reality, like the economic in Marx's thought. (Though a socialist, Mauss preferred the political thought of Jean Juarès to that of Marx or his bolshevik adherents in the PCF, and disagreed with Marx over the role of technique—it conditions the economy in Mauss—and had no taste for the idea of revolution, claiming that the tyranny of the proletarians is no less antisocial than that of the aristocrats. Whatever else they were, workers and bourgeoisie were both members of the same society, and could not but be saturated by the same ideas.)[38] It is due perhaps to its openness to a phenomenological interpretation that Mauss's gift has been given, received, and returned in the subsequent history of its reception in anthropological, psychoanalytic, and sociological discourse. Mauss simply presented his evidence, carefully drew comparisons, and suggested the direction of future research.

As a total social phenomenon the gift is, as Mauss puts it, a hybrid notion; it describes a central feature of archaic society that cannot be related to the individual act of giving because of the social constraint that governs the form. Nor is the gift-economy necessarily the circulation of things; it is also an economy of prestations: "They exchange . . .

courtesies, entertainments, ritual; military assistance, women, dances and feasts. . . ."[39] Thus, in Lévi-Strauss's terms, it is an economy of the exchange of signs.[40] Mauss's project, over and above the more disciplinary consideration, was to "rekindle the spirit of the gift" as a general social constraint in modern social formations, for "it is by opposing reason to emotion and setting up the will for peace against rash follies . . . that people succeed in substituting alliance, gift and commerce for war, isolation and stagnation."[41] To this end the work emphasizes the role of obligation in social exchange. There are three cardinal obligations in the gift-economy: to give, to receive, and to return the gift. This is perhaps the lesson relearnt in Mauss, and there is nothing particularly remarkable about it; it makes good sense. What is significant is that, as Michel Serres has said, it took the best sociological mind of the era to point out that the primitive other created by rationalist thought was evidence—among other things—of our own alienated social being, and that the importance of the kula, potlatch, mana, or hau is not that they are strange customs of strange people, but that they readily translate into institutions that have only recently slipped from the memory of European peoples and were, for Serres, the inspiration of art and literature.[42] But surely to invoke the hau (the spirit/animus that charges the gift) or mana (the power of prestige accrued, for example, through generosity), is to rekindle the wish for a return to an aristocratic conception of duty and obligation, a noblesse oblige? It is:

> We are returning, as indeed we must do, to the old theme of "noble expenditure." It is essential that, as in Anglo-Saxon countries and so many contemporary societies, savage and civilised, the rich should come once more, freely or by obligation, to consider themselves as treasurers, as it were, of their fellow citizens. Of the ancient civilisations from which ours has arisen some had the jubilee, others the liturgy, the choragus, the trierarchy, the syssita or the obligatory expenses of the aedile or consular official.[43]

Wishful thinking indeed! Lyotard's liquidation of all values has seen to that! The Mauss of the don speaks in the accents of an earlier epoch, in the tones of a radical humanism which says, with Durkheim, that "the ideal society is not outside the real society, it is part of it . . . for a society is not made up of the mass of individuals who compose it, the ground they occupy, the things they use . . . but it is above all the idea which it forms of itself."[44] These ideas are its collective representations, what Althusser called—in opposition to Marxist totality—a Leibnitzian, expressive totality.[45] A society is always present and present to itself in all its places. Whilst Mauss does not use the Durkheimian concept of "collective consciousness," there is, nonetheless, a notion of a "collective subject": "society is present in each of its parts and each institution expresses the totality of the social group."[46] Totality extends to this collective subject in *The Gift* where the intention is to "observe . . . minds as wholes and not minds divided into faculties."[47] (More wishful thinking: sociology and social theory since Mauss and Durkheim have tended to view the ideal as beyond the real and have witnessed the progressive fragmentation of minds divided against themselves. Perhaps here is the source of the malaise in sociology to which Denis Hollier refers.)[48]

Mauss's quest for totality is assisted by his discovery of two paradigmatic forms found in primitive society: the Melanesian kula and the Pacific Northwest Indian potlatch are the forms that coexist, a bit uneasily, as the metonyms for Mauss's totality. Extensive ethnographic research exists on these primitive institutions that are reduced to a single and total phenomenon,[49] and our attention must focus on the ambiguous alliance forged by Mauss between the aristocratic exchange system of the Triobriand Islanders and the "monster child of the gift-economy" of the Chinook Indians.

The kula is a form of inter- and intratribal exchange and commerce between the islanders. Geographically, the form produces two enormous concentric circles of ritual and ceremonial trading partners (it is only secondarily a commercial system) from which it derives its name, (kula=ring). It is composed of tokens—polished armshells and turned coral—which are the counterseals of the prestations, gifts, and feasts which circulate in opposite directions around the ring between the established exchanging partners. The exchange is aristocratic in the sense that it is the chiefs who give and receive prestations as representatives of the tribe; and though it is exchange between chiefs, the offerings received are distributed among the whole tribe according to a type of internal kula system. It is a form that stitches the fabric of intra- and intertribal relations and alliances, the distribution of information as well as the dissemination of goods, prestations, and gifts, and it is governed by the obligations referred to above. The existence of the kula provoked a reevaluation of these primitive societies:

> Thus the view which we must adopt regarding the Melanesian people is very different from the view normally taken. They have an extra-domestic economy and a highly developed exchange sys-

tem, and are busier commercially than French peasants and fisher-
men have been for the past hundred years. They have an extensive
economic life that cuts across geographic and linguistic boundaries. They replace our system of sale and purchase with one of
gifts and return gifts.[50]

It was Mauss's great insight, an event comparable for Lévi-Strauss to
the Newtonian revolution, to have theorized the existence of these
societies based on the pre-economic category of reciprocity, for in so
doing he broke with the premises of neoclassical economics and economic ethnocentrism. Maurice Merleau-Ponty argues that it was from
the systemic character of the social fact and the cycles of reciprocating
elements (signs) on many different levels that Lévi-Strauss was able to
construct a model of society as a "structure of structures."[51] Nonetheless, Mauss is elsewhere accused of "remaining a prisoner of the vocab-
ulary of the analyses of traditional political economy"[52] and for having
"passed over the question of production in silence."[53] There is, however, a sense in which *The Gift* is a critique of Adam Smith's political
economy, in that it opposes the notion of individual contract with a
system of total prestation.[54] Above all, and in contradistinction to
Lévi-Strauss's reading of Mauss's gift-economy, it is within the institution of the potlatch that we may discern the most radical consequences
of a primitive form capable of neutralizing the results of production:
the development of class society and accumulation.[55]

The partially nomadic tribes of the Northwest Pacific coast move in
family groups to their favored hunting and fishing grounds for the
spring and summer months. Despite the severity of the winter it was/is
a region blessed with favorable conditions, and the material culture it
could sustain was wealthy, like that of the Melanesians, even by European standards. In the winter the tribes would congregate in makeshift
towns: "During this period of concentration they are in a perpetual
state of effervescence. The social life becomes intense in the extreme."[56]
Certain occasions—marriages, initiations, deaths, and meetings—are
accompanied by the "reckless consumption of everything that has been
amassed with great industry from some of the richest coasts in the
world during the course of the summer and autumn."[57] Like the kula,
these occasions are constrained by obligations which, for Mauss, are
the flux that welds these institutions into a single great form. The
potlatch is characterized by its violence, its (ant)agonistic displays of
rivalry and prestations, including the ritual sacrifice of slaves. But it is,
like the kula, an open and collective display—"what we call simple

total prestations." Important for Mauss are the themes of honor and credit: "Nowhere else is the prestige of an individual so closely bound up with expenditure, and with the duty of returning with interest gifts received in such a way that the creditor becomes a debtor. Consumption and destruction are virtually unlimited. In some potlatch systems one is constrained to expend everything and to keep nothing."[58] So in the potlatch the themes of giving and destruction are wedded in the acquisition of honor; and on the indices of "wealth destroyed," rank, inheritance, and marriage are determined. Failure to observe the ritual obligations of giving and returning the gift with interest results in the loss of face or rank. But far from being an isolated phenomenon of these Indian tribes, the potlatch, like the kula, has a widespread distribution in primitive and archaic societies—Roman, Indian, and Germanic, for example—and it was on the basis of this distribution that Mauss constructed his theories of social morphologies.

In exploring these institutions of the kula and the potlatch Mauss provides a corrective to the ethnocentric and implicitly racist notions that view so-called primitive society as primitive. And by turning to linguistic evidence he contributes to the debate on the origin of the "economic," in pointing out that, for at least several primitive languages, there is "only a single word to cover buy and sell, borrow and lend." His archeology thus suggests that the economic did not evolve out of primitive institutions, in the model gift-barter-economic exchange, but indeed was always submerged in the institutions of the societies of the symbolic exchange. "Economic evolution has not gone from barter to sale and from cash to credit. Barter arose from the system of gifts given and received on credit, simplified by drawing together the moments of time which had previously been distinct. Likewise purchase and sale—both direct sale and credit sale—and the loan derive from the same source."[59] But in countering the claims of an evolving economy Mauss puts into place myths of his own, and in so doing creates his own contradictions: the myth that the indigene acted according to noneconomic factors opposes the idea that we are all of the species *homo oeconomicus*. (For Lyotard this is all too much; it is not a question of whether the primitive was economic or symbolic, but whether there is a primitive at all. "There is no primitive or savage society, we are all savages and all savages are capitalists and capitalized.")[60] The contradiction comes when Mauss celebrates the "venerable revolution" of the Greeks and Romans: the surpassing of the dangerous gift economy which was incompatible with the development

of the "market, trade and productivity." Michèle Richman claims that
it is because of this revolution that the totality so earnestly sought is
beyond us now; the autonomization of the economy has wrecked the
total institutions of the archaic society and their reclamation in Mauss's
ethical project is an impossibility.[61] Was Mauss incorrect in correlating
the demise of the gift-economy and the growth of hybrid notions and
their differentiations in linguistic expressions? Or did the primitives
always capitalize "affects" in the form of the symbolic lexicon as Lyotard claims (de parents et de paroles, de bêtes, de vies, de sexes) under
the sign of the less venal "great Zero"?[62] For the latter, Mauss should
be read not as the discovery of the precapitalist economy but as an
insinuation at the heart of that economy of an "indispensable comple-
ment" of "anteriority/exteriority": the fantasy of symbolic exchange
that haunts Baudrillard, and Marx too.[63]

Thus far we have attended to the basic features of Mauss's gift-
economy in attempting to outline its significance to theoretical concerns, particularly in relation to structuralist and phenomenological
interpretations in the field of social anthropology. At this point the
focus can now shift to epistemological questions, particularly those
concerned with theories of representation. In the next chapter the fate
of the gift-economy in the hands of one of its most important inter-
preters, Georges Bataille, will be examined. Richman, for one, argues
that Bataille is the major mediator of Maussian concepts for contemporary theory. The extent to which Baudrillard operates within the
field of a Maussian/Bataillian problematic will later become evident.
(It is possible that Richman's claim is too partial—since there are other
mediators: Caillois, Lacan, Leiris, or even an unmediated reception.)
There are certainly grounds for arguing that Mauss's concerns prefigured in some cases, and paralleled in others, research concerned
with a movement in epistemology which negatively mirrored the
growth of instrumental reason in tracing the progressive degradation
of the "symbol" into the "sign." As we said before this degradation, in
the minds of the sociologues we are examining, accompanies the autonomization of the partial sphere of the economy. Whereas once the
economic was but one effect of the symbolic exchange (the symbolic as
the ambivalent, the total social fact, irreducible to one of its moments,
always concerned with a multiplicity of levels: "legal, economic, religious, aesthetic, morphological and so on"),[64] it was now the "determinant instance," now the base on which the cultural superstructure
was erected (as vulgar Marxists have sometimes mistakenly inter-

preted Marx). It was now the orthodoxy of (materialist) economics in which

> man was believed to consist of two components, one more akin to hunger and gain, the other to honor and power. The one was "material," the other "ideal"; the one "economic," the other "non-economic"; the one "rational," the other "non-rational." The Utilitarians went so far as to identify two sets of terms, thus endowing the economic side of man's character with the aura of rationality. He who would have refused to imagine that he was acting for gain alone was thus considered not only immoral but also mad.[65]

Polanyi's passage brings us once again to the theme of the great *scission* of the anthropological field in a formula which repeats Foucault's famous dictum on the condition of madness as the "absence of work"— which is to say outside of the rational and measurable exchanges of the economy. In *The Order of Things* Foucault poses a homology between the discursive spheres of the economy (as the analysis of wealth) and theories of representation (in linguistics and semiology): he relates the introduction of labor as the general equivalent of all value to the degradation of the symbol into the sign in what he refers to as the "reduction" of the ternary structure of the sign [from Stoics to the Renaissance] to a binary relation of the signifier and signified in the seventeenth century (as expounded in the work of the Port-Royal Grammarians, and in the critiques of representation by Bacon and Descartes).[66] This reduction means:

> language was never to be anything more than a particular case of representation (for the Classics) or of signification (for us). The profound kinship of language with the world was thus dissolved. The primacy of the written word went into abeyance. And that uniform layer, in which the *seen* and the *read*, the visible and the expressible, were endlessly interwoven, vanished too. Things and words were to be separated from one another. The eye was henceforth destined to see and only to see, and the ear to hear and only to hear. Discourse was still to have the task of speaking that which is, but it was no longer to be anything more than what is said.[67]

In another context it is this "profound kinship with the world" that marks symbolic thought in both anthropological theories of the primitive and psychoanalytic (Freudian and Lacanian) theories of intersubjective relations. Thus Freud in *Totem and Taboo* reports on the sometimes severe injunction against uttering the name of the dead: "This taboo upon names will seem less puzzling if we bear in mind the fact that savages regard a name as an essential part of a man's personality and as an important possession: they treat words in every sense as things."[68] The notion of a shift from the symbolic to the semiotic is a recurrent theme in recent theoretical literature. Julia Kristeva, for example, extends the depth of the moment of transition to around the thirteenth century—though her interpretation is at odds with Foucault's.[69] For Baudrillard the growth of the counterfeit and fashion in the Renaissance is the origin of the competition of distinctive signs. Prior to this signs were restricted, subject to the interdictions of the first order of the simulacrum. The order culminates in the Baroque, and the stucco is its perfected form: "the triumphant democracy of all artificial signs, the apotheosis of theatre and fashion and that which translates, for the new class, into the possibility of 'doing it all' because it smashed the exclusivity of signs."[70] The transformations of the subsequent "order of production" have led to the "perfectly accomplished form of the species": the model. Here the sign is reduced to a set of coded differences and equivalences, and the simulation to the reference of the sign at the level of the code: the reinvention of the first order. (Baudrillard argues that the fabricators of stucco would envy the indestructibility of plastic but be horrified by the results: the weight of exhausted signs that pollute, like industrial waste, the social "imaginary.") The order that is placed by the counterfeit is essentially the Maussian archaic; it is constrained by obligation, by the reciprocity of symbolic exchange, and ruled by a ferocious hierarchy. Make no mistake, Baudrillard warns us; it is a cruel order "where any confusion of signs is punished as a grave infraction of the order of things."[71] In a telling remark Baudrillard refers to "the unbreakable reciprocity" and the "reciprocal obligation" of the archaic sign—what Wilden refers to as the classical symbol (the Greek *sumbolon* and the Latin *tessera* which, as the interlocking halves of a broken potsherd, signify a unique *relationship* rather than a *thing*).[72]

We have already noted the complaint of the structuralist Lévi-Strauss against the privilege accorded instrumental reason; humanity has always possessed vast quantities of positive knowledge (hence the equation of primitive thought and scientific reason in the *The Savage Mind*)[73] because this thought exists within the "closed totality" of language (which is, therefore, the *code* in which all knowledge can be articulated). Yet it is only recently that scientific knowledge has gained dominance: "choisie comme centre de référence de façon officielle et réfléchie."[74] For Lévi-Strauss there is an opposition between this knowledge "marked by continuity" and symbolic thought "which offers a character of discontinuity," and this opposition would seem to be the basis of Baudrillard's own opposition of symbolic exchange to the exchange of equivalences characteristic of the order of production. As an archetypical order, Lévi-Strauss's symbolic order is platonic, always implying a discontinuity between the original (the first order of the symbolic) and the second, third, or fourth orders—copies, reproductions, or the elaborations of the code. Baudrillard inherits this prejudice based on the hierarchy of logical types.[75]

Returning to the analogous relations between the economy and language, we can see that the conflict between the gift-economy and economic exchange had already been well constituted by the time they are confronted by Baudrillard's provocations. Indeed, on the evidence of Wilden for example, the polemical excesses of *The Mirror of Production* may have misconstrued their object: Marx and his de facto apologia for the order of production. In an archeological aside Wilden, disputing the claims of the Lacanian School to occupy the privileged ground of theory in the social sciences, remarks on the filiation of Lacanian theory of the Imaginary to Marx's theories of the valorization of commodities by the "general equivalent of exchange." It is worth quoting the passage at length:

> He (Marx) goes on to describe the valorization of the exchange-identities of commodities as a process by which "the body of commodity B acts as a mirror to the value of commodity A" [Marx, 1887:1,52]. In a "psychological" footnote, Marx compares this process of identification and valorization with the mirror-relationship through which a child comes to see himself as a human being by seeing himself "reflected" in others. (The common denominator in both Lacan and Marx here is, of course, the "desire for recognition" in Hegel's analysis of the relation between master and slave.) This correlation is quite surprising enough, I think, but it becomes even more significant when we reflect on Marx's thesis that under capitalism (symbolic) relationships between people are reduced to the status of (imaginary) relations between commodities or things. In this way . . . Lacan's theory of the Imaginary is given a socioeconomic foundation.[76]

3 THE ISSUE OF BATAILLE

The years pass, and people continue to entertain the illusion that some day they will be able to talk about Bataille. Because of this illusion they never really come to grips with his work which is of capital importance. . . . An earnest wish: may the younger generation do it for us, do what we did not dare to do, without waiting for one of us who will dare—to compete with youth.— Marguerite Duras, Outside: Selected Writings

Marguerite Duras was to wait six years until the silence erupted into speech and writing on Bataille, and appropriately, since the figure stalked him throughout his career, on the occasion of his death.[1] Age, however, prevailed over youth, and it was seventeen years before the younger generation risked their reputations in order to "confront the bull." By this time the generation of Barthes, Kristeva, and Sollers was fully engaged in a general campaign to articulate the project of a pseudo-philosophy of writing (*écriture*), using the analytic tools and orientation of the structuralism of de Saussure, Lacan, and Lévi-Strauss.[2] Thus it is against the background of delay in his reception that we come to address the issue of Bataille.

With the publication (1985) of a collection of Georges Bataille's writings from the 1930s, the reception of this man's work in the English-speaking West has been given new impetus. While there has been for some time now a quite intense interest in Bataille's texts, it has been somewhat confined to specialist journals of cultural theory.[3] The publication of *Visions of Excess*[4] marks a milestone for the further dissemination and reception of Bataille's writing, particularly in terms of his relationship to postwar theory. The aim in this chapter is to specify Bataille's contribution to this field both in terms of the framework (and its implicit narration) which we have already established, and in relation to the often remarkable claims which have been made about his work. Specification of his theory as either post-structuralist or post-modernist must be resisted in order to avoid the easy retrospective projection of Bataille into a seminal prehistory of these two categories; not from an aversion to the tautologically true, but rather as a result of a certain caution toward joining the rush to canonize writers and thinkers in the name of postmodernism—as this could be a repetition of the mistakes of modernism in the construction of a revised pantheon of universal culture.

Extensive biographical and historiographical research into Bataille has already attempted to situate him in the context of his immediate theoretical world; all the better to understand the general orientation of his writing, and all the better to limit the destructive movement of his text. (In this context two works should be mentioned: *Georges Bataille politique,* by Francis Marmande, and *Reading Georges Bataille,* by Michèle Richman.[5] These studies have attempted to specify Bataille's relationship to several discursive fields: anthropology, philosophy, psychoanalysis, Marxism, literature, and art.) This immediate theoretical world refers also to details of a biographical and bibliographical nature that relate to the charged interwar years and to the whiff of cordite and death that permeated the thought of the era, to the confused throng of emotions unleashed by the unprecedented brutality that had wiped out almost an entire generation of European men in the Great War. And, need I add, there was worse to come. To examine Bataille in relation to this world is not simply an exercise in historicism—designed to forestall his apotheosis in postmodernism (the fate reserved for him by Habermas[6])—nor a defiance in the face of those who might dismiss him from the forum of theory before the questions that might arise from a study of his texts have even been properly formulated. No, to examine Bataille in this context is to witness his critical engagement with, and his ultimate rejection of, major currents of modernist thought—Neo-Hegelianism, French sociology, and surrealism—from the standpoint of a prophetic return to Nietzsche.

That it is possible to simultaneously call Bataille a modernist, premodernist, and postmodernist says as much about our own theoretical tendency toward closure as it does about Bataille. The first thing to say about the discourse on Bataille is that it exhibits a certain tendentiousness; no less evident in Habermas's claim that French postmodernism embarked on the path of self-destruction when it followed Bataille,[7] than in Foucault's claim that Bataille's thought is a guiding light in the darkness of a new era of the *unthought.*[8] The second thing to say about the discourse on Bataille is that it never properly succeeds in appropriating his thought. In the psychoanalytic model of appropriation which is employed by Bataille, and incidentally borrowed from Freud, appropriation destroys the distinction between subject and object; in the "oral" phase the different (food) becomes the same (the "me"), but equally, excretion reestablishes the "different" in its expulsion from the body of that which cannot be assimilated.[9] If the bodies change, the process remains the same: Bataille consistently demands, and we cannot escape this demand, that we confront whatever is expelled; not because he is a philosopher locked in an anal phase of development— although he has been accused of this[10]—but because the theme of exclusion refers not to the myth of origin of humanity, but to its end. The texts of Bataille are a theater of the excremental in whose scenes one may glimpse golden threads: of textuality before the letter of Barthes; deconstruction before the letter of Derrida; and transgression before the letter of Baudrillard, or Foucault and his "return" to Nietzsche. And so the cat leaves the bag and tendentious thought demands speech: it is simply impossible *not* to imagine the centrality, were it to be a void, of Bataille's thought to an intellectual history of Parisian thought; impossible *not* to formulate questions that coalesce around this proposition. Quite correctly the rules of rational discourse discourage the exaggerated claim by their demands for evidence and qualification, and in the face of which such a claim may appear bizarre, if not certifiable. What is going on here?

How do we explain the delay of Bataille? Why, after the successive waves of French theory, starting with Sartrean existentialism, which have periodically been diffused through the English-speaking West, is it *now* (rather than twenty years ago as was the case for his reception in France), that Bataille finally emerges as one of the central figures in French thought? I think we can discount a conspiracy theory on the part of publishers desperately dredging the field to bring us ever more obscure figures from French literature: the enormous energy required for translation for little return would discount this scenario. The problems of translation would be much closer to the mark. Since translation is the interpretation of a text across the conventional frames of language, one could well imagine the translation of Bataille's texts as a formidable task indeed. The translators of *Visions of Excess* have made a valuable contribution. But this cannot be the whole story. Fashion is probably a factor here, and probably not an inconsiderable one. (But then, who is afraid of fashion? Those for whom fashion, like fetishism, is something that other people are afflicted with; how do you attack fashion without appearing as a vulgar moralist? As Lyotard reminds us, fashion/fetishism is a couplet well known to critical discourse which has always theorized it in pejorative terms.[11] False consciousness is likewise what other people have, for to admit that we are all afflicted and equal before its mystery would mean that criticism is itself a function of a fashion for critical thought, and that the object of analysis is itself fetishized in its relation to criticism.)

Yet fashion in itself, the play of an arbitrary code within the field of discourse, is insufficient to explain the delay of Bataille because it fails to account for a movement in discourse which *is* governed by an internal logic. For quite a while now we have experienced the effect of Bataille's thought in secondary literature without being able to specify its precise origins. It has been like the movement of a large dark body, maybe a black hole, whose presence in the heavens has been discernible in the erratic orbits of the visible planets: Foucault, Barthes, Derrida, Baudrillard, and the rest. To be sure these thinkers have made no secret of their interest in Bataille, nor indeed of the special place in discourse he occupies. One need only refer to the *colloques* (organized in the first instance by the *Tel Quel* group)[12] and to the reviews (such as *Critique* and *L'Arc*),[13] dedicated to the analysis of Bataille's text, to understand the intense interest spurred by the French rediscovery, at the heart of the modernist project, of a heterogeneous element that placed an entire tradition into a vertiginous relationship with its real and imaginary ends.

The "issue" of Bataille can be understood in three senses: as what has emerged from the theoretical and contextual background in the name of Bataille; as what issues from his text in the form of the impious, transgressive, and impossible; and as a metaphor for a fundamental philosophical exclusion. To put this another way, and to satisfy a desire for closure and continuity in a discontinuous realm, the issue of Bataille is the third term which he sets into play. Neither the result of a dialectical synthesis, nor the reference of a semiotic practice, the third term (or third order, since this is the project) has neither a Hegelian nor a structuralist origin but a Nietzschean, Sadean one—the "beyond" of good and evil—thus also a powerful ethic of the pagan.[14] It is toward these issues that this chapter is addressed within the context of the historical and anthropological schemas previously outlined.

To speak of Bataille's work, or works, is to refer to a very substantial body of writing, collected in nine volumes and written over approximately forty years until his death in 1962.[15] Largely ignored in the prewar years, the reception of Bataille was given impetus, as indicated, by the group connected with *Tel Quel*, including Philippe Sollers, Julia Kristeva, and Roland Barthes. For the latter, Bataille was particularly valued as a precursor to the general mutation of the status of literary and critical writing which challenged the traditional classifications and the claims to primacy of the original work of literature over its secondary criticism.[16] Bataille's texts transgress the boundaries of the old disciplines and in so doing produce a violent juxtaposition of the discursive and the discontinuous. They are thus also difficult and refractory texts, and this is evident in the matter of the voice in the text, an incessant shift of the designation of the *je* and the *moi*, in short, of the locus of subjectivity: it could be said that there are always at least two voices in the text. The one, the voice of the outlawed and prohibited Bataille, crosses the path of Bataille the continuous and discursive thinker, erupting as it crosses into an intense display of the sacrifice of meaning at the altar of a crucified (authorial) sovereignty. The act of writing is itself transgressive, perhaps ultimately the model of transgression in Bataille, in that the epistemological and linguistic foundations upon which the discrete disciplines are based are constantly put into question, and this is as true for the putatively scientific discourses of linguistics, anthropology, Marxism, or psychoanalysis as for the meditative and speculative discourses of philosophy or literature and criticism. For Barthes, Bataille's writing is the "exemplar of textuality": "What constitutes the Text is, on the contrary (or precisely), its subversive force in respect of the old classifications. How do you classify a writer like Georges Bataille? The answer is so difficult that the literary manuals prefer to forget about Bataille who, in fact, wrote texts, perhaps continuously one single text."[17]

Here too, we see another reason for the delay, noting, in passing, the contribution to the notion of écriture as developed by the *Tel Quel* group.[18] To classify Bataille is thus the same problem as "situating" him. That this is difficult to do helps to illuminate, by example, by the very act of writing itself, the process of the category and activity of the *heterogeneous*.[19]

Therefore, let us describe the first issue of the text as this category of the heterogeneous, for it is what is expelled from the *homogeneous* body; be this body political, textual, or corporeal. The figure of the sovereign leader, a narcissistic being-for-himself (borrowed from Freud),[20] forms, along with dangerous base elements, the mad, the criminal, and the revolutionary, the sphere of the heterogeneous in relation to the homogeneous social body. But for Bataille the preeminent category of social exclusion is the sacrifice. Likewise from the organic body are expelled the excremental and the sexual, bits and partial objects of the eroticized and fetishised body; and these elements, like the entire realm of the heterogeneous, are governed by ritual prohibitions which link, at an unconscious level, religious and profane practices subject to the rules of the symbolic. Above all, what must be kept apart is the body in death, in putrefaction, and this heterogeneous element is subject, like the other elements of the body, to the strictest taboos—giving rise to the universal practices that seek to purify the body of this contamination and profanation. (For Bataille the practices associated with this zone mediate the relationship between the living and the dead, between the profane and the sacred; for him they are the ultimate reference for literature and art as practices that seek to return to the homogeneous social body, in a purified form—*in the form of bleached bones*—that which nature and catastrophe have torn from human society.) From the textual issues the censored and the unspeakable in a perverse relation that associates the restricted discourse of divinity with the abject texts of pornography. (Here I think we should recall Bataille the pornographer, tirelessly and heroically carrying on the sovereign labors of de Sade. Bataille's pornographic works have been referred to as among the finest examples of the genre produced in the twentieth century.[21] We might also note that the reputation that Bataille earned as a pornographer—producing texts that never failed to cause a scandal—has, in many cases, preceded the reception of Bataille the social theorist, and this reputation may indeed be related to what we are calling his delay.)

The heterogeneous elements, and I give here but the barest account of them, are thus theorized as the realm of the unconscious, representing for Bataille the concrete and social expression of its structure and function. The analysis of the heterogeneous, which Bataille refers to as heterology, thus combines psychoanalytic categories (desire, transgression) with critical and philosophical concepts in a particular anthropological vision. This ironic "science" proceeds in its analysis according to a dream-like movement that associates the heterogeneous elements on the map of the unconscious: this movement is exemplified, for Barthes, by the declension and shift of the signifier, the eye, in the *Story of the Eye:*[22] *oeil, oeuf, soleil,* and *couille.* The movement is (over-)determined by mimesis (sphericity) and by the linguistic *glissement* (slide) that associates the word-shapes of the signifiers. In terms of a science, this process is clearly exotic, but this is precisely the point. For Bataille, the appropriating function of scientific analysis is a procedure of the homogeneous mind which is constitutionally incapable of theorizing the heterogeneous. Science itself represents a limit to the experience of the impossible.

But Bataille is not content to remain in the analytic stage of the heterogeneous and the limits which restrict experience access to its mysteries. On the contrary, in postulating the identity between sexuality and death, certainly demonstrable in psychoanalysis, Bataille takes a decidedly Nietzschean turn by linking the experience of the loss of subjectivity in ecstasy and sexual rapture with the philosophical loss of sovereignty in the death of God. With this death so disappears the transcendental guarantee of individual sovereignty, and what also disappears is that limit condition in thought that God represented; there is no exteriority of being. This lack of an existential guarantee, though hardly regretted, is associated with the demise of the "sacred" (a theme of the Durkheimian school), and leads in Bataille's thought to a strategy and a method (as opposed to a project) of going to the limits, of thoughts, notions, beliefs, and morals—and then transgressing those very limits in order to delimit their operation and the sovereign authority needed to exceed them by transgression.[23] This Nietzschean turn also places Bataille within the problematic of writing and death as addressed by the "philosophers of death," Maurice Blanchot and Pierre Klossowski.[24] It also brings us to the issue of transgression.

Foucault's essay on transgression furnishes one with an example of a text which challenges the privilege of the original (joyfully ceded by Bataille) in that one day (perhaps already) it will be impossible to consider transgression without first conceiving it in Foucauldian terms. In reference to this death of God, Foucault writes:

> Bataille was perfectly conscious of the possibilities of thought that could be released by this death . . . but what does it mean to kill God if he does not exist, to kill God *who has never existed?* Perhaps it means to kill God both because he does not exist and to guarantee he will not exist—certainly a cause for laughter: to kill God to liberate life from this existence that limits it . . .—as a sacrifice; to kill God to return him to this nothingness he is and to manifest his existence at the center of a light that blazes like a presence—for the ecstasy; to kill God in order to lose language in a deafening night . . .—and this is communication. The death of

> God does not restore us to a limited and positivistic world, but to a
> world exposed by the experience of its limits, made and unmade
> by that excess which transgresses it.[25]

In this fragment of Foucault's text on transgression we are led to
reduplicate the movement of thought in Bataille's text; from the Dionysian laugh to the profligate loss in the sacrifice; a movement from the
blinding light that was God to the dusk of a false consciousness that
opens on to the night of transgression, the night of *l'expérience intérieure,* the title of the work written on the darkest night of the Nazi
occupation, a work that celebrates abject despair and the acephality[26]
of *non-sens,* of the subject deprived of thought and discourse, of reason
and of subjectivity itself. This is the basis of Bataille's mysticism: this
will to self-loss in the transgression of sovereignty or, as Bataille expresses it, "the practice of joy before death."[27]

Of course, the thoroughgoing reference to Nietzsche has more than a
thematic significance since it defines an entire orientation at a political-
epistemological level. To specify this level, we must refer once again to
the "philosophy of death" as it were, and to ask what was the origin of
the surrealist disdain for bourgeois culture. Was it not of the same
origin as Nietzsche's vehement contempt for bourgeois mentality and
forms, his contempt for religion, and a feeble bourgeois art which had
betrayed their true supra-historical character by becoming confounded
with a utilitarian and mercantilist morality and with "the scientific
organization of social life which the Hegelian posterity had drawn as a
consequence from the agony of Christianity"?[28] Thus when Foucault
claims, in the "Orders of Discourse," that "whether it is through logic
or epistemology, *whether through Marx or Nietzsche* our entire epoch
struggles to disengage itself from Hegel,"[29] we must consider the place-
ment of Marx and Nietzsche on the same map as a commentary on the
political-epistemological orientation of this earlier generation of Bataille, Klossowski, and Blanchot. Foucault specifies this relation in the
"Preface to Transgression," in claiming that this category of transgression will one day "seem as decisive for our culture, as much a part of its
soil, as the experience of contradiction was at an earlier time for
dialectical thought."[30] For Foucault, Bataille was a key figure in the
escape from the Absolute Spirit. It is arguable whether modern philosophical thought has succeeded in this struggle, or whether we have
entered into the era of transgression, the Bataillean millennium. The
question we might pose: is what Foucault says as true for us as it is for

him? We should recall the circumstances of the appearance of "Preface to Transgression" in the double issue of *Critique* honoring the passing of the founder and editor of the review which held a privileged position in the world of French letters.[31] The list of contributors in this memorial issue forms a formidable group: in addition to Foucault, we read Maurice Blanchot, Pierre Klossowski, Raymond Queneau, Michel Leiris, and André Masson. Therefore, when Foucault writes that transgression will occupy this decisive role *for our culture,* it is pertinent to inquire *who* this collective subject is; is he referring to the intellectual culture of Paris, and can he speak for ours? Is the distinction valid any longer? Is there, for that matter, a strong tradition of dialectical thought that we must surpass in the English-speaking world?

There is a missing factor in Foucault's equation: contradiction is to dialectical thought as transgression is to x, x here representing modern thought. Does Foucault mean his experience, for if he does then this experience is precisely the experience of Bataille and his transgression, and the former age to which he refers is not a dim past but a recent, still-present past, in which the dominant mode of philosophical thought of writing would have been, and would still be, dialectical. Bataille, therefore, marks a moment—a milestone on the road from Hegel to Nietzsche, from dialectical (Koyré, Kojève, Merleau-Ponty, and Hyppolite) to genealogical, that is, Foucauldian thought.

In a universe stripped of all the means of transcendence in the form of religion or science, the destiny of the subject is forever immanent in experience. *Expérience* in Bataille's text is another one of those terms furnished with a specific and exclusive sense: experience is the experience of transgression, and thus has nothing to do with experience in general, except in opposition to the continuity and discursivity of its homogeneous existence. A word here on transgression: it is difficult to speak of transgression in terms of a definition, for the truth is that transgression in Bataille is a disposition, a "method of obstinacy" as Klossowski puts it,[32] rather than a more or less precise practice. As experience is the experience of transgression, transgression is the transgression of sovereignty, and sovereignty is related to pure loss, or dépense.

Sovereignty in Bataille is subject to a double usage. On one hand it can be read in its philosophical context as personal sovereignty (as inherited from Kant's transcendental and Hegel's transhistorical subjects), and on the other, sovereignty can be derived from a socio-anthropological origin, as a feudal concept which grounded the privilege of a social group (the aristocracy) in the dilapidation of wealth and the obligatory nature of conspicuous consumption. Moreover this is, for Bataille, an obligation which the bourgeoisie has historically avoided, preferring to conceal its expenditure, using it instead to "consolidate a symbolic code of distinctions between itself and the workers."[33] And thus Bataille struggles to strip sovereignty of its ideological associations with the bygone aristocracy without delivering it to a heroic bourgeois individual, since it is precisely this sovereign subject and its authorial forms which Bataille aims to annihilate by reserving it for a type of mystical experience of limits—of the poetic, the erotic.

The will to self-loss in sovereignty as the transgression of limits is thus related, in a general way, to the entire problematic of death that is inherited in French Hegelianism. In Hegel the crowning moment of sovereignty is victory or death in the wake of a risk of death in the struggle with the consciousness of the Other. But in a world purged of the battle of the masters, in which death returns as representation and spectacle and simulacrum, the negativity of the master is deprived of all historical meaning and is bequeathed to the slave as destiny through work. It is here that Bataille takes issue with the Hegelian anthropos and, by extension, with Marx's reworking and inversion of the dialectic of history. For Bataille there is an alternative to the negativity that positivises work: the operation of the process of the sacred and sacrifice.

The theme of the sacred, and its supreme category of the sacrifice, rejoins the science of heterology as a definition of the socially heterogeneous—of those things and practices which are subject to prohibition and censorship, excluded from contact and interest in the quotidianity of the workaday world. It is possible to locate this interest in the sacred and sacrifice within the tradition of French sociology—to which Bataille paid repeated tribute. But where Durkheim in *Elementary Forms of Religious Life* draws an irreducible discontinuity between the sacred and profane, Bataille finds it possible to reconcile them at the level of the heterogeneous. Durkheim had written:

> In all the history of human thought there exists no other example of two categories of things so profoundly differentiated or so radically opposed to one another. The traditional opposition of good and bad is nothing beside this; for the good and the bad are only two opposed species of the same class, namely morals, just as sickness and health are two different aspects of the same order of facts, life, while the sacred and profane have always and every-

where been conceived by the human mind as two distinct classes, as two worlds between which there is nothing in common . . . however much the forms of the contrast may vary, the fact of the contrast is universal.[34]

Bataille rejects this absolute division and Durkheim's impulse to read the sacred as heterogeneous in relation to the profane. For Bataille the sacred and profane have to be read together as the excluded in relation to the world of homogeneity, linked at a psychic and philological level.[35] Nonetheless, there is a common perspective of the two thinkers to view the sacred, and its expression in the sacrifice, as a (now lost) principle of social cohesion. For Durkheim the communication vivified and consciousness strengthened and quickened in the presence of the sacred—communion—forges the social bond. For Bataille it is "in the festivity of sacrifice and in its sacred violence that man attains that community in sovereignty which is lost in the social order founded on the primacy of production and acquisition."[36]

Therefore, whilst it is true that sacrifice must ultimately be theorized in the discourse of anthropology, its very absence from our contemporary social formations must also be accounted for in our anthropology about ourselves. This was the project of the College of Sociology,[37] the result of a collaboration of Bataille, Roger Caillois, and Michel Leiris between 1937 and 1939. In addition to a dedication to the exploration of the realm of the sacred, the substantive aim of this college was the analysis of the structure and function of secret societies in which no discrimination was made between secret groups in so-called archaic or primitive societies and those of the advanced societies: fraternities of warriors, initiatory groups, and heretical and orgiastic sects were considered alongside fascist and revolutionary organizations, terrorist groups, and crime syndicates. In the ways to which we have alluded, Bataille's project was antithetical to the French sociological school of Durkheim and Mauss. True to the spirit of the college, a secret group was formed associated with the review *Acéphale*[38]—a secret society, Nietzschean in outlook, dedicated, inter alia, to the experience of human sacrifice. (It is reported that the problem with the scheme was that while there was no shortage of volunteers for the role of victim, no one was willing to perform the act of execution. At a secret rendezvous in the forest the cult sacrificed a goat instead.) The college folded in 1939 under the pressure of the impending chaos, but not before it had organized several conferences, some of which attracted the exiled Adorno, Horkheimer, and Benjamin. At this juncture it is possible to specify common ground between Bataille and critical theory, particularly on the question of the sacred and its disappearance from modern social formations, and the relationship of this disappearance to the growth of instrumental reason and universal *mathemesis*, the world of homogeneity.[39]

We can note the parallel paths followed by the Frankfurt School, in the *Dialectic of Enlightenment*, and by Bataille, who stands here as a representative instance of a radical moment in French socio-anthropology. Their common direction could be expressed in terms of Adorno's and Horkheimer's "dialectical anthropology," in its critique of "equivalence," of abstraction, and of the ideological construction of "necessity" that is afforded a privileged status, as the basis for life, in both bourgeois and socialist societies.[40] Dialectical anthropology maintains a fidelity to Marx's critical model while at the same time surpassing the sub-Hegelian limitations of its understanding of liberation and domination. The parallel critique of homogeneity and production becomes all the more clear in the later exponents of the French anthropological critique, and particularly in the case of the theories of Pierre Clastres and Jean Baudrillard. To this critique—which, I argue, holds a key to the understanding of post-structuralist theory and which is deeply indebted to the thought of Bataille—we must now turn.

When Marx luxuriates, in *The German Ideology*, in his vision of life in communism as hunting in the morning, fishing in the afternoon, herding cattle in the evening, and criticizing late into the night, he is expressing an unconscious anthropology that is at odds with his own more explicit anthropology of the progressive development of modes of production.[41] For what this unconscious anthropology entails is a vision, admittedly slightly productivized,[42] of paleolithic society, of society prior to the great neolithic revolution, which, by establishing permanent human settlement based on the practices of farming and the ownership of land, confined and marginalized the nomadic paleolith. When it comes to the test, Marx, the champion of technique and industry opts—not without irony—for the decidedly unproductivist practices of the hunter-gatherer. Not for Marx digging coal in the morning and working the lathe in the afternoon; no, Marx in communism lives in a world of natural abundance. Now in a world of natural abundance nothing, properly speaking, is produced, and game and fish are there for the taking, dispensed, as it were, by a generous mythological moment of grace.[43] Of course, too much could be made of this apparent lapse in Marx's concentration, and it must be remembered that it occurred in the context of a discussion on the division of labor (a discussion that derides the German understanding of historical and prehistorical categories); but as Freud has taught us, loose talk has the capacity of revealing a repressed content of thought. What is set loose in Marx's dream is the (Baudrillardian) ghost of antiproduction, a ghost that haunted Marx the productivist, and all productivist thought, *as its true end*. Could Marx really have believed that the world of natural abundance, which would be communism, would be achieved by steam and steel, wheat and harvesters, plus the reunited organs of the original division of labor: the hand and mind? It would be a tall order indeed. A simulacrum of the very first order! It is, possibly, what he had in mind. At some point production in the form of its capitalist and socialist modes would have to be surpassed; at some point it would cease to be thought as the central category of human activity; at some stage humanity would stop producing its life so as to better live it.

Did Marx in fact glimpse an anthropological truth that has only recently been demonstrated on the basis of a reexamination of the evidence, and a revaluation of the perspectives, of a particular field of anthropology? This truth is that paleolithic society, far from being the site of a wretched struggle for existence and while knowing only few types of personal possessions and no ownership of land, was, nonetheless, a society of abundance. This, of course, is Marshall Sahlins's thesis in *Stone Age Economics,* and in *Culture and Practical Reason* (and which in some ways represents the basis for substantivist anthropology in both the U.S. and the French anthropological schools). What Sahlins suggests is that even were we to accept that paleolithic society produced its material existence—and this is precisely what is in question—then the time that was strictly necessary for production and reproduction was remarkably short. Not only was this labor-time brief, the actual tempo and intensity of the labor varied enormously. The process of the hunt involved many nonproductive activities including, one may imagine, criticizing. If one considers the concrete struggles of the contemporary working classes over wage and time conditions, then Marx's glimpse could only be disturbing in the extreme, and certainly a case for some type of sublimation. In truth, Marx's anthropology is an anthropology of scarcity where starvation "stalks the stalker" who is condemned, in the economic debate, to play the role of the bad example: the so-called subsistence economy.[44] (And playing the role of the bad example is the centerpiece of anthropological ethnocentrism, the most serious character disorder of all philosophies of totality.)

An anthropology based on an evolutionist vision condemns anterior society, beyond the idiocy of village life, to a grim ordeal of living in a blind nature, a nature indifferent to the cares of people who are themselves blind to the ordeal of their own nature. The *telos* of growth, the progressive development of social institutions, kinship structures, technology, belief systems, and the form and content of material conditions is animated by the same spirit that allows the Darwinian to express surprise that he (invariably a "he") is in the privileged presence of the "perfectly accomplished" form of the species, be it a tiger or tree or even Hegel. Somehow across the galactic wastes of evolutionary time the species have evolved, in the process of adaption for survival, for the sublime benefit of the scientific observer. It does not occur to the evolutionist that the tiger and the tree were always perfected forms, and of course their very existence attests to this: perfection in survivability is simply survival, and this was dealt with in the first fifteen minutes. So too with human survival; it simply never was indexed to the survival of individuals (what Marx refers to as the first "moment").[45] Human survival was always in terms of the group, and the collectivity was always the perfected form of the human; without it humans would die, or cease to be social, and this amounts to the same thing. If a discourse of anthropology imagines a so-called primitive communism as the repressed of capital and the order of production, then in its counter-discourse, in a schema in which time is reversible, production itself is the repressed, and primitive society is society against production.[46]

I would argue that the critical schema outlined above is representative of a political anthropology that characterizes certain species of post-structuralist thought. That structuralism is a discourse on anthropology, which takes its most developed form in Lévi-Strauss (and which, moreover, Foucault identified as the high ground of contemporary thought), permits us to specify certain conditions of the posterity of structuralism. To do so we might refer to an example of structuralism's antithetical moment which appeared in its conceptual firmament from the very beginning. This moment is to be found (by no means exclusively) in the double reading to which Mauss's *The Gift* is subject, setting in motion two related, but ultimately conflictual, anthropological and epistemological models. As we argued earlier, Mauss's work split on the question of "production." In failing to theorize this realm, Mauss created the *aporia* within which the divergent theories took shape. On one side, the structuralist inherits the gift in the form of the Melanesian kula, a single and total form which circulates as a vehicle for messages of categorically different types: symbolic, political, economic, and strategic. In Lévi-Strauss the kula exemplifies the exchangist character of human society: for him primitive society is society-for-exchange, as it is through the exchange of gifts, words, and women (his categories), that the social bond is sealed and the symbolic discourse of the interrelated structures nourished and maintained. It is a homeostatic principle par excellence. But there is, claims Pierre Clastres, a silence in Lévi-Strauss's text on the question of war. From its origins, anthropology has divided over the definition of the character of primitive society. And it is here that Clastres parts company with his former mentor. Against the model of the primitive society as society-for-exchange, Clastres opposes primitive society as society *against* war. This is an inversion of the classical view of primitive society as society-for-war, but one which nonetheless maintains the centrality and ethnological reality of a level of fundamental violence which is constitutive of the social. Exchange as potential war averted, or war as the issue of a bad exchange or an *échange manqué* as Lévi-Strauss supposes, "is contradictory to the sociological reality" of primitive society, since war is logically *prior* to exchange: "war implies alliance and alliance implies exchange. War is not failed exchange, but exchange is a tactic of war."[47]

If the kula is the metaphor for exchange in Mauss, then the potlatch is the metaphor for war, and it is here that Bataille's reading of Mauss has proved crucial for the development of structuralism's countertradition. The potlatch is the gift of excess, the *prestation* that is accompanied, on occasions, with a display so antagonistic that it is indistinguishable from an act of war. The significance of the potlatch for Bataille, however, is not as a pure celebration of destruction, but due rather to its normative function. The potlatch society prevents accumulation by the immediate sacrifice of the surplus, la part maudite, in an active principle of consumption which ensures an undivided social body and forbids the development of class society. This is, I believe, the central message in *La Part maudite*,[48] and its value to social theory is that it sets into motion the analysis of society based on modes of dépense. This latter term must also be understood in a restricted sense, in that it refers to expenditure which is dedicated to unproductive practices: war, sex, death, art, and literature. In this analysis it is precisely the means of disposing of the surplus—which even the most reputedly subsistence economies will produce—that characterizes the nature of different social formations. Thus, societies of production, capitalist or socialist, distinguish themselves from the rest by their reinvestment of the surplus into the machinery of production. So contrary to appearances, industrial society is society which defers consumption, preferring, in the terms of the situationists, to substitute the spectacle for the festival, reserving "consumption" as a private and rational principle: the privatization of wealth.[49] To draw the thread tighter, we could say that Baudrillard's critique of the systems and modes of productivist thought are filiated, via the agency of the situationists and the critique of the spectacle, to Bataille's analysis of modes of dépense.

A period of sixteen years separates Bataille's major works on "the notion of expenditure" which appeared in the review *La Critique sociale* in 1933,[50] from *La Part maudite,* the "accursed share" or the "damned part" of 1949. This latter work Bataille considered to be his major theoretical contribution, a systematic exposition of his vision of the world: his philosophy of man, nature, and history.[51] Here Bataille returns to many of the themes previously explored in the "Notion of Expenditure": to the critique of the classical principle of utility; to the social function of sacrifice in the potlatch (the victim as the quintessential part maudite); and to a general theory of the potlatch which inverts the terms of classical and critical political economy by giving priority to the "dilapidation," rather than to the accumulation, of wealth. In theorizing the restricted economy of use values (political economy) *together* with the sacred economy of sacrifice, Bataille arrives at the theory of a *general economy.*[52] This theory sets out to go beyond the limits which bound "economic man" and economic reason. The general economy is an expression of Bataille's cosmology which holds a preeminent place, like the Aztecs with whom he felt so much affinity, for the figure of the sun. For the sun is the source of a boundless and generous superabundance of growth and energy. It is the gift without return which "shines on us with the energy of the sun."[53] Just as Bataille claimed that Mauss had misread his own evidence, so Baudrillard claims that Bataille "has misread Mauss," since the "unilateral gift does not exist":

> He who had so well explored the human sacrifice of the Aztecs should have known, like them, that the Sun gives nothing, and it is necessary to nourish it continually with human blood to keep it shining. It is necessary to defy the gods with sacrifice so that they will respond with profusion. Put another way, the root of sacrifice and the general economy is never simply pure *dépense* or some sort

of drive of excess delivered to us by nature, but an incessant process of defiance.[54]

(One might note in passing a basis for Baudrillard's symbolic exchange—as the counter-gift—within the Bataillean problematic.) For Baudrillard it is not, therefore, in the notion of dépense ("too much like the inverted figure of the prohibited"), that Bataille's response to his "true question" must be sought. That question was: "Why is it that people have always experienced the need and felt the obligation to kill living beings ritually? In failing to know how to respond, all men have remained in ignorance of what they are."[55] It is rather below the level of the text, at its interstices, that Baudrillard locates the answer; in the mythic assertion of the existence of the sacred. Bataille's mythic force is, for Baudrillard, as for what seems to be an entire generation, constituted by "a subject of knowledge" always "at the boiling point" which is retrieved "at the height of death": the sacrificial force of writing.[56] Knowledge confronted at the height of death returns us to the preface of Hegel's *The Phenomenology of Mind* and to Alexandre Kojève's Marxist construction of the philosopher in his famous initiatory readings to the rising generation at the Sorbonne in the 1930s. Kojève's *Introduction to the Reading of Hegel* produces a thoroughly Marxist conception of the philosopher on the eve of the battle of Jena, and conversely, a thoroughly Hegelian Marx, and it is from Kojève that Bataille inherits these two conceptions.[57] Without going into the peripatetics of the Hegelian schema of history again we can say simply that what appealed to Bataille, and for that matter Lacan, was the primordial basis of history in the master/slave dialectic, a dialectic that is translated in the psychoanalytic discourse into the father/son relationship, and in Marxism into the conflict between the bourgeoisie and proletariat. Hegelian negativity is given a specific value in both cases, that is, the value of the proletariat, the value of the son, as the negation of negating action of the bourgeoisie and the father. In addition, the master/slave dialectic reserves a preeminent role for the irrational principle of violence in the formation or constitution of consciousness: historical consciousness in the case of Marx, and individual consciousness in the case of Freud is finally taken or prized (in a *prise de conscience*) in the violent action of revolution and the symbolic violence of Oedipus.[58]

The conflict between Bataille and the project of history, outlined in Hegel and Marx, can be understood as one further episode in a conflict that has shadowed all philosophical thought when it claims to speak in the name of some higher authority, be this reason, the state, or history. Jacques Derrida tells the story of Kant's disapproval of those he described as mystagogues—the imitators of the true philosophical overlords. These people are given to the display of poetics and prophecy, they ironize and subvert the original significations of philosophy as a rational *savoir-vivre* by announcing, in a particular tone, "something like the end of philosophy."[59] In the parliament of philosophy the voice of reason is ridiculed by the mystagogue who places the gift in opposition to work, the intuition in opposition to the concept, the genius in opposition to the scholar, and the aristocracy in opposition to the democracy. By replacing evidence with "analogies and verisimilitudes," they "resort to poetic schemas." One supposes that this is no more or less than what Derrida himself achieves in drawing the analogy between Kant's struggle with his mystagogues and Derrida's own struggle against the contemporary mystagogue. Derrida might indeed be his own bête-noire when he remarks that there is something of the mystagogue in each of us, and that all discourse is ambiguous to some degree. Naturally Derrida refuses to take sides—in his characteristic doubledealing—by arguing that there is a collusion between the foes, and that to play Aristotle against Plato, as Kant is happy to do (for Plato is guilty of a superstitious theophany) simply puts another head beneath the crown of the sovereign. But before Derrida returns the crown to the prop box of philosophy, he lingers a moment and gives it a little buff, a gentle frisson, against his better instincts, in order to conjure up its power before its fall from grace, its transformation from an authentic auratic symbol, commanding in its own right, into a simulacrum of the once sovereign character of the philosophical overlords. Yet before philosophy is definitively screwed by this perverse doppelganger, before the parliament of the overlords is converted—or should I say reconverted—into the theater of who knows what (the theatre of the apocalypse?), there must be staged the scenes of the discourses of the end, featuring those of Hegel, Marx, and Nietzsche, which combine and multiply in a bewildering profusion. Derrida:

> I tell you this in truth; this is not only the end of this here, but also and first of that there, the end of history, the end of class struggle, the end of philosophy, the end of God, the end of religion, the end of Christianity and morals (this [ça] was the most serious naïveté), the end of the subject, the end of man, the end of the West, the end of Oedipus, the end of the earth, *Apocalypse Now*, I tell you, in the cataclysm, the fire, the flood, the fundamental earthquake, the

napalm descending from the sky by helicopter, like prostitutes, and also the end of literature, the end of painting, art as a thing of the past, the end of psychoanalysis, the end of the university, the end of phallocentrism and phallogocentrism, and I don't know what else.[60]

Even to declare the end of the end is to "participate in the concert," as it is the "end of the meta-language on the subject of eschatological language."

Now, to put an end to the apocalyptic babble Kant, in his exasperation, calls for a "scientific police" who would rout the chapel of "arrogant philosophy" and would return the debate to a rational discourse on *practical* reason.[61] The first motion of practical reason, in the philosophy of modernism (for we may as well start with Kant as anywhere else), is this expulsion to the poetic, the prophetic, and the discourse on ends. This scene, rehearsed at the philosophical level with Kant, is played out in the cultural formations called modernist, including, let it be said, in the discourse on capital.

We will call this philosophical expulsion the final issue of Bataille's text. In writing pornography that is philosophy and vice versa, the text is rendered as beyond use value, except as a negative reference, for the systems of thought that constitute the philosophies and sciences of the human. Yet the fact that Bataille's thought resonates in a particular field of French (and not so French) theory—whose scope I have tried to indicate in a limited way in this chapter—must cause us to reflect on the conditions of our own appropriation and exclusion of species of thought and knowledge, some of which are indeed forms of this French theory. Thus we must ask the question: how do we deal with Bataille's fictive philosophical meta-narrative? Would it be good or bad to take Bataille seriously? What would it mean to take Bataille seriously?

To subject the text to a pious critique or a rational *détournement* would surely be a case for laughter to one, I suppose Nietzschean, way of thinking; yet to ignore the text would be a refusal to drink at the waters of Lethe that Bataille so generously offers to those in pursuit of history and society. This water is writing, but writing without time or memory, writing that returns from its source to an oceanic tradition that affirms itself as thinking the impossible, of "opening notions beyond themselves."[62] It is writing which affirms, as Foucault has written, that before anything else, thought is "a perilous act." He goes on to say:

Sade, Nietzsche, Artaud and Bataille have understood this on behalf of all those who tried to ignore it; it is also certain that

Hegel, Marx and Freud knew it. Can we say that it is not known by those who, in their profound stupidity, assert that there is no philosophy without political choice, that all thought is either "progressive" or "reactionary?" Their foolishness is to believe that all thought "expresses" the ideology of a class; their involuntary profundity is that they point directly at the modern mode of being of thought . . . [which advances] towards that region where man's Other must become the Same as himself.[63]

On the issue of Bataille one is compelled to conclude paradoxically, since the burden of his argument and criticism is never to foreclose discourse, but, on the contrary, to expose thought by opening it up to the condition of its own impossibility. Bataille's method and practice—heterology—ineluctably concern a meta-discourse on writing. This, as I have tried to show, is recognized by those thinkers called poststructuralist: Foucault, Derrida, Barthes, Baudrillard, and Lyotard. The project of writing would claim Bataille as an exemplar who, in setting into play a third term beyond the habitual dualisms, good and evil, left and right, material and ideal, literature and pornography, thus also sets into motion a project of the critique of criticism—hence the paradox. I would like to suggest that this discourse on writing is subject to a dialectical movement which co-polarizes the antiproductivist discourse with the nonpositive affirmation of production which we find in the writing of Jean-François Lyotard.

4 THEORIES OF THE THIRD ORDER

"Now look here . . . we have said that this process of representation deals with something at third remove from reality, haven't we?"—Plato, The Republic

We are cautioned by Plato against the seduction of the "third order representations" of the poet and the painter of scenes. It is a moral injunction, for the third order is the order of shams, of reflections and shadows. It is the order that is one remove from the real world that is made by people—the second order—which itself is at one remove from the "essential reality" of the "ultimate nature of things." We are cautioned not only because the artist's representation is at two removes from this ultimate reality, but also because it does not appeal to reason—all in all "a thoroughly unsound combination." To these three orders of representation there corresponds a parallel hierarchy of practices—of use, manufacture, and representation. "Use" is the privileged category, for it is only with reference to use that the "quality, beauty, or fitness of any implement or creature or action can be judged." "Manufacture" is compelled to be at the service of use (where knowledge of the object is formed) and it is, therefore, a dependent practice, a fact that banishes it to the second order. But the practice of mimesis, of representation, including all painting and tragic poetry, is irredeemable: the artist has neither knowledge of the object in use (ideal practice) nor of the object in manufacture. And even though representations can reproduce everything "they never penetrate beneath the superficial appearance of anything."[1] We might be tempted to conclude, therefore, that the "crisis of representation" which is heralded as one of the conditions of postmodernist thought[2] has already been acted out in the theaters of antiquity, as Plato's fears suggest—confirming that there is nothing new under the sun, or that Western philosophy is but a footnote to the Greeks.

Perhaps of all the modern thinkers involved with the question of this crisis, the thought of Jean Baudrillard comes closest to operating within, and on, the epistemological framework of this Platonic discourse. For, without a doubt, Baudrillard is a theorist of the third order, of an order of representational phenomena composed of such figures as the simulacrum, simulation, model, and the hyperreal.[3] But unlike Plato—who would like to draw a categorical distinction between the second and third orders, because the latter "does not appeal to reason"—for Baudrillard the entire second order, which is the order of Plato's production, along with the immense edifice of its theoretical, philosophical, and cultural discourses, has collapsed into the third order. Reason itself has ceased to appeal to reason, and is henceforth to lead a phantom existence in an apocalyptic vision. The evidence of this collapse, it is argued, is around us: choose an object of any discourse or practice and it will be discovered that its logic and finality—its operational field—is structured according to the principles of representation. Metastable but paradoxically at the point of implosion, the third order, which is now confounded with the order of production, inherits, in all its phenomenal forms, the strategies of the object.

The project has thus been the articulation, encouragement even, of this collapse (implosion, involution) of the values and referents of Western epistemology and culture. Fascinated, as Marx was with capital, with a perverse object of desire and armed with wit, hyperbole, and a "pataphysical" logic, Baudrillard strips the object (in its theoretical permutations) of its metaphysical presuppositions and theatrical disguises to expose the rules of its game, to lay bare its false transparencies, its strategies of mirroring and simulation, of dissuasion, deterrence, and dissimulation. For the treacheries of the object are not at all epiphenomenal but structural: they return to the heart of the episteme and refer to a structural shift in the relationship between the sign and its referent, between the representation and the represented. They are evidence of a profound crisis in the utopia of progress and of the contradictions within the totalizing character of the universal culture. And like Plato who had founded an entire ethic based on the maintenance of a strong symbolic order and hierarchy of representation and on the suppression of dangerous and ambiguous authority (as in the case of writing and in the parable of the cave), so too Baudrillard expresses an ethical position. But this position seems to have a Nietzschean, rather than Platonic, origin in an ethic—or an aesthetic—which says with Nietzsche that the sham world is the real world,

whereas the real world is the world of illusion. This would be, therefore, to locate Baudrillard's text (adopting the terminology used in
relation to Bataille) within the tradition of French Nietzscheanism
which, as we have already noted, must be understood in reaction to the
dialectical formulations of Hegelianism. The debt to Bataille is considerable: conceptually in terms of the general economy and transgression
and in terms of the vehement anti-productivism and the formulations
on death in "La mort chez Bataille";[4] and methodologically in the form
of a radical and reckless gesture which condemns Baudrillard, like
Bataille, to exist on the line of impossibility, in the transgression of
which Bataille had sacrificed authorial sovereignty. The debt is returned symbolically: in a similar refusal of the rules, as delivered in the
theoretical patrimony, which place science above experience, and in a
similar willingness, a duty almost, to transgress the disciplinary boundaries, but this time without the useless and heroic gestures or sacrificial
excess of acephality, but *coolly* in a deadly game whose charm is its
pretense to complicity.

Unremitting in his condemnation of this totality, Baudrillard nevertheless posits the existence of a massively repressed social principle
that haunts rationalist, pragmatist, and functionalist thought and the
social systems and structures they have spawned: symbolic exchange. If
there is an optimistic moment, admittedly of joyous destruction, in the
"early"[5] Baudrillard (up to *L'Echange symbolique et la mort*), then it is
to be found in this problematic category of symbolic exchange. It
operates as his meta-position in the critique of political economy and
its contemporary avatar, semio-linguistics; as the order excluded from
contemporary social consciousness, an ideal and lost social principle;
and as the basis of an (unconscious) political and (conscious) theoretical strategy: the return of the repressed. The counter-gift is its privileged moment, above all other moments of exchange, since it is the gift
returned as excess, poison and defiance, the response which "raises the
stakes," ensures communication and is its guarantee. And contrary to
Marx's conception, the first historical act is not the movement of the
hand to mouth but an outstretched hand offering food. There is no
"communication without response."[6] The genealogy of the symbolic
exchange is a complex reworking of the Maussian gift via Bataille and
Lévi-Strauss, "re-read while crossing Freud without the warrant of
Lacan."[7] As *thanatos* it achieves its ultimate status as a weapon in the
battle against production in all its transformations. That Baudrillard
does privilege the counter-gift underlines the parallel to the drawn

between la part maudite and symbolic exchange, or between Bataille's
general economy and Baudrillard's generalized political economy. In
pursuing a Bataillean anti-productivism, Baudrillard resolves the ambiguous relationship Bataille established with regard to Lévi-Strauss's
structuralism, by identifying structuralism as the imaginary of the
system of political economy. It is thus that Baudrillard joins structuralism's antithetical countertradition.

The critique of the sign, of its logic and political economy, is the form
that this theoretical movement takes in the writings of Baudrillard—
from the attempts in *Le Système des objets,* and *La Société de consommation ses mythes, ses structures,* to uncover a systematic logic governing the circulation of the objects of consumption based on linguistic
and psychoanalytic models—to the proposition in *For a Critique of the
Political Economy of the Sign* and *The Mirror of Production,* that the
sign has achieved the status of a type of perverse "total social fact,"
the universal form in a generalized political economy. In the later
L'Echange symbolique et la mort the critical framework is jettisoned in
favor of the revolutionary anthropology which had been foreshadowed
in the earlier works.

In the early works on consumption, *Le Système des objets* and *La
Société de consommation,* Baudrillard seeks to demonstrate that the
logic governing the circulation of objects is a pure logic of differentiation—a sign logic—whose formal coherence rests upon its articulation
of differential values within a code. In a very strong sense his analyses in
these works operate within a semiological/structuralist paradigm.[8]
This sense is reinforced by Baudrillard himself. For example, he starts
Le Système des objets with the claim that the house is a faithful image
of the family and of the social structures of an epoch. Whereas the
bourgeois house is the image of "patriarchal order" and "hierarchical
etiquette," the modern house is structured like a body—as an integrated field of organic functions abstracted from the body—which
itself has become the ideal schema for the integrated social structures.
The familial object, too, lives out this life of the structural homology. In
the bourgeois house: "The clock is a mechanical heart that reassures us
about our own hearts . . . the clock is the equivalent in time of the
mirror in space."[9]

Without denying the debt to structuralism which is evident in the
operation of homology, and in the binary opposition ancient/modern,
it has been argued that even at this early stage there was an implicit
break with semiolinguistics in the attempt to employ semiology both

historically and critically—producing a type of critical semiology[10] or, as Charles Levin puts it, to initiate, in *Le Système des objets*, a particular type of "phenomenology of reification" and a "phenomenology of structuralism itself."[11] Critical semiology thus attempts to go beyond the mechanistic analysis of semiology, interpreting the historical system of reference as a mythical structure. The binary ancient/modern is nourished by the binary myths of origin and function: the bygone object (l'ancien)[12] assumes a place in the general system as a "hot" object in a "cool" society. (This is both an inversion of Lévi-Straussian terminology which refers to the primitive as cool and the modern as hot, and an ironic reference to McLuhan. Baudrillard is not above parodying the prophets of technology—particularly if their message is subvertible.)[13] Authentic or not, the bygone object is the locus of (libidinal) investments: "More and more, statues and paintings of the virgin or the saints disappear from museums and churches. They are bought on the black market for wealthy property-owners for their deep satisfaction. Finally a cultural paradox but economic truth: only the counterfeit can satisfy this thirst for authenticity."[14] In its "myth of origin" the bygone object derives power through its proximity to a romanticized past, and by extension, to its production in the hands of a creator. This power—itself mythologized—is prized from the object in three analytic glosses: psychoanalytic, linguistic, and anthropological.

In the first, a picture is painted of the object in an Oedipal family portrait. The object is "sublimely filiated" with the father, to the source of power and authority who achieves his preeminence in the system as the "fantasy at the heart of reality where all mythological and individual conscience resides—the fantasy of the projection of a detail which is the equivalent of 'I' and around which the rest of the world is organized."[15] In its linguistic gloss the bygone object achieves a "perfect tense" by its flight out of the present and everyday (and a flight, what is more, that is to be found in every aesthetic sentiment): "Epochs, styles, models, or series, precious or not for none of this changes its lived specificity: it is neither genuine nor fake, it is 'perfect.'"[16] And, properly speaking, the bygone object is neither synchronic nor diachronic, but anachronic—the structuralist framework shakes. In the anthropological analysis Baudrillard uses an inverse projection of the bygone object in Western societies: the technological object in primitive society. As the broken television in the jungle has the virtue of power (*mana*) as fetish, for us the fetish is reversed. Stripped of its function—in rite and ceremony—the bygone object (of anterior or primitive

society) ramifies our own myth of origin, of the continuity and survivability of our own society. For Baudrillard this myth is crucial, for it
relates to a genealogy of power and to the logic of its discrimination.
Encapsulated in the short discourse on the bygone object is the critique
of the social logic that has reduced the object to the status of signifier
(later referred to as the "semiological reduction").[17] For when blood,
birth, and titles lose their prestige qua signifiers in the democratizing
processes of the eighteenth and nineteenth centuries, their ideological
value flees to material objects: to objets d'art, furniture, and jewels that
have been gathered from all points of the globe.[18] Thus the stage is set
for the extension of an Althusserian concept of ideology as a material
process in which the "material" is sign and the "process" is exchange.

Opposed to the bygone object is the functional, modern object which
is charged with its own mythological significations: of nature, work,
and progress. Where the bygone object is "heavy," the functional/
modern object is "light." The former is significant but useless, the latter
useful but insignificant. It is also a historically specific form:

> The object only begins to truly exist at the time of its formal
> liberation as sign-function, and this liberation only results from
> the mutation of . . . industrial society into what could be called
> our techno-culture, from the passage of a *metallurgic* into a *semi-
> urgic* society . . . when the problem of its finality of meaning . . .
> begins to be posed beyond its status as a product and a commodity.
> This mutation is roughed out in the 19th Century, but the Bauhaus
> solidifies it theoretically. So it is from the Bauhaus' inception that
> we can logically date the "revolution of the object."[19]

The object is thereby liberated from the theatricality and ritual function
of the bygone object, and rededicated to the role of technical and
rational function of problem solving,[20] and is then surpassed by an
order whose hyperrationality becomes the principle of its very irrationality: production produces in order to produce production. Or,
more provocatively: production is one of the modes of reproduction.[21]
(The movement from the *metallurgic* to the *semiurgic* signifies the
absent *demiurgic* of gnostic fame, the prime creator and mover of
matter, of the fundamental division of light and "base matter," to
maintain the reference to Bataille, and thus of the irreconcilable principles of good and evil.) The object, now the conflation of commodity
and sign, is not, however, devoid of anthromorphic characteristics; it is
charged with the imperative—work! In this respect, Baudrillard ar-

gues, it shares with the subject an analogous destiny, of the liberated individual in the bourgeois era free to sell labor power. When the object is broken (or the subject sick) or when the object is outmoded (the subject is redundant) it has moved beyond its social (and this means productive) finality. So subject and object become confounded and are capable of being read each way. In an inversion of terms the historical development of one acts as the theoretical model for the other.

Epistemologies are often based on spatial models, and one that readily comes to mind is Foucault's extraordinary structure outlined in *The Order of Things*—a sort of crystalline matrix of the intersecting planes and axes which constitute the discursive field.[22] Baudrillard, for his part, employs a dynamic model whose form is an immense spiral movement—fashioned, in a mischievous aside, on Ubu's bloated stomach (*la Gidouille*).[23] As profoundly unconscious as the movement of the stars in the heavens, the system keeps an appointed round with destiny; in the case of the modern object liberated from the univocality of function, this involves a movement to a "higher logical type," but lower order.[24] In a drastic "semiological reduction," the object as commodity, drawing its referents from the organic sciences and rational calculus of the nineteenth century, mutates at the very time when there no longer exists a finality of needs for which it functions as a use value. And needs themselves mutate to a new form that has little to do with the necessary reproduction and satisfaction of the cherished subject of nineteenth-century ideology, but are rather commanded by the needs of system reproduction alone. What are henceforth consumed are not use values, but the signs of use value. The persistence of the referent function is explained in terms of one of these "scientific" myths. In a parody of psychoanalysis, what might constitute the structuralist mentality is characterized by

> a relationship of fecality which requires the conductibility of internal organs. These will be the bases for a characterology of technical civilization. If hypochondria is the obsession with the circulation of substances and the functionality of primary organs one can, in some ways, qualify modern man, the cybernetician, as the cerebral hypochondriac obsessed by the total circulation of messages.[25]

In the obsession with the circulation of messages we can clearly detect a reference to structuralist Lévi-Strauss, but even more clearly it is a reference to that obsession called streamlining which, as an "aesthetics of consumption,"[26] prefigured the universal mode of consumer engineering with which we are all now familiar. In the 1930s in the United States "fluid dynamism" represented an important and baroque variant on the modernist, functionalist style. Truly the Americans were obsessed with fluid movement, not only in relation to the nascent aviation industry, but with the shape of cars and of consumer objects generally. The great designers of streamlining sketched out a utopian vision of a society in fluid movement: of cars down the arterial highways; of the fluid movement of goods through the economy (and thus the depression strategy of the economic planners—to increase the rate of social metabolism). People, goods, objects—the laminar schema was conceived with military precision. In this schema the call to arms was a call to objects (gadgets, white goods, appliances, and cars), and the army to be mobilized was the reserve army of consumers, whose captains mapped out strategies on flow charts where phallic arrows predicted market penetration against consumer resistance.[27] (It is indeed relevant here to recall the identification which Bataille proposed between "military" and "industrial" society in *La Part maudite*, as two modalities of the same form of homogeneity.)[28] Among other things, Baudrillard argues that the curved forms of streamlining are related to gestural forms, particularly of work. The "formal accomplishment" of this stylization masks a basic loss—of symbolic relationships established in work—by means of a simulacrum of energy reinvented by the force of signs.[29]

But as if the logic of function and its referent myths is insufficient to carry the system, it is redoubled by the entire discourse of publicity which, inventing some of its own myths, imposes a relatively coherent collective vision, not simply of objects, but of a chain of signifiers "to the extent that they signify one another as a complex super-object, luring the consumer into a network of the most complex motivations."[30] It is in this way that the entire system of objects and its attendant discourse of publicity reinvents, presents, and represents to the consumer a banal version of natural abundance—not perceived as the product of labor, but as the inheritance of a "generous mythological moment" of progress, technology, and growth.[31] The "miracle" of the system is given its own anthropological dimension: according to Baudrillard in the West we live out our own version of the Cargo Cult. For just as the primitives expected Western aid as a natural delivery of ancestral cargo—in the form of gifts—via the agency of the whites, so we too accept consumption as a natural effect, something that successive generations inherit as a "natural right to abundance." Thus we find a stubborn resistance in the West to the idea that our prosperity is gained at the expense of a global rip-off—for this prosperity has been assumed as a sort of right. Like the Melanesians, who attempted to entice the planes (loaded with this cargo) by constructing models of them on the ground, (carefully lit at night, because this is what the whites did), so we too are under the sway of a belief in a magical cathexis: "It is a mentality of the primitives, in the sense that it has been defined as based on the belief in the omnipotence of signs." And that the images do (miraculously) descend into the television is insufficient to render our world the real and that of the indigene the imaginary: they are both of the latter order.[32] The television is the vehicle of our own mythic cargo—publicity—which has no need of the rationality of proof, information, or sense simply because it is assumed like the fable of Father Christmas. Television is the chimney of the imaginary—a rationalist fable that people reserve for their second childhoods of perpetual gratification by fabulous parents![33]

The referent myths of abundance and needs and the complementary categories of growth and scarcity are subjected by Baudrillard to a kind of class analysis which attempts to unlock their ideological baggage with the key of their master concept—equality. (In passing it is interesting to note that even in these early works Baudrillard eschews the categories of classical Marxist sociological theory—simultaneously attempting to preserve their critical tenor while replacing their conceptual framework. In the present case this involves the analysis of power based on a semiological discrimination, rather than on economic domination or exploitation.) The "society of abundance," so popular a few years ago among the prophets of growth, is exposed as a compromise between democratic egalitarianism and the social imperative of privilege and discrimination. What these (extinct) prophets of growth failed to see, according to Baudrillard, was that even if growth absorbed poverty, discrimination would not cease to exist. What Galbraith and the others failed to see was the fact that the problem ceasing to exist was itself a problem. For at the level of the object and the discourses which surround it, discrimination still occurs where obvious poverty has been eliminated; it is no longer economic, but semiological. Those unable to possess, or dispossessed of, the latest object of fashion, the authentic bygone object, or the other indices of privilege—the signs of Veblen's "invidious distinction"—live in an "immediate past," in an indifferent and timeless world that is neither truly ancient nor contemporary, a world that is not their own but a simulation of last year's fashions—"a time that is the equivalent to space in the suburbs."[34] The discrimination extends infinitely to any value produced so long as it possesses a correlative need (miraculously recognized by desire!). At work here is the Veblen-effect; it states that the most expensive and the rarest commodities will be purchased exactly because of, rather than despite, their cost and rarity. In the effort to achieve (invidious) distinction the progressive flight of value can be traced—having arrived at the level of the object in its journey from blood, rank, and titles, it then goes on to seek new rarities: air, water, space, and greenery, and ultimately ends up at even more subtle and abstract indices of privilege: work, education, and culture, for "*knowledge and power are the rarest goods.*" Progress in capitalist societies is the progressive transformation of all natural and concrete values to productive forms for economic profit and social distinction.[35]

The attempt to provide a comprehensive and rational model of systems of thought and the transformations of cultural forms places Baudrillard in the tradition of the Enlightenment; and the critical tenor of his writings place them in the line of the non-Marxist radical tradition of French socialism. There is, however, a very clear purpose in these early works (*For a Critique of the Political Economy of the Sign* and *The Mirror of Production*) to integrate such insights into a Marxist problematic. That he ultimately finds this impossible to do—and we shall see the reasons why—should not prevent us from recognizing Baudrillard's debt to Marxist critical sociology. In *For a Critique* Baudrillard seeks to place his analyses of consumption and the object into a project outlined by Lukács, who thought that "(T)he problem of commodities must not be considered in isolation . . . but as the central, structural problem in capitalist society in all its aspects. Only in this case can the structure of commodity relations be made to yield a model of all objective forms of bourgeois society, together with all subjective forms corresponding with them."[36] *For a Critique* attempts to demonstrate that the structure of the commodity, and the phenomenology that it engenders in late capitalism, is precisely homologous to the structure and lived reality of the sign; that the entire realm of commodity relations referred to by Marx and Lukács constitutes the political economy of the sign, thus addending the Marxist moment—when the object as commodity becomes the general form—with a later moment when this form mutates to a new level of abstraction as sign.

Marxist in intent—insofar as Marx promoted the critique of political economy—Baudrillard's analysis of the sign is something more than visiting a semiological method on Marx's commodity. In the same way that Marx's critique of political economy produced his own radical version of it, so too Baudrillard's critique of semio-linguistics produces his own critical version of it in the form of a critical semiology. The analogy is certainly plain to see—semio-linguistics is to the latter as political economy was to the former. Both, in their noncritical modes, are positivisms of a sort, both make claims to have isolated the laws, structures, and behaviors of their respective systems; political economy by sticking to the facts of supply/demand, labor/exchange; semio-linguistics (and structuralism) by its mechanical manipulation of the terms of the analysis and thus "autonomizing and reifying partial systems"[37] and avoiding meaningful contextualizations in a purely relativistic exercise. They are both psychologistic. But as Levin points out, as early as *Le Système des objets* Baudrillard was aware of structuralism as an accomplice—as the "mode of the imaginary"—corresponding with the stage of the system's technological development: "One can make out in it aspects, or perhaps structures, of an animist imaginary, followed by an energist imaginary. Will it be necessary to study the structures of a cyberneticist imaginary whose focal myth will no longer be that of an absolute functionalism, but of an absolute interrelationality of the world."[38]

It is, of course, precisely this interrelationality which characterizes Lévi-Strauss's epistemological model based on the structures of mind, kinship systems, and language:

> Every culture can be considered as an ensemble of symbolic systems on the first level of which are placed language, the rules of marriage, economic relations, art, science, and religion. All of these systems aim at expressing certain aspects of social reality, and more, the relations which these two types of reality maintain between themselves and the others.[39]

So Baudrillard's debt to Lévi-Strauss is ambiguous. We can see that Baudrillard's reading of the symbolic is radically different to Lévi-Strauss's, a rejection of the functionalism implicit in the latter's "model of reciprocity." Yet such a model is not without a use value to Baudrillard since it is consignable to the world of homogeneity as the "cybernetic imaginary." And while the aim might be to erode the centerless web of structures, the model which is nonetheless employed for the communication network of the system of consumption is based on kinship systems: "The circulation, purchase, sale, and appropriation of goods and differentiated signs constitutes today our language, our code by which the entire society *communicates* and speaks to itself."[40] It is, however, a language with a difference: at the conclusion to *Le Système des objets* Baudrillard argues that the discourse of objects is like a language, but only in the sense that a dictionary contains the possibility of speech but is radically other than speech. For the "immense paradigm lacks a syntax," it is an impoverished language—"a lexicon that covers walls and haunts consciousness"—but one that nevertheless has the efficacy of a code, as "a scale of distinctive criteria more or less arbitrarily indexed to a scale of stereotyped personalities."[41] From code to language to speech, the theoretical object of the discourse assumes ever wider statutory powers to assure its adequacy, an adequacy that is vigorously defended. What is instituted by consumption is an esperanto of signs, a universal impoverishment of language as *parole,* and the tentacular and spectacular spread of this esperanto is so complete that its counter-discourse—critique—is totally recuperated to the extent that "only the two versions together constitute the myth." Baudrillard gains enormous mileage from this methodological trope: the work of denunciation, be it the discourses on alienation, the exposures of the mechanisms of the sign, the derision of pop and anti-art are themselves, as he puts it baroquely, part of the mythic labor which "plays the counter-chant in the formal liturgy of the object."

> Just as the society of the middle ages equilibrated itself on God AND the Devil, so ours equilibrates itself on consumption AND its denunciation. And whereas heresies and sects of black magic were organized around the Devil, our own magic is white, for heresy is no longer possible in abundance. This is the prophylactic whiteness of a saturated society, of a society without vertigo or history, without any other myth than itself.[42]

Here is reached, at the close of *La Société de consommation,* an *aporia,* a limit condition of critical discourse where the critique itself is implicated as the accomplice of the object of criticism. For even to criticize the positive and negative versions of a discourse as twin mythologies only relocates the critique while at the same time maintaining the centrality of the object as well as a critical distance from it. In this way demystification itself is furnished with its own mythological status as a structural component of an entire system of thought. But apart from the phenomenological skepticism, a passage such as this demonstrates a poetic process at work: a work of allusion and connotation in which the textual fabric is overlocked with the stitch of reference that draws on and draws together a multitude of sources. It is a form of writing that cannot, according to its own logic, be critical; but it nonetheless takes the form of criticism as a literary genre akin to poetry. It resonates with the traditions of writing in which it is embedded, from which we might single out Adorno and his critique of the culture industry, its ideological categories of needs and equivalence in enlightened rationality, and his critique of cultural criticism;[43] or Georges Bataille's heterological sociology and its category of the general economy—composed of its homogeneous (ideological) and heterological (transgressive, critical) moments;[44] or the reference to Robert Jaulin's anthropological critique of the West's totalization of cultures in *La Paix blanche*.[45] The ultimate critical reference is, of course, Marx's. A dialectical transformation of the concepts at hand? Perhaps, but only up to the point of the disappearance of modes of critical thought; in truth Baudrillard is impassioned by the disappearance of the great categories of sociophilosophical thought, and exhibits something like and more than that condition of incredulity which Lyotard identified as postmodern.[46] In this respect he seems to owe a debt to the Frankfurt school—acknowledged in the essay "Sur le nihilisme."[47] In musing over the "mode of disappearance" (and touching at the same time on a theme addressed by Paul Virilio)[48] of the "real," "history," the "social," "meaning," and so on, as the obsession of the nihilist, Baudrillard detects traces of this radicality in Benjamin and Adorno—mingled with whiffs of nostalgia for the dialectic and with a melancholy for its lost systems.[49] In this essay it is argued that just as in the nineteenth century "appearances" were destroyed for the benefit of "meaning," now the situation is reversed: meaning disappears under the weight of its own profundity and saturation to be replaced by appearances which (surprise!) were never really destroyed. And in this we discover another methodological trope that is regularly employed: when something is everywhere, it is nowhere—what we might term as the Baudrillardian doctrine of immanent reversibility. (It is perhaps what Lyotard refers to as the "theatricality" of the sign, the game of hide-and-seek played by the signifier, the referent, and the meaning.)[50]

To return to the object and its analysis, in *For a Critique* Baudrillard attempts to disentangle the various significations of the object that render it such a difficult category for analysis by arguing that, despite its various significations, the object in its social operation assumes a singular ontology, an ontology dependent upon its social operation. Thus we never "possess" a "tool" (for example), for the social operation of the tool is in use, not in possession. Likewise, the object tool in its economic expression, "commodity," the object of economic exchange, is a commutable value, but not commutable with use value, but only with other exchange values. But the sign-object is the object of a "sign-exchange" whose operation is based on the differential values established in a semiological system, or code, which autonomously affixes individuals on a register of status ("This scale is properly the social order").[51] It is argued that the sign-object is a kind of mutation and fusion of two practices, economic exchange and symbolic exchange. The object of symbolic exchange is neither a use nor an exchange value, but the unique expression of a relationship whose model is the gift which, of course, can be relatively arbitrary. But this is the paradox of the gift: while it is arbitrary, once *given* its meaning is a specific, and no other, relationship. Unlike the symbolic object, which signifies absence and presence according to a logic of lack and desire, the sign-object signifies precisely the absence of any relationship at all. It signifies rather a reified relationship incarnate in the sign between people and the index of social status based on an ever-commutable and exchangeable code.

What has to happen here is for the sign-object to simultaneously disengage itself from the commodity as the new form corresponding to the general phase of socioeconomic formation while at the same time preserving the political-economic relations of power inherited from an earlier phase, namely exchange relations of capital. The sign-object must also disengage itself from the *obligation* that inheres in the archaic sign, its attachment to a more or less fixed hierarchical social order. (This means that the revolution of the sign in overturning the etiquette of feudal symbology is, like the revolution of the commodity, a paradoxical phenomenon: progressive in the sense that it smashes a ruthless and powerful order of signification, reactionary in that it ushers in a new, but no less discriminatory, structure of commutable values. "Fashion" is the paradigmatic form of this new structure.)[52] In the first instance, the disengagement is accomplished by a critique of use value as the referent alibi, of use value as the signified and the epistemological guarantee of exchange value. The aim here is to demonstrate that an economic rationality which is based on the unproblematic relationship between the commodity and its use value is simply a fantasy and what is more, a fantasy which is inherited by Marx in his critique of political economy. Released from its function of satisfying real needs, the commodity assumes its place in the generalized system of commutable signs. Even the arch-commodity, money, has become one sign among many in this extended scenario.

It may be worthwhile to recall Marx's reading of capitalist exchange here: exchange value is an equivalence between two commodities on the basis of a third value, typically money (famously expressed in the formulas M-C-M and C-M-C). While these exchanges are always based on an ideal equivalence, Marx detected a contradiction in the way that the value of the commodity labor power was established. Put simply, it was Marx's contention that there was a fraction of labor time that was systematically withheld in the equation that fixed the value of labor power, and that this fraction was translated into surplus value at the point when the commodity entered the system of consumption. It was through this mechanism, this variability of the cost of labor power against the value it realized in exchange, that capital exploited, for the benefit of an entire class, the surplus value that was derived from an unaccounted-for surplus labor power (in the medium of time). The governing principle at work in the system is the extension and universalization of exchange value, such that labor, in its definition as capital and as the supreme commodity, is itself reduced to the reified, abstract relations of commodity exchange. The emancipation of the individual (capital) from the feudal obligation of serfdom thus involves a recognition of an identity between exchange value and freedom. This freedom to exchange one's labor is transformed into an obligation to enter and remain prisoner of the system of exchange value, which reduces labor to the status of commodity and the subject (who labors) to the status of an economic cipher: an empty place of value.[53]

It is not solely, however, the labor theory of value implicit in this analysis that Baudrillard wants to question (although he does formulate a critique of labor-as-essence in *The Mirror of Production*); rather he seeks to extend the Marxist critique of the labor/capital exchange process to an area that had formerly escaped the purview of political economy, namely, use value, a sphere that Marx himself had declared "outside the sphere of investigation of political economy."[54] "To define the notion of commodity, it is not important to know its particular content and its exact destination. It suffices that before it is a commodity, in other words, the vehicle (support) of exchange value—the article must satisfy a given social need by possessing a corresponding useful property. That is all."[55] Use value is posited by Marx as an unproblematic sphere, characterized by Baudrillard as "beyond the market economy, money and exchange value, in the glorious autonomy of man's simple relation to his work and his products."[56] Marx thus stands accused of harboring an idealism which proposes use value as beyond history (though with its historically specific forms—this changes nothing) and beyond commodity fetishism, which is the fetishism of exchange value alone. Marx had failed to account for this entire realm of use value, which Baudrillard will discover to be a realm bound by its own equivalences and fetishes: of utility, functions, and needs.

What Baudrillard proposes in answer to this breach is a parallel critique of use value as an ideological guarantee of exchange value. Central to this critique is an analysis of the system of needs as the equivalent of abstract social labor (in the analysis of exchange value), on the basis that use value can likewise be fetished as a "systematic abstraction." It is the two spheres together, exchange value and use value, that will henceforth constitute the reunited object of commodity fetishism.[57] This proposal is supported by the claim that to be exchangeable products first have to be rationalized in terms of an equivalence of utility (and contrary to Marx's incomparability of use values) which is of the same origin as the "general abstract code of equivalence" that reigns over the equation labor power—exchange value. There is thus an equivalence of use values and needs, in which the preeminent category is the use value of labor power, production. This equivalence is given an anthropological dimension:

> There is a homology between the "emancipation" in the bourgeois era of the private individual given final form by his needs and the functional emancipation of objects as use values . . . henceforth secularized, functionalized and rationalized in purpose, objects become the promise of an ideal (and idealist) political economy, with its watchword "to each according to his needs."[58]

The discussion of the object and its liberation in the modern era starts to take shape in terms of the extended critique. As we can see, it is the concept of needs which plays the villain's role in the piece—dissimulated in the mask of a natural, satisfying anthropology. Far from being the objective and natural effect of the commodity system, (or any system for that matter), needs themselves are the product of a system that inscribes utility at the heart of the object and a productivist mentality in the individual—who is "nothing but the subject thought in economic terms, rethought, simplified and abstracted by the economy."[59]

When the enormous structures of political economy and semiology are posed as the homology: exchange value/use value to signifier/ signified; and political economy/critique of political economy to "discourse of communication"/"rational decoding and distinctive value," irresistible forces of attraction conflate the two material spheres of economic production and semiosis. What is required by Baudrillard is a magical thread to suture them. That thread is ideology—no longer considered in the light of an artificial distinction between base and superstructure, but as "*that very form* which traverses the production of signs and material production."[60]

> This partitioning of the object domain obscures even the simplest realities. If any progress is to be made at this point, "research"— especially Marxist research—must come to terms with the fact that nothing produced or exchanged today (objects, services, bodies, sex, culture, knowledge, etc.) can be decoded exclusively as a sign, nor solely measured as a commodity; that everything appears in the context of a general political economy . . . the object of political economy is quite simply the *object,* the object form, on which use value, exchange value and sign value converge in a complex mode that describes the most general form of political economy.[61]

But before this new super-object (we can recall the object and its discourse from the critique of consumer rationality) can emerge from the profane liaison of the sign and commodity, the sign itself must be exposed as deeply implicated in the logic of political economy. Here the analysis of the sign focuses on a critique of the arbitrary relationship between the signifier and signified and between the sign and referent as explained in Ferdinand de Saussure's semiology.[62] For Baudrillard the arbitrary character of the system is not to be found in the commonplace that signifieds are arbitrarily affixed to signifiers, as Saussure might argue, but rather "arbitrariness arises from the fundamental institution of an exact correlation between a given 'discrete' signifier and an equally 'discrete' signified." Even if the structure is complicated by the existence of more than one signified for a given signifier—or vice versa—the principle of equivalence "which roots the arbitrariness of the sign" remains intact, and is merely transformed to an equally arbitrary polyvalence. (The principle of ambivalence, however, is reserved in Baudrillard's hierarchy of representational practices for the category of symbolic exchange, which should be understood in part, as "transgression.")[63] Emile Benveniste, in his critique of Saussure, locates the arbitrariness of the sign between the sign and its phenomenal referent—which means that arbitrariness is removed from the logical intention of the linguistic sign.[64] To Baudrillard, both schemes are idealist and on a par with the proposition that use value has an objective, essential finality in the order of production.

> The scission (*coupure*) does not occur between a sign and a real referent. It occurs between the signifier as form and, on the other side, the signified and referent which together are registered as content—the one of thought, the other of reality . . . the referent in question is no more external to the sign than is the signified: indeed it is governed by the sign.[65]

Like use value, the function of the referent is to act as the guarantee—the content, alibi, and rationale for the respective systems which are structurally and logically weighted toward exchange value and the signifier. And just as the system of political economy requires some wizardry to unite subject and object, so too semiology requires something similar to unite the sign and reality, and it is our old friend "needs" in the guise of "motivation." But like the concept of needs, motivation describes nothing: "behind the formal opposition between two terms" (exchange value and use value, sign and referent) runs a "specular and tautological process between two modalities of the same form, via the *detour* of a self-proclaimed content."[66]

The practical consequence of this reductive homology is that the entire field of semio-linguistics is implicated in the extension of the commodity form to those formerly unalienable areas, as identified by Marx, of virtue, love, knowledge, and consciousness. Semiology thus naively colludes with political economy, but masks its complicity by claiming to be a scientific and objective discourse. And in an analogous manner to the formation of the myth of consumption (composed of the positive and negative versions) so too semiology is composed of its mechanical (Saussure, Benveniste, Eco, and early Barthes) and critical (Derrida, Kristeva, and *Tel Quel*) perspectives. The latter, who argue on behalf of the signified (the idealism of meaning) against the arbitrary chains of signifiers, only confirm that separation which establishes the logic of the sign by making "the 'real' the ideal alternative to the formal play of signs."[67] For Baudrillard, the radical critique of the political economy of the sign is to grasp it as *form* in the same way that Marx grasped the commodity as a form. The approaches are different to the extent that in order to get at the mysteries of the commodity Marx privileges one of the terms, use value, whereas for Baudrillard the privileged term, symbolic exchange, stands outside of the structural arrangement of the sign of exchange value.

In his introductory remarks translator Levin describes *For a Critique* as "literally a commotion of ideas, sometimes inconsistent, issuing from a period of intense critical activity in which nothing was resolved."[68] While it is true that there are aspects of this work which are perplexing, it is resolved in one important respect. In "For a General Theory," Baudrillard locates the critique of the commodity/sign form (generalized political economy) within an enlarged discursive field. The model is represented schematically:

$$\frac{\text{Economic Exchange Value}}{\text{Use Value}} = \frac{\text{Signifier}}{\text{Signified}} \left| \begin{array}{l} \text{Symbolic} \\ \text{Exchange}^{69} \end{array} \right.$$

The schema is the basis for a revolutionary anthropology which privileges the term beyond the (vertical) line of exclusion (as opposed to the horizontal lines on the left of the equation which are lines of structuration in the respective forms, commodity, and sign.) In a way the schema is remarkably familar, since when taken as a totality, it appears to be a reworking of Bataille's model of the general economy (composed of those homogeneous elements based on equivalence together with the heterogeneous elements—transgression, sacrifice, and death—which are unassimilable to the homogeneous sphere). In choosing to remain on the side of symbolic exchange, on the side of an idealized communication, Baudrillard repeats Bataille's impossible sociological gesture of arguing from the position of the excluded term; and in this way he links up with the tradition of heterological and anthropological thought. Indeed, this idea of a revolutionary anthropology underpins his analysis in the subsequent works, *Le Miroir de la production* and *L'Echange symbolique et la mort*.

The argument in *The Mirror of Production* is with the anthropological Marx and Marxist anthropology. Key concepts of historical materialism are questioned, particularly the preeminent category of production and all its axiomatic projections in Marxist epistemology. Baudrillard asks: "What is axiomatic about productive forces or about the dialectical genesis of modes of production from which springs all revolutionary theory? What is axiomatic about the generic richness of man who is labor power, about the motor of history, or about history itself, which is 'only the production by men of their material life' "?[70] In a provocative excursion through materialist and structuralist anthropology (Engels and Godelier) and epistemology (Marx and Althusser)

Baudrillard concludes: very little. By submitting their key concepts to a rigorous logic ("corrosive beyond measure" as one reviewer puts it)[71] he seeks to radically put into question claims to the universal application in the study of primitive, anterior, or even our own culture, of such concepts as survival, scarcity, production, necessity, and objective labor. Even the work of the unconscious dear to the Freudo-Marxists is questioned. The bar of exclusion works both ways (see figure above). If the whole structural system of value excludes symbolic exchange, then symbolic exchange is vigorously protected from any hint of instrumental reason or rationalist eschatology.[72] Although this is not the place to entertain the possible counter-defense that could emerge from Marxists, it is interesting to note a general silence which reigns in critical literature. Has Baudrillard, in his mole-like work, unearthed a point of strategic weakness in this body of theory, producing a Gödel theorem to the latter's mathematics? Or has he merely delivered a symbolic coup de grace to an exhausted body of theory?[73]

To return to the commodity/sign form. In spite of what becomes an increasingly hostile attitude to Marx, Baudrillard, in *The Mirror of Production* is still keen to explore his theories in relation to Marxist epistemology. Take, for example, his reading of the development of this new form against Marx's three phases of political economy.[74] Between phase 1 and phase 2 Marx identified the revolutionary process and progress of capital and the changed social structures that this entailed. However, between phase 2 and phase 3 he only foresaw an extension of the infrastructural changes of phase 2 taking place in the superstructure in phase 3. The result of this, according to Baudrillard, was that Marx failed to project the revolutionary changes between phase 1 to phase 2 on to the mutations between phase 2 to phase 3. To be fair to Marx, Baudrillard acknowledges that phase 3 was not fully developed in his own time:

> In Marx's projection this new phase of political economy . . . is immediately neutralized, drawn into the wake of phase II, in terms of the market and "mercantile venality." Even today the only "Marxist" critique of culture, consumption, of ideology, sex, etc. . . . is made in terms characteristic of phase II and though reaching their full value there can only serve as a *metaphorical reference* when transferred as a principle of analysis to phase III.[75]

The upshot of this analysis is that a revolution may have occurred "without our Marxists knowing it"—a formal revolution that replaces the form-commodity with the form-sign, that replaces the general law of equivalence ruled by exchange value with the reign of the sign and with the structural law of value.[76] Far from being a mere connotation of the commodity, the sign form institutes "an operational structure that lends itself to a structural manipulation compared with which the quantitative mystery of surplus value appears inoffensive."[77] Thus the critique of the generalized political economy is clearly rooted in an analysis of power, for what else can be inferred from the notion of "structural manipulation"? Structural manipulation might here be illustrated with what occurs in the progress of capitalism: when the competitive era of capital gives way to monopoly capitalism, the concepts that fueled its competition and struggles (between capital as well as between capital and labor), the very terms of political economy and its Marxist critique lose their references. Thus the era of false needs and "consumer engineering" is ushered in,[78] a new heroic struggle of the productive system to leave nothing unproduced for the satisfaction of needs freely chosen in the market—having been carefully insinuated there by the discourses of consumption and advertising. So too the heroic struggles of labor cease to be the terms of a dialectical process and become instead the referents of a system that administers them in homeopathic doses—so as to disguise their disappearance by means of simulating their operations. In an analysis of contemporary strikes (post-May 1968) Baudrillard identifies the unions themselves, and particularly their representative authorities as forces of dissuasion subverting the radical and maximalist demands of workers into the parameters of sane negotiation.[79] In this way, Baudrillard provides a political dimension to the crisis of representation.

To the phases of Marx's model of the development of the modes of capitalist production Baudrillard addends the "modes of signification"—a parodistic structure to be sure—under the sway in our own era of an omnipresent code which, perhaps not unsurprisingly, takes its reference from the model of DNA where all possible mutations and transformations are preinscribed as it were at the level of the code. If one of the helixes of this structure is Marx's model of stages, then its double is constituted by this model of the modes of signification. We are leaving the classical era of the sign where the signifier refers to a distinctive value in a vertical structure

$$\frac{\text{(Sg}}{\text{/Sd}}$$
$$\text{/Rft),}$$

leaving that era of the sign which corresponded to an early stage of capital when the commodity had a real referent—use value—and entering the next stage, the competitive era of signs: "the signified and referent are now abolished to the sole profit of the play of signifiers, of a generalized formulation in which the code no longer refers back to any subjective or objective "reality" but to its own logic."[80] This transformation from the "commodity law of value" to the "structural law of value" is a radical interpretation of Saussure's brief remarks in the *Course in General Linguistics* concerning the relationship of economic values (value-in-exchange) in economics to the exchange of meaning (signification) in linguistics.[81] The sign, in Baudrillard's schema, is liberated from any archaic obligation to designate anything at all—and "finally liberated for a structural game, or 'combinatory,' according to an indifference and total indetermination which succeeds the former rule of determined equivalence"[82] (a movement from the classical, to the functional, and ultimately to the structural stage of the sign). But with this structural transformation also comes the eclipse of the earlier analyses of the object and the critique of the political economy of the sign—because it is couched in the terms of a surpassed anterior discourse. The former critique is regarded, in *L'Echange symbolique et la mort,* as a pis aller (as something which had to do) and that was only really useful as an allusion. For what is in play is the progressive destruction of social relations ruled by value, which is a political phenomenon, and not at all economic. Political economy and the political economy of the sign cease to exist, yet lead a secondary existence, in simulation, as a "phantom principle of dissuasion."

[It's the] End of the dialectic of the signifier and signified which permitted the accumulation of knowledge and meaning, the linear syntagm of cumulative discourse. [It's the] Simultaneous end of use value and exchange value which alone allowed accumulation and social production. End of the linear dimension of discourse. End of the classical era of the sign. End of the era of production.[83]

The contention here is that the discourses and critiques of Marxism and semiology cease to have a truth referent in reality. If Baudrillard appears to destroy them, it is only in their existence as simulacra. When all references are shorn from the determinist and objectivist sciences, or from the dialectical visions of history and knowledge, then they themselves are reduced to the status of those bygone objects, declined in that past-perfect tense and sustained as alibis for the hyperreal sciences of the third order: genetics, cybernetics, and the aleatory mutations of the indeterminancy principle. And the subphilosophical literary genre of

Alfred Jarry finally comes of age: "Against a hyper-realist system, the only strategy is pataphysical, a sort of 'science of imaginary solutions' which is to say a science-fiction of returning the system against itself to the extreme limit of simulation, of a reversible simulation in a hyper-logic of destruction and death."[84]

5 LYOTARD AND THE JOUISSANCE OF PRACTICAL REASON

*The enemy and accomplice of writing, its Big Brother (or rather its O'Brien), is language (*langue*), by which I mean not only the mother tongue, but the entire heritage of words, of the feats and works of what is called the literary culture. One writes against language, but necessarily with it. To say what it already knows how to say is not writing. One wants to say what it does not know how to say, and what it should be able to say. One violates it, one seduces it, one introduces into it an idiom which it had not known. But when that same desire to be able to say something other than what has been already said—has disappeared, and when language is experienced as impenetrable and inert rendering vain all writing, then it is called Newspeak.—Jean-François Lyotard,* Le Postmoderne expliqué aux enfants

The struggle against totalitarianism—against totalitarianisms—has taken and takes many forms. The forms of this resistance are contingent upon the techniques and forces deployed by the despotic organizations, the big brothers. As political totalitarianism gives way to complex new forms—technoscientific, commercial, and linguisitic dominance of modes of life and everyday life—so new means of combating them must be invented and thought. For Jean-François Lyotard they are conditions that preclude a recourse to common sense and everyday language,[1] since the events of the twentieth century, for which Auschwitz and Hiroshima stand out as horrifying beacons, have done something more than delay the progress of emancipation set in train by the Enlightenment: they have clouded its very ideals. For Lyotard it is not a case of abandoning the project of modernism—which is the charge leveled by Habermas against him[2]—but of the project having been liquidated by such events. The postmodern (or postmodernity) is instituted and initiated by a new species of historical crime, that of "populocide."[3]

Lyotard is, therefore, skeptical and resistant toward simplifications and "simplifying slogans," resistant too toward the call and desire for "the restoration of sure values,"[4] by which he means the call to renew the project of modernism (*le project moderne*). Slogans and simplifications are the product of doctrine and the doctrinaire mind which is incapable, and unwilling, to accept the singularity of the event which irrupts into the order of "fixed meaning." And yet the experience of art and writing in modernism is anti-doctrinal, and, for Lyotard, has borne witness to the irruption of meaning, to the irruption of the event, no matter how lowly or earth-shattering. Thus Lyotard affirms writing which, like Winston Smith's journal, bears witness to the infamy of bureaucratic Newspeak; he affirms that we must be "guerrillas of love" against the code of feelings: "The labor of writing is akin to the work of love, since it inscribes the trace of an initiatory event in language, and thus offers to share it—and if not a share of knowledge, then a share of the feeling which it can and must hold as communal."[5]

By way of introduction to this chapter, let us say that the problematic of writing is by no means surpassed in Lyotard's theoretical propositions, and occupies a central, even meta-critical position in his oeuvre (his Text). It is a position that might be described as an aesthetic which, in correlating the practices of art and writing as resistance, defines his postmodernism as a direct continuation of the radical hypotheses of modernism.[6] The purpose of this chapter is threefold; to contextualize Lyotard's discourse on the postmodern; to place Lyotard's thought in relation to the tradition of discourse that we have examined thus far in this book, and particularly in relation to the transgressive text; and to specify, via the analysis of a particular text, Lyotard's relationship to the thought of Jean Baudrillard. In the opening chapter use was made of Lyotard's well-known and often repeated discussion of the crisis of the meta-narratives[7] in order to initiate a discourse on the fate of history in the post-Hegelian era in French theory. Against this historical horizon of crisis several themes have been outlined. In the interest of a certain reciprocity, it is now necessary to return to that crisis and to place it in the context of Lyotard's own theoretical development.

Such a contextualization will, perforce, demonstrate both deep continuities within Lyotard's work, and equally, in the most recent texts,[8] the tendency toward a style that results in an aphoristic discontinuity reminiscent of Nietzsche's writings. The rapid dissemination of Lyotard's later texts in English also provides a historical contingency; since his interventions are being recognized on questions concerning postmodernism, desire theory, language theory, and post-Marxism—including an exchange with the Habermasian version of critical theory.[9] (This exchange itself attests to the condition of transnationalization of contemporary theoretical discourse.)

In light of this complex field of debate, the aim of this present chapter is not to engage in a close analysis of the positions which have been ranged for and against the work of Lyotard in English language criticism. The reader familiar with the reception of Lyotard's work (and the reception of French post-structuralism generally) will be aware that some of the finest theoretical minds in the anglophone world have turned their pens and energy to the critical examination of these texts. Some of this response and reaction is extremely provocative and significant in its own right; postmodernism is the object of a fairly intense contestation, and sometimes the locus for the desire for revenge, vilification, and vindication.[10] The confession here is that, while a comparative analysis of the relative merits of competing epistemological systems is an important continuing project, its appearance here would be premature, and in a sense dangerous, even vaguely pompous. Rather my aim is to continue the narration of the heterodoxical tradition of French thought, this cartography of a ruptured and abyssal territory.

We have, throughout this work, noted certain features of the landscape and the tracks connecting them; these features would be those writers and theorists, the "thinking heads" and intellectual capitals invested in the conceptual labor of producing new figures, of discourse, for which the gift economy, transgression, the general economy, and symbolic exchange serve as representatives. These figures have been discussed in the context of several themes—the anthropological critique, the theories of writing (écriture), and the theories of representation. In addition to an examination of Lyotard's crisis with the metanarratives, the desire now is to situate his thought without fixing it within this ensemble, in order to grant it a measure of free play.

Bataille's thought provides a context for this situation. When Foucault imagined a new era of transgression he suggested that its hopeful beginnings were readable in the "calcinated roots" of Bataille's thought. Transgression, and the thought for which it was a rhetorical figure, would ultimately come to replace the dialectical thought of contradiction. Transgression is the game of limits: a play at the conventional frames of language, at the border of disciplines, and across the line of taboo; in writing, transgression involves the sacrifice of signs, for Bataille a potlatch of the genres of writing and the forms of authorial sovereignty. Bataille wrote, "*il faut le système Et il faut l'excés,*"[11] in an expressive formula which indicates the line of taboo which the transgression seeks to cross and then to recross. Transgression maintains the taboo, since without it it would lose its fundamental violence. A society without taboos would be outside human society. And the taboo also maintains transgression, since the concept of a limit, such as a taboo, is only possible on the condition of its infringement: an unpassable limit would require no social constraint to prevent its crossing. Transgression is very close, therefore, to the figure of the Aufhebung, in which the contradiction which is surpassed is sublated as a trace and readable in the new structural arrangement of the dialectic. There is an irony in Foucault's prediction.

It is hardly a large conceptual leap to suggest that what Lyotard calls "impiety" can be related to the "method of obstinacy" described by Klossowski apropos Bataille, and that Lyotard's attempts to subvert and to intervene in the systems of thought, theoretical discourse, and belief systems owe something to the example of Bataille.[12] Now if Bataille, in following the example of Nietzsche and de Sade, exulted in the profanation of religious beliefs and bourgeois morality, even if this was to remain ultimately religious, then it might be said that Lyotard's transgression is directed at that sphere which is held to be an heir of religion: political faith. Perhaps in this sense Lyotard's text remains political.

In the preceding chapter we noted the outlines of Baudrillard's vehement anti-productivism. In a sense, Lyotard's thought might be opposed to Baudrillard's as a nonpositive affirmation of the productive system. It is important to be clear about this, since when they are lumped together under the rubric of postmodernism (see Guattari, "The Postmodern Dead End"),[13] a level of violence is delivered to their texts. Whilst linked at a thematic level, in terms of a "critique" of criticism (and in this way post-Marxist), the texts of the two writers, particularly those produced in the 1970s, are, nonetheless, opposed in several respects. The most important of these is over this question of production, expressible in terms of a contest between the concept of "symbolic exchange" and the "analytic of desire" employed by Lyotard under the title of the "libidinal economy." But before we turn to this arena, let us first examine the context of Lyotard's development as a theorist.

Trained as a philosopher, Lyotard published his first book, *Phénomenologie* in 1954; it was not until 1971 that he published his next book, *Discours, figure,* being a version of his *doctorat d'état* on the subject of psychoanalysis and art. Since 1971 a very large number of books have been published over a spectrum of theoretical concerns: art theory, psychoanalysis, philosophy, and political and social theory. A glance at the bibliography explains something here; in the seventeen years separating the first two books Lyotard's output is in the form of journal articles which are largely concerned with the Algerian struggle for independence from colonial rule, (predominantly published in the review *Socialisme ou barbarie*); there are also several critical pieces in *L'Art vivant,* passing reference to Marxist and psychoanalytic theory, and a critique of Lévi-Straussian structuralism ("The Indians don't cook flowers").[14] But what seems to dominate in this period is the connection with *Socialisme ou barbarie,* a militant Trotskyist tendency which represented, along with other splinter groups, a tradition of non-PCF Marxism and socialism in France. The group was committed to militancy and to workers' power, committed thus to theoretical practice defined as praxis philosophy. Lyotard wrote in this period, in a deeply productivist formula: "Man is the work of his works."[15]

In this context we can assert that the incredulity which Lyotard expresses toward the narrative of Marx, the emancipation of the subject of history, and the historical accomplishment of socialism, was by no means so sublime as *The Postmodern Condition* might suggest. After two decades of praxis philosophy, Lyotard had, in a manner, lost his belief in the revolutionary program represented by *Socialisme ou barbarie.* Why?

This is a complex question, since in part we must consider Lyotard's militancy against the background of a countervailing tendency toward Nietzsche which had taken hold in contemporary philosophy—in the work of Foucault and Klossowski, but perhaps above all, in the work of Deleuze.[16] But as Lyotard himself avers, he is not above fashion; he is a philosopher *dans le vent:* phenomenology, praxis philosophy, Nietzscheanism, postmodernism, language games, desire theory—Lyotard is an opportunist, in a way a *promiscuous* thinker.

Vincent Descombes, in *Modern French Philosophy,* argues that the militant Lyotard had availed himself of revolutionary theory that recounted the story of the contradiction of the mode of production; a contradiction which would lead either to war (or generalized fascism) or—through the mobilization of a latent revolutionary potential at the point of capital's crisis—to socialism. But, according to Descombes,[17] Lyotard made two discoveries: first, that the truth which he thought himself to be speaking was in fact "no more than a moral ideal. . . . It was therefore not *the truth* at all, but only the expression of a *desire for truth.*"[18] Second, that this collapse of the truth referent of revolutionary Marxism was not the result of a movement in a philosophical game, but rather the result of an analysis of concrete historical conditions.

These discoveries can, however, still be generally related to the critique of Soviet state socialism generated by the *Socialisme ou barbarie* group.[19] The major thrust of their analysis developed from a perception that the character of Stalinism was counterrevolutionary because it subverted the Bolshevik ideal of world socialism. Therefore, it followed that the Communist parties in the West which followed the Moscow line participated in the travesty. The perception was itself grounded in Cornelius Castoriadis's critical analysis of the mode of production in the putatively socialist economy of the USSR.[20] In a complex argument Castoriadis claimed to demonstrate that this socialist state, which acted as a concrete reference for socialists throughout the world, was in fact involved in a betrayal. Far from following Marx's formulae for the equitable redistribution of the surplus, the state was, in effect, still involved in the construction of new forms of exploitation and domination in the sphere of political economy. The mechanism, and beneficiary, of this domination was, of course, the Stalinist bureaucracy. In Lyotard's terms this organization incanted the narrative of emancipation while at the same time setting itself above the terms which it narrated, above the worker-citizens, above the idea of the people from which it drew its legitimation. Alas, was Althusser tragically correct in asserting the existence of ideology in socialism? This narrative of emancipation was ruthlessly enforced by a paranoiac organization which could brook no counter-chant, no counter-narrative. The evidence of this, for Lyotard, was the historical suppression of what he had come to consider as a vital sphere of liberationist thought: art and literature.

For the disenchanted militant who had regarded theoretical practice as an important source of the critique of capitalist totality, it was an intolerable and hypocritical situation. For Lyotard it revealed a pious morality which inherited the Stalinist condemnation of art and literature as elitist practices. It was a morality which authorized a search for the *salvation* and a *revenge* on the guilty. In this sense, the morality of militant Marxism began to represent, for Lyotard, a thoroughly messianic religious metaphor. And as though this was not a bitter enough pill to swallow, it had to be washed down by the experience of the events of May 1968. These events, to a certain way of thinking, demonstrated the near-total failure of the organized militant left to participate in the ludic insurrection of the May Days. These organizations had failed to anticipate the sectors of contemporary society from which the rebellious urge would spring, and were unprepared for the sceno-dramatic effects of the critique of the spectacle. The situationists had been altogether closer to the mark. All in all, it was a very bad month for theoretical practice.

In 1964 Lyotard had split with *Socialisme ou barbarie* on questions of theory and practice. This break, combined with a similar break from Freudian psychoanalysis, conspired to set Lyotard adrift, hence the title of the collection of essays of 1973: *Dérive à partir de Marx et Freud* ("Adrift from Marx and Freud").[21] In this work Lyotard attempts to specify his relationship to the central practice and methodology of Marxist theory: the critique. Lyotard writes: "If reason, which has been handed over to the air-conditioned totalitarianism of the very disputatious end of this century, is not to be relied upon, then its great tool, its very mainspring, its provision of infinite progress, its fertile negativity, its pains and toiling i.e. critique—should not be given any credit either."[22] Reason, critique, power—they are all one to Lyotard. To criticize is to know better—but this critical relationship can only operate in the sphere of knowledge, and hence in the sphere of power. We have come across this critical crisis before, though not in identical terms, in the theory of the heterogeneous as expounded by Bataille. His mystical expérience of thinking and exceeding thought at the same time, lurching at the edge of the abyss of *unreason* by activating the heterogeneous elements, stands outside the critical relation. The rejection of the critical relation is also found in Baudrillard's critique of the critical mirror—the reflection of capital in Marxism as the formal accomplishment of identity in the thought of production.

When the name Lyotard becomes hitched up to an idea and an entire problematic of the postmodern (a term which avoids the specificity of postmoder*nity* or postmodern*ism*), it becomes possible to suggest that the "crisis of the meta-narratives" can be read as a narration of Lyotard's own crisis with the meta-narratives of Freud and Marx, and a type of loss of political faith. The major text on postmodernism, *The Postmodern Condition,* is in many ways atypical in relation to Lyotard's other works. Published under commission from the Council of Universities of Quebec in 1979, and subtitled "Report on Knowledge,"[23] the work is a sustained analysis, among other things, of the conditions of the legitimation of knowledge in contemporary science, a discourse thus following in the wake of the new physics, and indeterminacy. This analysis focuses, and even exaggerates, the relationship between the narrative and knowledge, and Lyotard devotes much energy to the analysis of the pragmatics of speech acts, since it is within their structure that conditions of authority of modern science is to be found in the philosophical meta-narratives such as Kant's transcendental idea of freedom and the potential perfectability of the rational, purposive subject of the enlightenment, or in Hegel's culmination of world history, and Marx's inversion of the same. The legitimacy of science is thus based on the deferred idea of the "promised community."[24] Perhaps above all others, it is this narrative of the promised community, which "remains beyond reach like an horizon," which is fractured and liquidated by the irruption of the event—for which Auschwitz serves as such a potent sign. "Reason" in the service of the idea of humanity, in the service of its achievable end through history, stands crossed and double-crossed at the threshold of *post-history* by the signs of its historical failure. Lyotard writes:

> The enthusiasm aroused by the French Revolution represented for Kant an eminent example of the unforeseen opportunities which such an event can grant us. In it he discovered the "historical sign" of a moral disposition in humanity, and the index of a progress towards an ultimate goal for the species. If our feelings are not the same as Kant's it is because we are confronted by a multiplicity of historical signs—in which the names of Auschwitz and Kolyma, Budapest 1956 and such as it is, May 68, are evoked in their heterogeneity—each emphasizing in their way the dispersion of ends and the decline of Ideas established in the Enlightenment.[25]

The critique of "semiological reason" thus rejects the positivities of science and the enlightenment ushered in by Kant's thought, and stands, before the collapse of their ideas, in the condition of incredulity. One is in the postmodern if and when one is incredulous; to be reductive, to be incredulous is the condition of the postmodernist.

Lyotard got it drifting—from philosophy to militancy into art via psychoanalysis, back through Wittgenstein on his way to the Greeks, ethics, and paganism. Lyotard revels in a heterogeneous experience of knowledge—leading him to privilege the little narrative which proliferate in the space of the fallen idols, in the demise of transhistorical and transcendental values. Thus also a Nietzscheanism which reaches quite a fervor:

Here is a course of action: harden, worsen and accelerate decadence. Adopt the perspective of active nihilism, exceed the mere recognition—be it depressive or admiring—of the destruction of all values. Become more and more incredulous. Push decadence further still and accept, for instance, to destroy the belief in truth under all its forms.[26]

The situationist, Raoul Vaneigem, in *The Revolution of Everyday Life*, repeats Nietzsche's description·of the difference between active and passive nihilism. The passive nihilist believes simply in nothing, and passive nihilism is an overture to conformism. On the other hand, the active nihilist "criticises the causes of disintegration by speeding up the process. *Active nihilism is pre-revolutionary: passive nihilism is counter-revolutionary*. And most people waltz tragi-comically between the two."[27] Lyotard would, in this sense, have to be classified as a pre-revolutionary thinker.

The game of drifting, however, dissimulated certain intensities in Lyotard's text—up to the point of their violent eruption in the work of 1974, *Economie libidinale*, a work which Lyotard later describes as a "scandal" and "devoid" of dialectics in the Aristotlean sense of the term, "because it is all rhetoric, working entirely at the level of persuasion."[28]

A difficult and refractory text, *Economie libidinale* nonetheless represents a crucial text to the unfolding of Lyotard's own narrative. (The relative absence of reference to this work in English-speaking discourse is understandable and regrettable; taken as a whole it is an enormous work and written in a highly idiomatic style, and thus not easily rendered into English. It is, if you like, a Deleuzian text in the sense of being schizophrenic and nonnegotiable in a poetic way: the reader is left little room to move except in the direction of the flow. What it lacks in the clarity of its outcome is replaced by the intensity of its expression, its irrepressible antagonism and agonism.[29]) Lyotard does allow, however, that the work can be taken as a series of theses whilst admitting their inconsistency, eschewing the manipulation of the reader in the Platonic dialogue. These would rather be the ends of reason, making sense at the expense of experience, in the sense of expérience, in this instance in the name of the *intense* sign read at the surface of the social, *la grande pellicule*.[30] (*Pellicule* read here in both its senses: as a membrane capable of transferring here and obstructing there the flows and investments of a *desire* which is of the order of production, the libidinal economy; and as a photographic film surface, a screen or gel, a thick holographic plate capable of registering the multiple traces of this movement of desire as a *phantasm*.)[31]

What we have here, in the framework of a polemic and contestation is a fusion of a Freudian theory of drives with a Marxist political economy—applied as an "analytic of desire," a deconstruction of the intense sign lodged in the text of desire, or the desiring text. What I would now like to do is to present, to re-present, an example of this operation—bearing in mind Lyotard's own caution in terms of the articulation of theses. While the libidinal economy is primarily concerned with texts, both as a theory of writing and as an analytic of texts, it can also be applied to any psychic apparatus, be it a written text or a work of art. In this respect, the libidinal economy has an aesthetic dimension, since it evolved in Lyotard's thought (writing) in relation to his early studies of psychoanalysis and art.[32]

Before we turn to the analysis of Marx's text in the *Economie libidinale*—chosen for its thematic and methodological content—we need to turn briefly to Freud's general theory of the libido, which he characterizes as the sexual drive. This meaning, as the sexual drive, is always present in Freud both in the noun and the adjectival "libidinal." However, there is a second sense expressed by the difference and *différance* of the terms libido and *libidinal relations*. For the child, as Freud tells us in *Group Psychology and the Analysis of the Ego*,[33] the sexual drive is initially directed at one or the other parent. When eventually it becomes obvious to the child that this drive will lead nowhere, because it transgresses that fundamental prohibition and the symbolic code of the father, then the child will produce affection instead. "Libidinal" thus refers to the affection which is produced in the inhibition of the sexual instincts. This theory is, however, more interesting in terms of its dysfunctional aspects, in terms of a theory of perversion in which the abnormal arrangement is one in which sexual attraction is expressed for those who are despised, while affection is reserved for those who are (merely) respected. This dysfunctional sense of the libidinal is, as I presently argue, of some consequence for Lyotard. In the same text, Freud remarks on the lack of criticism which is directed toward the loved one, and which he calls *idealization*.[34] This is particularly developed in terms of the psychoanalysis of the leader: the affection which the members of a group express toward a leader, and the feelings the leader has toward her or himself (the narcissistic type) or, more rarely, the feelings of the leader for the group (Jesus), are all likewise libidinal.

Therefore, when the analytic of desire is applied to the Text of Marx, we can see that for the militant Lyotard there will be powerful effects to witness, particularly in terms of the dysfunctional psychoanalytic arrangement of libidinal relations. But we must not stop here without an idea of what animates the model, of what gives it a pretension to the economic. This is another Freudian motion found in the later theory of drives in the "Metapsychological Essays."[35] For Lyotard these works, which introduced the death-drive and the Nirvana principle, permitted Freud's theory of a libido "to escape from thermodynamism and mechanism": his theory of the unconscious would avoid closing in on itself as a theoretical system. The Nirvana principle remained an expression of the undecidability of the dualism of the principle of life and the principle of death. "Freud brilliantly said that the death drive works silently in the rumor of Eros."[36]

Once again, in order to grasp Lyotard's understanding of an economic psychic function, we need to refer to his work on psychoanalysis and art—which will demonstrate the way in which he plays the later Freud against the young Freud in the grip of the representational model. From this analysis will arise the replacement of the metaphor by the metonym, which is a legacy of the Saussurian theory of communication. The sign becomes, in Lyotard's analysis, a metonym of substitution, rather than a screen on which the subjective reference is simulated and dissimulated, and for which the sign serves as a substitute. This is very close to the way that Lyotard conceives exchange in the discourse of political economy; signification is deferred, interminable, "meaning is never present in flesh and blood"—so that even the materiality of the sign is insignificant and not valuable in itself. Lyotard calls this process dematerialization and relates it to Adorno's work on serialism. Material in serialism is not valuable in itself, but in the relationship of one term to the next. The rejection of the Port-Royal semiology—a "Platonism of the theory of ideas"—is thus related to the privilege of the libidinal relations and libidinal economy over the libido and the theory of sexual drives, and to the condition of this dematerialization. This is a fundamentally modern phenomenon, and is not simply the equivalent of capital in the realm of sensibility; it is the fragmentation and abstraction of signs and the fabrication of new ones. Recurrence and repetition are installed as basic traits within the system, and a new region, "a pulsional strip"[37] is colonized: the sculptural, political, erotic, linguistic—"offering the libido new occasions for intensifications."

The problem with Freud's aesthetic theory, explains Lyotard in the essay, "Psychanalyse et peinture,"[38] was that he (Freud) had privileged the subject of the work of art over its plastic support which, in the process of mimesis, is rendered transparent to the inaccessible scene behind it. In a further process, one discovers a latent content dissimulated in the object represented: the trace or silhouette of a form which is determinant in the painter's unconscious. Put simply, for Lyotard, Freud's schema made it impossible to analyze anything but the representational painting or work of art. Impossible, therefore, the analysis of the nonrepresentational painting in which "the traditions and space of the QuattroCento tumbled into ruins" and in which the function of representation, so crucial to Freud's theory, is rendered insignificant. To address the lacuna in Freud, Lyotard decides to "read Freud against himself," by availing himself of the theory of drives and the libidinal economy. Lyotard expresses great hope for the new analytic arrangement, for it might free the object from a dubious psychoanalysis without a subject. It might also free aesthetic theory from its Platonism in which the object takes the form of a mimetic representation in the unconscious modeled as a screen or palimpsest and interpreted according to the law of the father and his symbolic code. The object, which is now free to be itself, can become the locus "of libidinal operations engendering an inexhausible polymorphy." Lyotard muses "maybe the hypothesis should be extended to other objects, objects to produce and consume, ones to sing and to listen to, objects to love."[39]

So it is in this context of a disengagement from Freud, from the Freud of the Leonardo studies at any rate, that the discussion can now turn to an aspect of the *Economie libidinale,* itself a vast psychic arrangement where Lyotard gives rein to his affections and disaffections. Specifically, I would like to turn to what for my purposes is the central piece of the work; "The Desire named Marx." Three reasons can be advanced: the essay gathers up, in an intensely rhetorical way, Lyotard's orientation in respect to Marx and the militant legacy he left behind; the essay serves to highlight Lyotard's own deconstructive practice of writing the impious by applying the analytic of desire, with its *topoi* of repetition, delay, and ambivalence to the text of Marx, thereby giving form to his incredulity before the latter's meta-narration; the essay establishes Lyotard's negative relation to (actually another nonpositive affirmation of) the thought of Jean Baudrillard.

The intention, declares Lyotard, is to "take Marx as though he were an author" full of affects, to take "his text as a folly and not as a theory," but without hate or devotion, to activate Marx's desire in the complex libidinal volume called his text. This desire is to be found not simply in the major theoretical works but equally in the margin "at the edge of the continent," in notes and letters, in *lapsi* and in the figures of repetition and delay in the machinery of theoretical analysis. To uncover this desire is also, in a sense, to uncover Lyotard's—the militant's desire to unmask the process of capital, the desire to bring an end to its reign. It is additionally thus the desire of the idealist to bring about a harmony of people in nature, the love of people for others, of men for women and vice versa. All very well and proper these desires we might say; what is the problem? The problem is that these are not the only figures of desire at play in the militant idealist.

To awaken these closeted desires, Lyotard caresses a metonym borrowed from Bataille—Marx's beard—a partial object in a Lacanian sense,[40] eroticized as a channel for the transference and countertransference of libidinal energies, which is to say the object of a desire which is never directed toward the genital figure of *jouissance,* but toward a prolongation, through repetition and substitution, of an endless *deferral* of accomplishment.

The libidinal Marx is a polymorphous creature, a hermaphrodite with the "huge head of a warlike and quarrelsome man of thought" set atop the soft feminine contours of a "young Rhenish lover." So it is a strange bi-sexuated arrangement giving rise to a sort of ambivalence: the old man and the young woman, a monster in which femininity and virility exchange indiscernibly, "thus putting a stop to the reassuring difference of the sexes."[41]

Now the young woman Marx, who is called Alice (of Wonderland fame), is obfuscated by the perverse body of capital because it simultaneously occasions in her a revulsion and a strange fascination. She is the epicurean Marx, the Marx of the doctoral thesis, the aesthetic Marx. She claims a great love for this man of thought who offers to act as the Great Prosecutor of the crimes of capital. He is "assigned to the accusation of the perverts" and entrusted with the invention of a suitable lover, the proletariat, for the little Alice. The bi-sexed Marx is composed of stereotypes; the chaste young woman is a dreamer, dreaming of a reconciliation with her lover, while the man of thought is irascible and domineering. All the better to underline Lyotard's sentiment: this theoretical practice is really a very *male* thing,[42] as it concerns the formulation and the handing down of laws. Thus the beard is a metonym for the desire for law, the desire of the patriarch (Abraham, Moses, Marx, and Freud). And so Lyotard is led to say that theoretical practice is also about power, and not simply or not at all the power of the narrated proletariat, but the power which the militant assumes when the kid gloves are removed or, in default of the revolution, the power which is capitalized on behalf of the oppressed, which is also Alice's desire for something different and better.

So the beard belongs to the man of law, the prosecutor of the crimes of capital in the court of history. And yes, we agree, this is a great and important undertaking. Like a permanent crimes commission the law-yer works overtime in the British Museum, methodically considering every instantiation of capital's infamy. And it is a very beautiful thing, this dossier on the accused, and it attests to an admirable force of intellect and invention, itself passably libidinal. But lodged in the mas-sive machinery of theoretical elaboration is a figure of delay. For here there is an aesthetic figure which delays the appearance of the text on capital: sentences become paragraphs, and paragraphs become chap-ters in the cancerous process of theoretical articulation. The non finito of the text is evidence, for Lyotard, that what is being produced is a work of art, in this case a text. A psychic apparatus.

But Alice is restless, and she wonders why it takes so long for the intellectual head to produce the healthy body of socialism in the obstet-rics of capital. Why does the prosecutor take so long to sum up? What is it about theoretical discourse that makes it so interminable? It is, for Lyotard, because the result of this investment of time and grey matter can also be considered a *jouissance differé*, a jouissance of the same order as the jouissance of capital—which is as a channel for libidinal intensities in its prostitutive arrangement. What is more, capital will never give birth to the healthy infant of socialism because its body is barren, and Lyotard's (or is it Marx's?) task is phenomenological, to bear witness to the stillborn birth of socialism. Alice will be forever condemned to dream of that reconciliation, when she and her lover will meet in a different time and place.

Put another way, when something approaching the desired reality of the socialist body suddenly appeared on the scene, at the International of 1871, Marx was to write to his Russian translator, Danielson:

> It is doubtless useless to wait for the revision of the first chapter, as my time, for quite a time now, has been so taken up (and there is little prospect for amelioration) that I can no longer pursue my theoretical works. It is certain that one beautiful morning I will put a stop to it, but there are circumstances when one is morally

obliged to be concerned with things much less attractive than study and theoretical research.

And Lyotard translates into the libidinal: " 'Not very attractive,' says the equivocal prosecutor, 'your beautiful proletarian body, let us return our gaze once again to the unspeakable prostitute of capital.' "[43] So here is the reason for the delay and the cause of Alice's unhappiness. The old man is cheating on her, besotted as he is by the object which he loves to hate.

We could recall Alice's complaint: "Jam yesterday, jam tomorrow, never jam today!" And this too can be translated: "There was communism in the undivided social body of the 'primitive,' there will be a reunification of the alienated body in 'advanced' communism, but today there is only alienation from the memory and dream, the alienation which marks my body." Everybody is going to pay for this, Alice with her eternal misery, the prosecutor in a mass of words, articulations, and organized arguments—a theoretical torture with which he will martyr himself for Christ the proletariat, whose suffering will be the price of its redemption.[44]

Lyotard admits that it would be possible to use this religious metaphor in a critique of what is religious in Marx and in militancy; guilt, resentment, and morality. But he argues that this reunified body, which is to act as the reference for the sacrifice of the martyrs or the agony of the proletariat, has never and will never exist. In any event, what would be the use of another critique, even if it was to be an atheist one, and apart from the fact that there are already a hundred thousand of them? It would be to reinstall himself "armed with bi-focal lenses, like some sort of Lilliput . . . on a small piece of the giant's posterior."[45] Lyotard has something else in mind, "something beyond religion and atheism, something like the Roman parody."[46] He would rather evoke the pagan in all its heterogeneity, including the Clastrian idea of pagan society as primitive society, as society against the state, dialectically sublated in the parody—a joyous science of the social . . .[47] So we come to the central propositions of the text: that all political economy is libidinal economy, and the symbolic exchange is likewise a libidinal economy. Lyotard argues that, in referring to a "prostitutive" arrangement of labor/capital, Marx presents a libidinal figure of the proletariat. Capital, the pimp, extracts value by alienating the erogenous zones of the prostitute, labor. In the analogy, the disconnected fragments of the body are linked to the fluid transformations and exchanges of intensities and signs in an endless account of in-comings and out-goings. Lyotard understands that while such a regime gives rise to exploitation, to the domination and regulation of the body, it also involves another species of jouissance, to what I have referred, in the title, as the jouissance of practical reason.

The ancient formula of Hegel—work or die, which means also die or die *in* or *of* work—is refuted by Lyotard:

> And if one does *this* [work], if one becomes a slave of the machine, the machine of the machine, the screwer screwed by it, eight hours a day, twelve in the last century, is it because one is forced to do it, constrained because one clings to life? Death is not an alternative to *that,* it is part of it, it attests that there is a *jouissance* in it. The workless English did not become workers in order to survive, they were—buckle up tightly and spit on me later—delighted [*joui*] by the hysterical exhaustion, masochism, who knows, of *staying* in the mines, in the foundries and workshops, in hell. They were delighted in and by the insane destruction of their inorganic body which was of course imposed on them, delighted by the decomposition of their personal identity which the peasant tradition had constructed for them, delighted by the dissolution of families and villages and delighted by the new and monstrous anonymity of the suburbs and the pubs in the morning and evening.[48]

In the libidinal economy there is thus an affection for the prostitutive arrangement imposed by capital. To claim that this is perversity changes nothing, because, according to Lyotard, it was always so—and hence the impossibility of speaking of alienation; there never was and never will be a productive, artistic, or poetic metamorphosis without the dissolution of the body. There will never be a resolution of the hermaphroditic text. Alienation itself springs out of the fantasy of such a body, a strange combination of the erotic, hygienic Greek body and the erotic, supernatural Christian body.[49] For Lyotard, the militant's resentment (*ressentiment*) derives from a desire for the return of the whole body, the reunification of the "(in)organic body" of the earth with the body without organs of the socius and the body with organs of the worker. Nor is alienation related to castration, nor to the "foreclosure" of castration as Baudrillard's symbolic exchange might have it. Castration has no part in the fundamental schema which, as Baudrillard himself will point out, is deeply economistic, deeply exchangist. The fear of alienation is not the fear of loss, but the fear of not being able to give, of not being able to enter into the flux of exchanges and the investment of energies, even the deferred, strange, and partial jouissance of partial bodies: the autonomization and metamorphoses of the fragmented body in production, their investment in the labor-time of the system. The metaphor of the unified body, whether in mythic communism or the "pre-economy," is ultimately religious, since "the only way of not being alienated since Hegel, and no doubt Jesus, is to be God."[50]

Lyotard directed this last remark at Castoriadis who, "justly tired of rehashing the problems of historical materialism," proposed replacing it with a theory of generalized creativity. Giving full rein to his disaffections, Lyotard reserves for this theory a parenthesis of hate. Because, when Castoriadis, the militant, renounced militancy, he became a "valet" of the people—still secretly and ambivalently continuing with the adultery of knowledge and power.

> Finally it was not necessary to say: let us restart the revolution, rather . . . it was necessary to say: let us eliminate the idea as well, since it has become and perhaps has always been a little idea about nothing, the idea of a reversal of position in the sphere of economic and political power and thus the idea of the preservation of this sphere. . . . "Thinking heads are always connected by invisible threads to the body of the people," wrote a delighted Marx to Meyer (1871).[51]

The parenthesis occurs in a general discussion of the thought of Baudrillard, for whom Lyotard reserves some fraternal criticism. From our point of view "The Desire Named Marx" is a significant text because it is one of the few places in contemporary French literature where Baudrillard's thought is examined in any detail, and it is especially significant in that it occurs in the context of Lyotard's rendezvous with desire in Marx.[52]

Lyotard describes his relationship with Baudrillard as co-polarized and synchronized, but claims that the latter's thought is burdened by theoretical and critical hypotheses—even though Baudrillard's denunciation of "the critical" and "the theoretical" (in *The Mirror of Production*) are made in formulae which Lyotard would "joyfully countersign." The problem for Lyotard is that Baudrillard still aims at the "true" when he reproaches Marxism for censuring or debarring social relationships commanded by the symbolic exchange—relationships centered on the exhaustion of libidinal energies "of love and death."

Lyotard's critique amounts to a sort of critique of Baudrillard's anthropological critique. For Lyotard it is a fantasy to imagine a society without political economy and without the unconscious, or to imagine that political economy or the unconscious appeared, *sponte sua*, from thin air and then to be imposed on the social body which had not known them; or to imagine that political economy was not present "in filigree, in embryo" in archaic society. Just like the commodity in Marx, Bataille's potlatch is emphatically as much a figure of order as the former: they both compose the semiotic surface of the social. Mauss understood this in terms of the interest which accrues in the cycles of the exchange of gifts. That the symbolic exchange is charged with powerful effect changes nothing for, as Lyotard tells us, to have a "lack" is the same thing as having any other sort of "have." In this way, Lyotard distances himself from the alibi and lost reference of the gift-economy:

> Why can't he [Baudrillard] see that the whole problematic of the gift and symbolic exchange, as he receives it from Mauss, with or without the deflections of Bataille, Caillois and Lacan, pertain completely to imperialism and Western racism—that it is the good savage of ethnology, slightly libidinalized, who he inherits with the concept.[53]

Just as there is no time, neither is there space or place for the reference of the symbolic exchange—which will amount to no more than an enactment of representation in the theater of the sign—the setting aside of an ideal reference. It is a similar fantasy, for Lyotard, as believing there is a human nature which is good to the degree that it is rebellious, the same dream as Plato's when he sought "a source for his Atlantic Utopia among the ancient savages of Egypt"; the same dream as Marx's when he invents the proletariat as the negation of negation and the place of the absence of contradiction and alienation; the same as Baudrillard's when he discovers, positively, the subversive reference in today's "marginals." The dream is one of a nonalienated region which would be able to escape the law of capital. But there is no region which can escape the regimes of power, "regime and reign, sign and apparatus." To have faith in one recommences religion, and this will assure us of being desperate: "Perhaps," writes Lyotard, "in terms of politics, our desire is to be, and always remain, desperate.[54]

Let us conclude here on a note of the co-polarity in the thought of the two postmodernists. It's possible, if in the circumstances parodic, to call this thought dialectically opposed, a dialectic in, and of, postmodernism. Lyotard's ironic affirmation of the system of production and exchange which champions the inventive moves it enables in technology, science, and the realm of sensibility, the potentiality of artistic and linguistic expression in cultures of the avant-garde is momentarily mirrored in Baudrillard's denunciation of the same, in his fascination with the "perverse polymorphy" of signification. But in spite of their rejection of critique and dialectical thought, they carry on the critique by other means. The continuity of their thought on writing—instituted by Bataille—can be instructively compared. In *Just Gaming,* Lyotard remarks: "The difference between what I write and poetry and literature is that, in principle, what I write is not fiction. But I do wonder more and more: is there a real difference between theory and a fiction? After all, don't we have the right to present theoretical statements under the form of fictions? Not *under* the form, but *in* the form."[55] In an interview on the publication of his book, *L'Amérique,* Baudrillard says something similar: "I do not really think of myself as a philosopher. Criticism [*critique*] has come to me through a movement of radicality which has a poetic, as opposed to philosophical, origin. It is not a function of distantiation or I know not what dialectical critique of phenomena: it would rather be the attempt to seek in the object a path of disappearance, a disappearance of the object and the subject itself at the same time."[56]

In proposing a relationship between theory and fiction—between philosophy and poetry—the postmodernists have underlined, in a way, the continuity of their thought and writing with the thought and writing of Bataille. They are simultaneously witnesses (no doubt phenomenological) and participants in an aesthetic movement, instituted by the critical surrealism of Bataille, which introduces into the "philosophically serious" the figures of the game: an indeterminacy and a disintegration of the certainties and positivities of so-called theoretical thought—radically questioning the function of criticism and the role of writing and art, and the very position of the other in Western thought. In the next chapter this process of dissolution, which is one of the hallmarks of modernist culture, is linked to the elaboration of (theory of) the death drive. On this note, which will attempt to account for the destructive tendencies in modernist art and postmodernist theory—in the forms of exchange exemplified by Bataille's potlatch, Clastre's warrior society, Baudrillard's symbolic exchange, and Lyotard's micronarratives, the current investigation will conclude.

6 REVENGE OF THE MIRROR PEOPLE

The possibility that fiction is more fantastic than reality is infinitely remote, and this said, one can invoke a writer such as Borges with equanimity, since even his most fantastic stories would fail to match the reality for which they can serve as an exemplary metaphor. One such metaphor, or allegory, "The Fauna of Mirrors" has already been canonized, as the literary historian might put it, in contemporary discourse. The fact of its popularity should not prevent its appearance here, since what it expresses in terms of the problematic of identity in Western metaphysics in the space of a couple of hundred words far surpasses many learned tomes. It is to this theme, its permutations in the body of writings examined in this book, that this concluding chapter is directed. Since it is a short piece, it can be quoted in full:

In one of the volumes of the *Lettres édifiantes et curieuses* that appeared in Paris during the first half of the eighteenth century, Father Fontecchio of the Society of Jesus planned a study of the superstitions and misinformation of the common people of Canton; in the preliminary outline he noted that the Fish was a shifting and shining creature that nobody had ever caught but that many had said that they had glimpsed in the depths of mirrors. Father Fontecchio died in 1736, and the work begun by his pen remained unfinished; some 150 years later Herbert Allen Giles took up the interrupted task. According to Giles, belief in the Fish is part of a larger myth that goes back to the legendary times of the Yellow Emperor.

In those days the world of mirrors and the world of men were not, as they are now, cut off from each other. They were besides, quite different; neither beings nor colours nor shapes were the same. Both kingdoms, the specular and the human, lived in harmony; you could come and go through mirrors. One night the mirror people invaded the earth. Their power was great, but at the end of bloody warfare the magic arts of the Yellow Emperor prevailed. He repulsed the invaders, imprisoned them in their mirrors, and forced on them the task of repeating, as though in a kind of dream, all the actions of men. He stripped them of their power and of their forms and reduced them to mere slavish reflections. Nonetheless, a day will come when the magic spell will be shaken off.

The first to awaken will be the Fish. Deep in the mirror we will perceive a very faint line and the colour of this line will be like no other colour. Later on, other shapes will begin to stir. Little by little they will differ from us; little by little they will not imitate us. They will break through the barrier of glass or metal and this time will not be defeated. Side by side with these mirror creatures, the creatures of water will join the battle.

In Yunnan they do not speak of the Fish but of the Tiger of the Mirror. Others believe that in advance of the invasion we will hear from the depths of mirrors the clatter of weapons.[1]

This fabulous tale gathers together, and juxtaposes, three significant themes which can be related to the concerns that have been addressed in this book. These themes are the myths of origin and end, the theory of an instinctual aggressivity, and the principle of nonidentity. The myth of origin here, of course, is one of harmony in difference: "neither beings nor colours nor shapes were the same. . . . you could come and go through mirrors." The origin is moreover a time of pre-identity menaced by an unaccounted-for malevolence on the part of the mirror people: "One night the mirror people invaded the earth." Tantalizingly, no reason is provided for the aggression of the mirror people, but one might surmise that it was to forestall the magic arts of the Yellow Emperor which were to imprison and to compel them to repeat "as though in a kind of dream" the actions of men. And having been reduced to the status of "mere slavish reflections" the mirror people must wait until the power of the emperor's magic arts has worn off, and thus the myth of the end: "this time they will not be defeated." What will be the outcome of this final victory of the mirror people? Will it be to reestablish harmony in difference?

To take the "Fauna of the Mirror" as an allegory—as a narrative about a subject under the guise of another (OED)—raises questions of intentionality and interpretation. Surely there is a charm in the multi-valency of Borges's text; it can be interpreted as a masked discourse on Lacan's psychoanalytic theories of the mirror stage. But equally it can be taken as a discourse on power—in a Foucauldian sense—or then again as an allegory for the movement of aesthetic sensibility in modernism, in the form of the critique of representation, of iconicity, and mimesis. It can be interpreted in these different ways, to be sure, but this in no way guarantees that Borges had any intention that it should, and here is its charm—whether through artifice or innocence, the simple narrative has a childlike profundity. The fauna of the mirror are denizens of Borges's *Book of Imaginary Beings*. He wrote in the preface to the 1957 edition that in the "zoo of mythology" there "is something in the dragon's image that appeals to the human imagination, and so we find the dragon in quite distinct places and times. It is, so to speak, a necessary monster, not an ephemeral or accidental one, such as the three-headed chimera or the catoblepas."[2] It might be argued that a figure such as the bi-sexed Marx, a modern centaur, is likewise a necessary monster which has appeared in quite distinct circumstances of time and place. So too, perhaps, are Baudrillard's "transpolitical" figures of the obese, the hostage, and the obscene, the mirror images of a scene of politics in the path of disappearance. Or again like the improbable dionysian figure of the *Acéphale*.

Acknowledging that there are dangers in interpreting the tale as an allegory, or rather as a series of allegories, in what sense can it be said to be an allegory of psychoanalysis? The signs to such an interpretation have already been posted: the overall structure of the tale refers to a type of social mirror-phase. The mirror people represent the instincts, the Yellow Emperor represents the force of law, that is, repression; the mirror a bar to the unconscious where the instincts are obliged to conform with the images, the *imagos,* ordained by the symbolic law of the father. If, at a theoretical level, what is being described is the process of self-identification as a "coercive unification" of the subject through the control of the instincts so as to transcend an aggressivity constitutive of a primal subject—a Lacanian scenario—then the liberation of the instincts, the revolution of desire, the smashing of glass and metal would prophesy the radical impulses of the anti-Oedipus.

The second impulse is to read the text as an allegory of power—in no way contradicting the psychoanalytic reading, on the contrary, reinforcing it—which can be related to Foucault's discourses on power and to the anthropological critique which has been raised in the course of the book. The power which is exercised over the mirror people is not simply coercive or violent but disciplinary—since the task of the imprisoned is "to repeat the actions of men," to exercise a mimetic control of the body. What is more, and the metaphor of the mirror serves to emphasize this, the actions and movements of the incarcerated are subject to a gaze, to a surveillance by a paranoiac and narcissistic state apparatus. But the transition is nonetheless there, a movement from brutal suppression to self-control, to the minute regulation of the body in the name of normality.[3]

Bearing in mind the psychoanalytic and genealogical axes of the space of interpretation and without leaving them, there remains an aesthetic dimension, an allegory—reductive interpretation though it may be—that must be crossed. This dimension represents, in a sense, the absent heart of our study—a vacuum of unthought which has attracted, without foreknowledge or prejudgment, a number of theoretical propositions and machineries. But before we touch on this dimension, it would be worthwhile making use of other anecdotal material in order to place the entire discussion in the harsh light of history—since it is the historical instance, the negative in negative dialectics which renders enlightenment aesthetics problematic.

At Dachau there is a permanent exhibition dedicated to the victims of the Nazi brutality, recording and documenting the infamy of the regime. It inspires a vertigo of horror. In the display of collected artifacts, there is a chart which sets out the meaning of the insignia that the incarcerated were obliged, under pain of death, to wear on their sleeves and lapels. By no means complex, the matrix permitted a series of evaluations to be made at a glance about the bearer. The code specified at least three factors: the crime (of being Jewish, gypsy, gay, or political); the national origin (also a sort of crime, of being Polish, Czech, or Russian); and the prisoner's status (slaveworker, simple criminal, experimental subject, recidivist, or the dangerous and instantly expendable). Represented by a combination of basic colors, shapes, and bands, the system provided a simple and visible means of assisting the control of the captive peoples.

Such a semiotic system, which crudely affixed the brute details of biographical fact onto the arms of the interned, and which was arranged to be read by the gaze of the exterminating machine, represents, in the discourse of power, a type of ultimate system for the reduction of individuals to the *identity* of an abstract code of difference. It will be readily appreciated that individual characteristics of subjects—colorings, accents, and idiosyncracies of every description—were simply effaced by the substitution of an *identification* of the subject with a model constructed in the matrix of the semiotic chart.

The imposition of this identity was not, of course, the result of irrationalism, nor even an example of the irrationality of reason which, through a historical somersault, comes to signify its opposite. The genocide of the European Jews, as Clastres points out, was the logical result of a racism which was allowed to develop freely.[4] That the ends or the goals of this enterprise were irrational or paranoiac should not prevent the recognition of such a system as the quintessence of rationality, defined in the terms of the organization and administration of state power. Instrumental reason at the service of humanity, authorized by the people (Volk), is crossed, double-crossed by the signs of its historical failure: Dachau, and Auschwitz.

Auschwitz. Such a sign evokes two names among many in (critical) theory: Theodor Adorno and Jean-François Lyotard. The former for his famous dictum that there can be no more poetry after Auschwitz,[5] and the latter who, in following Adorno, claims that the crime of Auschwitz—populocide—opens up the new historical era of postmodernity.[6] For Lyotard, the destruction of the sovereign figure of the people—as the legitimate and legitimating authority—repeats at another level and another time the crime that opened up the era of modernity, the regicide of Louis XVI, the legitimate and legitimating monarchical sovereign. The legitimating authority in the democratic era enabled by the French Revolution, however, is no longer vested in the figure of a person—as it was in the body of the monarch, but in the idea of the people, the idea of emancipation and of the promised community. With the destruction of a people (the Jews) by the people (the Volk), what is destroyed is the idea of the people as the legitimating authority, as what gives right to the idea of rights.

The example of Auschwitz serves to illustrate the proposition that the fiction of the fauna of mirrors is in no way more fantastic than historical reality.

Let us now return to the allegory and to the aesthetic dimension. "Little by little they will differ from us; little by little they will not imitate us." If we were to take the work of Manet and Courbet as commencing a new historical era of art and to trace this movement through all its permutations in impressionism, postimpressionism, and subsequently the avant-gardist movements of the twentieth century, a slightly formalist schema admittedly, it would be possible to characterize the movement as one toward abstraction, toward the total dissolution of the representational space and the conventions of mimesis which had been established over four centuries. In refusing the space of the mirror and the function of mimesis, modern art embodies a principle of nonidentity. This refusal takes many forms, including the active destructive tendencies associated with the dadaists, the surrealists, and their neo manifestations. It is this destructive tendency which provides the revenge in the "revenge of the mirror people." In order to grasp this tendency at a cultural level—the relationship of the death drive to modernist aesthetics—it is necessary once again to turn to psychoanalytic theory and in particular to Freud's metapsychology and Lacan's reworking of its basic tenets.

"Revenge," Jacques Lacan tells us, is an example of a "paranoiac knowledge" which can correspond to "certain critical moments that mark the history of man's mental genesis"—namely, as the last aggressive reaction in a long series of motivations. (The genetic character of these motivations suggests a possible psychoanalytic structure of the history of modern art as, in Lacan's terms, a case of a curable, self-punishing paranoia where the "aggressive act resolves the delusional construction."[7] Lacan's work on aggression, "Aggressivity in Psychoanalysis" is involved with an aspect of Freud's metapsychology which has largely eluded application in the practice of psychoanalysis, yet which in Freud's later writings constituted a significant avenue of theoretical and philosophical research. Claiming that Freud's conceptual system remained open, Lacan focuses on

> the enigmatic signification that Freud expressed in the term *death instinct,* which, rather like the figure of the Sphinx, reveals the aporia that confronted this great mind in the most profound attempt so far made to formulate an experience of man in the register of biology. . . . That is why the metapsychological nature of the death tendencies is continually being discussed by our theoreticians, not without contradiction, and often, it must be admitted, in a somewhat formalist way.[8]

The reader will appreciate that theoretical interest in the aporia of the death drive is still great; indeed, I would argue that it forms a major underlying thematic in the fold of theoretical literature which we have examined in this book. The aporia remains necessarily unclosed, and still subject to contradiction and formalism. The intention of this concluding chapter is not to cross the continent of the death drive, since that would involve another book, but to mark the space of its elaboration, and to suggest its pertinence to the discourse of the postmodern. (Having started on the note of Hegel's "iron law of our time" in the conflict of the master and slave, it is possible that we have already sleepwalked across this continent; the articulation of the themes found in the work of Bataille, Baudrillard, and Lyotard has perhaps obscured the common ground from which the themes have emerged, or on which they may be situated.)

It was noted in the previous chapter that Freud supplemented the dualistic theory of drives with the Nirvana principle, which for Lyotard remained an expression of the undecidability or indeterminacy of both the origin and the goals of the drives, but also what kept the system open as it had for Lacan. Throughout the work on the instincts, but perhaps more particularly after the introduction of the death drive in *Beyond the Pleasure Principle*, the systematic framework of the drives was always threatened by this indeterminacy.[9] In *Beyond the Pleasure Principle* (which introduced the concept of the compulsion to repeat as a manifestation of the death instinct—Borges: "and forced on them the task of repeating, as though in a kind of dream, all the actions of men"), the indeterminacy is expressed by a continual shifting of the ego instincts and the sexual instincts in their assignation to the principles of life and death, successively employing the dynamic, topographical, and economic models of the entire system. The situation is clarified somewhat in the subsequent works, *The Ego and the Id* and "The Economic Problem of Masochism" in which the death drive was much more clearly associated with aggressivity and with the tendency to destructiveness.[10] In *Civilization and Its Discontents* the death drive forms one of the countervailing tendencies in the progress of civilization, perpetually threatening it with disintegration.[11]

Civilization copes with the threat of disintegration, according to Freud, in a manner analogous to the functioning of the super-ego in the individual, through the suppression and restriction of aggressive and self-destructive tendencies by the production of a "sense of guilt." For Freud this social conscience produces an anxiety, a malaise which is the source of the "discontent" with the process of "civilization."[12] In adopting a vitalist and progressivist conception of civilization, Freud accepted this discontent as a necessary evil to be endured in the formation of larger communities of humanity, the goal of which, through the libidinal bonding of individuals through *identification,* is "in mastering the disturbance of their communal life by the human instinct of aggression and self-destruction."[13] To his credit, Freud was also disturbed by the aggression of the cultural superego itself, to the extent that he listened, "without indignation" to arguments that the goal of such culture is not worth the efforts—in terms of what the individual will tolerate—concluding that "man's judgements of value follow directly from his wishes for happiness—that, accordingly, they are an attempt to support his illusions with arguments."[14]

In Lacan we discover a similar ambiguity, but with different outcomes. He, on one hand, appears to reject the evolutionist schema, writing, "Darwin's success seems to derive from the fact that he projected the predations of Victorian society and the economic euphoria that sanctioned for that society the social devastation that it initiated on a planetary scale, and to the fact that it justified its predations by the image of a laissez-faire of the strongest predators in competition for their natural prey."[15] But equally he rejects the humanitarian ideals which Freud had noted approvingly in *Civilization and Its Discontents*. Lacan reveals himself as an enemy of normal morality which transforms aggressivity into the virtue of strength, indispensable in the development of the ego, an entity which Lacan is to excoriate as that "emancipated" man of modern society, that "pitiful victim" and "being of nothingness" of Hegelian and existential repute.[16] There is also an archaic moment in which Lacan evokes the "saturations" of the superego and the ego ideal "realized in all kinds of organic forms in traditional societies, forms that extend from the rituals of everyday intimacy to the periodical festivals in which the community manifests itself." In the context, this endorsement of the archaic appears almost reactive, even reactionary when it bemoans the abolition of the "cosmic polarity" of the "male and female principles" and the "battle between the sexes" which leads to "democratic" anarchy of the passions "and their desperate levelling down by the 'great winged hornet' of narcissistic tyranny."[17] At other times, of course, Lacan is far more scathing in his reference to Freud's superego when he writes, in "The Freudian Thing," about "that obscene, ferocious figure in which we must see the true signification of the superego."[18]

Lacan's theory of aggressivity, like his other psychoanalytic speculation, is ultimately anchored to his theory of the mirror stage—this at least is the conventional wisdom[19]—as the site of a primordial process of identifications which, passing through fragmented body images and orthopaedic projections, leads to "the assumption of the armour of an alienating identity, which will mark with its rigid structure the subject's entire mental development."[20] This identity, the perfect counterpart of the subject, is a transformation of the "specular *I*" into the "social *I*," which, entering into the "dialectic of desire" is turned into an "apparatus for which every instinctual thrust constitutes a danger," thus an apparatus for censorship and cultural mediation exemplified by the Oedipus complex. For Lacan it was this conception, so closely related to Freud's work on narcissism, which helped to explain the destructive and death instincts and the aggressivity which the *I* releases "in any relation to the other."

To return to the death drive: for Freud in *Beyond the Pleasure Principle* the dualistic theory of drives was complicated by the feelings of pleasure that can occur in the heightening of tension, and, correlatively, the feelings of unpleasure that can accompany a relaxation of tension. The idea of pleasure in pain, of a destructive instinct in the service of Eros, he related to the phenomena of sadism and masochism, in which the destructive tendencies are alternately directed toward the other and the self, both "strongly alloyed to eroticism." He found, in humans, an undeniable inclination to aggression, to badness and evil. But he also discovered that the more aggression toward the outside world is checked, the more severe becomes the superego. In "The Economic Problem of Masochism," Freud postulates the existence of a sadistic superego and a masochistic ego where a "*cultural suppression of the instincts*" produces a sense of guilt and an increasingly severe conscience.[21] The severe conscience is, in the current interpretation, the power of the Yellow Emperor, and the mirror identity, which is forced on the mirror people, is that fictive structure, postulated by Lacan, assumed by the ego in the subject's asymptotic coming-into-being. In the temporal dialectic this figure, termed the ideal I (Lacan) or the ego ideal (Freud) is both the illusion of past and future unities, and as such the first and "classic gesture of the self: *méconnaissance,* misprision, misrecognition."[22]

In coming to the elaboration of the death drive in the thought of Lyotard and Baudrillard, it will be understood that in fact their use of the concept is considerably opposed. In the case of Lyotard it forms part of the ensemble of drives constituting the libidinal economy: the investment and reinvestment of the "fragmented body" in the channels of the desiring economy is a type of compulsion to repeat and an attempt to return to the "inorganic body."[23] The indeterminacy of an aesthetic based in the libidinal economy, the result of the Freudian reading of Marx, produces, it should be argued, an aesthetic based on metonymy, on the figures of repetition and substitution (see chapter 5). Such an aesthetic has much in common with the aesthetic sublime—expounded by Kant—precisely in terms of this indeterminacy. And thus a simple, (unconscious?) *glissement* from the subliminal into the sublime. Lyotard's aesthetic of the sublime represents one of the stakes in postmodern thought, and surely another is symbolic exchange and the aesthetics of the spectacle. But before turning to the aesthetics of metonomy, let us turn once again to the symbolic exchange and its part in the death drive.

Baudrillard's concept of symbolic exchange, which, as an analysis of Mauss's gift tends toward Bataille's interpretation of the potlatch, seems to involve a deeper notion of reciprocity than that implied in its structuralist conception, deeper than the principle of economic exchange for which it might represent an ideal reference. Neither an economy nor a pre-economy, the principle of symbolic exchange in fact opposes any exchange of identities, either mediated or unmediated. But Baudrillard's refusal to take the recourse of an economic metaphor—either to describe the structure or the contents of this exchange—has presented a nearly insuperable problem of definition. Coupled with this are problems posed by those habitual conceptions of the symbolic in a host of discourses, in iconography, semiology, anthropology, and Lacanian psychoanalysis (where the various significations appear to converge). Against this background the difficulty of securing this deeper sense of reciprocity involved in symbolic exchange, even deeper than that employed by Lacan,[24] is considerable. As we have already seen, one of his strategies throughout his work, and in the wake of Mauss and Bataille, has been to link the concept to primitive and archaic notions and practices. The use of archaisms of any kind is a dangerous move in theoretical discourse, invariably giving rise to specific accusations of reactionary thought or romanticism.[25] Baudrillard, however, pursues a return to the archaic in the face of enlightened consciousness with great tenacity; pursuing it, let us say, to the deep recesses of psychoanalysis in order to discover a symbolic Freud to oppose to the interpretative machinery of Freudianism.

Baudrillard celebrates the death drive as a radical concept which breaks with Western thought, in which the "domination of nature and sublimation of aggressivity in production and accumulation characterize themselves as constructive Eros."[26] The problem with Freud's conception of the death drive is that it is conceived biologically and psychically. Biologically it is the result of a decree of science which marks it off as a form of inorganic death toward which the drive (and the organism) are headed. In a literal sense science, in producing itself as code, projects death as an excluded conceptual object: the nonliving, the nonsentient, and the inorganic. And this is also true of psychoanalysis which reproduces the same discrimination at a different level, drawing a line between the organic/somatic and something else. The conception of the drives, according to Baudrillard, is an attempt to bridge this gap, which is a repetition of the metaphysics of the mind/body split. The something else, of course, is the unconscious. It is into this sphere (which is formed in the separation of the spheres in the order of science), where all "wild, errant and transversal" processes are placed "in order to be domesticated *in the name of the unconscious.*" The death drive for Baudrillard must, on the contrary, be opposed to the positivity of the psychoanalytic apparatus elaborated by Freud in the economic, energetic, and topographical metaphors employed through-out his work. The principle of death must be turned against the entire interpretive machinery. As with Marxism, Baudrillard aims at the definitive resolution of psychoanalysis:

> Neither their "synthesis" nor their contamination—only their re-spective extermination—can provide a foundation for radical the-ory. Marxism and psychoanalysis are going through a crisis. We must telescope and precipitate their respective crises rather than using one to support the other. They can still do each other a great deal of harm. We must not deprive ourselves of this spectacle. They are only critical fields.[27]

In his engagement with the "critical fields," Baudrillard finds a fellow observer, an ally and mentor, in Bataille, and particularly in the latter's figure of luxurious and sumptuous death. For against the economic metaphor Bataille opposed a paroxysm of exchange, a libidinal exhaus-tion rather than a libidinal investment—communication is only possi-ble on the condition that it irrupts into the order of death and its signifying chain: excess, ambivalence, gift, sacrifice, dépense, and par-oxysm. So, in Bataille, Baudrillard discovers a vision of death and an antieconomic principle; the luxurious character of death conjoins sex-uality as communication, as the loss of *identity* in death and in the erotic *"mis à nu."* Baudrillard writes:

> There remains, in the excessive and luxurious vision of death in Bataille, something which tears it from psychoanalysis, from the

individual and psychic influence of psychoanalysis—the possibility of derailing the economic, *of smashing not only the objective mirror of political economy but also the inverted psychic mirror of repression, of the unconscious and the libidinal economy.*[28]

More than a return of the repressed, and not simply a critique of an armor-plated (super-)ego, but a provocation and act of defiance in the face of the entire interpretative machinery, Baudrillard's writing is an enactment of a symbolic violence, and an escalation of the stakes in his exchange with contemporary discourse—unmasking the simulacra one by one, first Marx, then Freud, and all of their derivatives: libidinal economy, schizoanalysis, and deconstruction—by smashing their mirrors. Surely this is the form of the aesthetics of the spectacle, and for that an archaism at one with the noble *flaneur* mentality. A passive nihilism, as it is said. "Put something in my place," is the mute response of theory, and I think I agree with Lyotard when he says that Baudrillard still aims at the truth, whether this is in the symbolic or the symbolic exchange.[29] But I would also argue that the truth in Baudrillard is no more than a metaphor—for which the lie is a specific signifying absence. Thus there is an anti-interpretative machinery in Baudrillard's thought, a creative/destructive affinity with the spectacular world and its avatars of simulation: the counterfeit, ruse, alibi, and lure; mirror figures which obscure the truth of the absence of truth, like the icon which exterminates the idea of God. Speaking of the iconoclasts, Baudrillard writes:

> Had they been able to believe that images only occulted or masked the Platonic Idea of God, there would have been no reason to destroy them. One can live with the idea of a distorted truth. But their metaphysical despair came from the idea that the images concealed nothing at all, and that in fact they were not images . . . but actually perfect simulacra forever radiant in their own fascination.[30]

The symbolic exchange is no longer mentioned after *L'Echange symbolique et la mort*—though it does seem to live on in the concept of a fatal strategy. Like the theory of the libidinal economy, it is perhaps a phenomenon of the 1970s when both theories were drawn into the wake of the events of 1968 and the political face of theory was unmasked in the iconoclasm of the worker-students. Still too hot for the cool 1980s! There is a story here; but whether it is one central to that era, to the climate of thought, and the spectacle of the end of discourse, or a minor and clearly eccentric hallucination of the sacrifice of systems of thought—Marxism, psychoanalysis, and semiolinguistics—it is too early to judge. In relation to the magisterial unfolding of the Hegelian schema, or the good productive practice of the Marxist machinery, or altruistic machinery of psychoanalytic interpretation, the thought of the 1970s is lilliputian, micro-narrational. But like an irritant medium, or a pataphysical sneeze in Nebraska which causes the hurricane in the Ukraine, it is not any less for all that: *ça dépend*. Of course, to the highminded and serious, Anglo-Saxon world of theory it is an anathema. In response to contemporary French thought, it monotonously trots out its hobbyhorses on to the parade grounds of positivism before dispatching them into a battle with an adversary *qu'ils ne connaient point*. Rejection of universal laws in favor of the rules of heterogeneous formation implies, at a political level, the incommensurablity of legal and ethical frames, but it does not dispense with them. "Difference" is not simply a fugitive category pursued for the fun of the paradoxical, but a concept of great philosophical depth; this is the lesson that Derrida and Foucault and, more recently, Lyotard have taught.

Another means of expressing heterogeneity, as we have seen, is in the privilege which Lyotard grants the little narratives,[31] over the meta-narratives. They are afforded a certain hegemony as knowledge, "a little sovereignty" which permits them to escape the crisis of delegitimation. "They escape, that is certain, but only on the basis that they no longer have the value of legitimation." What then is the status of the little narratives? On this question hangs a considerable stake, not simply in terms of the reception of Lyotard's thought, but by dint of the generic similarity of the whole of French thought after 1968. The battle which is joined over the reception of this thought is by no means a unique or recent phenomenon, and can be thematized in a number of ways: anti-foundationalism versus foundationalism, unreason versus reason, and so on.[32] Anti-philosophical thought, criticizing the foundations of philosophy, renders an aesthetic judgment on the subject of the philosophy of consciousness—this we find in Lyotard: a rejection of the ideology of universalism by the claims of particularities. Habermas has called this movement one of affirmation of the "growing pluralism of 'gods and demons' [*Glaubensmächte*], existential modes of being, myths, value attitudes, and metaphysical or religious world views" which vitiate against the philosophical procedures which maintain, "at a higher level of abstraction, the unity of reason."[33]

This brings us to a minor event, a contest which is by no means spent, between Lyotard and Habermas. If Habermas has put into question the relativism of the thought of post-1968, then conversely, what is also at stake is Habermas's dream of "completing the project of modernity" through the reunification of the spheres of science, art, and morality (unconstrained interaction of the cognitive with the moral/practical and aesthetic/expressive elements), as a cure to a "reified everyday praxis." Such a goal, implies Lyotard, in "Answering the Question: What is Postmodernism," would be to revive the aesthetic ideal of the beautiful. For Habermas to achieve his goals involves removing those contemporary tendencies which he identifies as: "the anti-modernism of the young conservatives"; the "pre-modernism of the old conservatives," and the "post-modernism of the neo-conservatives."[34] One may well imagine Lyotard's surprise as he finds himself grouped in the first category. For surely anti-modernism would be a rejection of the very tradition of the avant-gardes which he seeks to champion in his concept of the postmodern as the aesthetic sublime—the concept of the post-modern as the founding moment, the alpha and omega of modernism. Under the aegis of the sublime he exhorts us "to wage a war on totality; let us be witnesses to the unpresentable; let us activate the differences and save the honour of the name."[35] Would the name be postmodernism?

It would not be difficult, on the basis of a survey of this deeply divided discourse, to arrive at the depressing conclusion that the aesthetic horizon is still defined within the terms of the Kantian aesthetic categories of the sublime and the beautiful. Meaghan Morris, in her astute and critical study on Lyotard and the sublime, suggests something like this.[36] Lyotard's move to the aesthetics of the sublime, claims Morris, is both ingenious and banal. Ingenious because it quite successfully retrieves Kantian aesthetics from wafting about in the forms of the ideally beautiful, mediated by the principles of understanding and the *sensus communis,* of say practical reason, by privileging the moment of the "presentation of the unpresentable": the sublime. But in claiming the sublime for the aesthetics of the avant-garde and for postmodernism, Lyotard repeats the "familiar description of the status quo" by prescribing the "moral encouragement to artists to keep on experimenting for the sake of the pure Event. . . . And it is in the prescription of this pursuit . . . that there are echoes of the story of Speculation."[37] Lyotard could be reminded of his rebuke of Baudrillard for having remained in the place of criticism, since it is the place and not simply the contents of criticism which have to be avoided. Lyotard could be reminded because, according to Nietzsche, the place of the aesthetic judgment is at the level of the spectator, that is, at the level of art criticism but not at the level of art.[38] Such a critique of Lyotard's sublime repeats, in a way, Nietzsche's critique of Schopenhauer's understanding of Kant's version of the aesthetic problem. Nietzsche argues that the introduction of the spectator into the concept of the beautiful exposed the danger of arguing the beautiful in art while lacking familiarity, in a personal way, with the "abundance of vivid events, desires, surprises, transports in the realm of the beautiful" and in which "a lack of subtler personal experience reposes in the shape of a fat worm of error."[39] The error for Nietzsche is found at the basis of Kant's definition of the beautiful: "That is beautiful which pleases us *without interest,*" which in Schopenhauer is translated as operating "precisely against *sexual* 'interestedness.' " Schopenhauer "never wearied of glorifying *this* liberation from the will as the great merit and utility of the aesthetic condition."[40]

At this point the psychoanalytic concept of sublimation and the aesthetic sublime beautifully condense, since in Freud sublimation is the process of replacing the aims of the libido, sexual interestedness and activity, by the urges of research and artistic creation.[41] The sublime would be that which is sublimated by the process of inhibition: the unpresentable and the unpleasurable. Pleasure in pain, love in hate, beauty in ugliness—these are all features of the Kantian sublime for which the exquisite agony of tragedy represented an exemplary case. Even though Lyotard warns against this condensation, "confusion" he calls it,[42] it nonetheless underwrites his analysis of the libidinal Marx—his presentation of the unpresentable Marx.

For Lyotard, the aesthetic judgment in Kant demonstrated that, in matters of taste, it is impossible to judge on the basis of determinate concepts, which is to say, to found a judgment on the basis of a given universal principle ready to be applied, in order to arrive at a stable consensus. It is necessary to judge on the basis of a singular given in an unforeseen case "without rules in order to establish the rule." Moreover, while it is possible to *discuss* disagreements it is not possible to dispute them: this is the basis, according to Lyotard, of the *reflective* judgment in Kant. On this reflective judgment, writes Lyotard, "is based the activity of the artist and the critical philosopher, 'republican' politics—any inventive step which, on the path of the unknown, of the unacceptable, breaks with constituted norms, shatters consensus, and revives the meaning of the *différend*."⁴³ Thus somewhat paradoxically a notion of the avant-gardes is retrieved in the moment of aesthetic indeterminacy in Kant. In the antinomies of aesthetic judgment in Kant, Lyotard finds it impossible to arrive at a consensus on the question of beauty, and on the question of the sublime the possibility worsens.

> To be sure, in appealing to some universal, each aesthetic judgment, according to Kant, carries the promise of an ideal community, where my particular opinion would be shared by all. But, precisely because it is immediate, because it operates "without the mediation of any concept," aesthetic judgment can only claim a subjective universality, "the *indeterminate* norm of common sense." . . . And this troubling of common sense worsens with the consciousness of the sublime, which attests to the unpresentable, to the incommensurable excess of the Idea before the real. Then the community comes apart, to the point where it is connected by no more than a thread to the Idea of our destination.⁴⁴

Therefore, and again paradoxically, postmodern aesthetics *à la* Lyotard valorizes the tendency in modernist thought—which was already there in Kant's aesthetics—to shatter consensus. In this way Lyotard retrieves the legacy of the avant-gardes from the bathwater of modernism. When this is done for the sake of art, it is of course yet another manifestation of the formalism which has discredited much of modernist culture—including some of its postmodern variations—as a fundamentally conservative phenomenon. But when it is done in the name of heterogeneity, that is, from the point of view of the mirror people, a subjugated other either internal or external to the consciousness of the West, then it remains, like the best examples of the modernist avant-gardes, a progressive and potentially radical phenomenon. It reveals an ethical dimension in postmodern thought which cannot and must not be ignored.

Let us now employ the metaphor of the mirror in a slightly different way in order to draw the battle lines differently. To suggest, in effect, that despite the obvious differences and the heterogeneity of the sources and the aims, the thinkers whose work has been considered in this study are representatives of the mirror people. Granting that a metaphor is necessarily inadequate to its object, such a metaphor is perhaps less reductive than amalgamating the whole lot under the heading of post-structuralism or postmodernism, because it maintains the differences of approach (the harmony in difference) to the question of identity. There are indeed generic similarities, family resemblances perhaps. There is a coincidence of Lacan's critique of the ego, "in conformity with the utilitarian conception of man that reinforces it,"[45] and Bataille's critique of homogeneity, and Baudrillard's later critique of the economism of the sign. Likewise, Foucault's critique of the modern Western episteme as the advance of the same into the realm of the other, destroying it in the name of a quest for a universal conception of the human, can be related to Clastres's critique of the state as possessed of a "will to reduce difference and otherness" and propelled, in its modern form, by the economic regime of capital which knows no frontiers. Equally Clastres's work on the autarky as a unit of social, as opposed to self, sufficiency, idealized as the undivided social body, shares with Bataille's sanguinary vision of the primitive an ethical perspective based on a principle of violence and evil, by defining an obligatory level of aggression in the figure of the warrior vowed to a noble death, who spares the social body of a division which pits one portion of the society against and over another by his own death. The relativization of sociology, as Lacan puts it, by the "scientific collection of cultural forms which we are destroying in the world" has a corollary in the structure of the epistemological field, the unforeseen consequence of an imperialism of thought. Like the primitive world, the collection of autarkies, this modern thought has been divested of an imperial center. This is the revenge of the mirror people.

NOTES

Introduction

1 Alexandre Kojève, *Introduction to the Reading of Hegel's Phenomenology of Mind*, p. 160.
2 Ibid., p. 161.
3 Jean-François Lyotard, *The Postmodern Condition: A Report on Knowledge*, and *Economie libidinale*.
4 Fredric Jameson, "Postmodernism and Consumer Society," in Hal Foster (ed.), *The Anti-Aesthetic: Essays on Postmodern Culture*, p. 111.
5 Ibid., p. 125.
6 Ibid.
7 Félix Guattari, "The Postmodern Dead End," *Flash Art* 128, May/June 1986, p. 40.
8 Ibid., p. 41.
9 Ibid., p. 41.

1 W(h)ither History

1 Attributed to Friedrich Nietzsche.
2 Louis Althusser, *Lenin and Philosophy and Other Essays*, p. 162.
3 Alfred Jarry, *Selected Works of Alfred Jarry*, pp. 9, 13.
4 Ruy Launoir, *Clefs pour la 'Pataphysique*. The literary/artistic phenomenon of 'pataphysics, the invention of the pre-dadaist, protosurrealist Jarry, occupies the place of a comic intermezzo in the mise-en-scène of modern, primarily modernist, French thought. As a minor and absurd movement of infinitessimal brevity, pataphysics (to drop the absurd apostrophe) represents an obverse and parodic mirror to the philosophically and scientifically serious. Yet it has, nonetheless, led a certain life at the edge of the machinery and has been maintained as a reference for every type of philosophical and epistemological pretension. These references are widespread. The phenomenon of pataphysics is of interest to the history of surrealism. In addition to dressing itself in an impossible version of technical language, pataphysics also furnished itself with the trappings of an institutional bureaucracy in the form of the College of Pataphysics, publishing—irregularly—the proceedings of the college's conferences and meditations (for example, in the now rare *Cahiers du Collège du Pataphysique, Dossiers,* and *Subsidia*). The life-tenured "office-bearers" called *satraps* (the name of the provincial governors of the Persian Empire!), included Ray-

mond Queneau, Marcel Duchamp, Max Ernst, Joan Miró, Eugene Ionesco, Michel Leiris, Réne Clair, Groucho Marx, and Man Ray . . . quite a lineup. In 1960 the *Evergreen Review* devoted an entire issue to pataphysics, prompting a response in the *Intérnationale Situationniste,* which accused the Americans of erecting an authority in pataphysics. The idea of an authority is "to go against the spirit of pataphysics" which in fact forbids the pataphysical mind, if we can refer to one as such, from organizing a social movement around an idea that has been turned into a religion. Pataphysics is an aesthetic nihilism and a will to crisis, and it is small wonder that it is taken up by the situationists. Like them, it advocated the path of active nihilism. For the situationist Jorn, the pataphysician must choose either a "situological" method or nothing. To choose nothing, Jorn argues, is to choose the "perfectly adapted religion for the modern society of the spectacle: a religion of passivity and pure absence." Asger Jorn, "La Pataphysique, une religion en formation," *Intérnationale Situationniste* 6, 1961, p. 31.

5   I. -L. Sandormir in Launoir, *Clefs pour la 'Pataphysique,* pp. 86–87.
6   Friedrich Nietzsche, *A Nietzsche Reader,* p. 278.
7   Lyotard, *The Postmodern Condition,* p. xxiii.
8   Ibid., p. 60.
9   Anthony Wilden, in his book-length introduction to Jacques Lacan's *The Language of the Self,* relates Sartre's notion of lack and Lacan's theory of desire ("the metonymy of desire") to a common source in Kojève's lectures, claiming that there are "in fact few contemporary readings of Hegel which do not owe a considerable debt to Kojève's commentaries, and he himself owes an equal debt to Heidegger." (Jacques Lacan, *The Language of the Self: The Function of Language in Psychoanalysis,* p. 193.) Mark Poster, in *Existential Marxism in Postwar France from Sartre to Althusser,* argues that the whole of postwar theory in France takes as its bases the thematics and problematics expounded in the readings of Hegel in the 1930s— which is to say, the combined efforts of Jean Wahl, Alexandre Kojève, and Jean Hyppolite to translate, comment, and teach Hegel. Poster considers Hyppolite's contribution to the propagation of Hegel to be of greater significance than Kojève's project in the sense that he (Hyppolite) used his reading of Hegel as a mutual interrogation of such fields as psychoanalysis, Marxism, and existentialism. See Jean Hyppolite, *Studies on Marx and Hegel.* Hyppolite's Marxist readings of Hegel were seminal not only for the reception of Hegel, and particularly *The Phenomenology of Mind* (which Hyppolite translated, with commentary in 1946 in *Genèse et structure de la phénomenologie de l'ésprit de Hegel),* but also for the reception of the early Marx. (The English edition of *The Phenomenology of Mind* was translated by J. B. Baillie.) Hyppolite writes: "In this *phenomenology,* as Marx understood it, Hegel often described with great fidelity some of the fundamental characteristics of the human condition, in particular those of the alienation of man through his conditions of work and existence. Marx's *Economic and Philosophic Manuscripts* are nothing other than a commentary on *The Phenomenology of Mind (Studies on Marx and Hegel,* p. vii). The philosopher Vincent Descombes in his history of *Modern French Philosophy* (originally published as *Le Même et l'autre,* 1979), commences his study with Kojève's commentaries by quoting him: "It may well be that the future of the world, and thus the sense of the present and the significance of the past, will depend in the last analysis on contemporary interpretations of Hegel's works" (p. 9).

10   Michel Foucault, "Orders of Discourse," in *Social Science Information* 10 (1971): 28. In this essay, which is the transcript of his inaugural address delivered at the Collège de France, Foucault pays homage to his mentors: Dumézil, Canguilhem, and especially to Jean Hyppolite. Foucault said "I think this work [in reference to Hyppolite's contribution] articulated in a small number of books . . . has traversed and formulated the most fundamental problems of our age. Many of us are infinitely indebted to him" (p. 30). Foucault's debts are based on what he calls Hyppolite's "alterations" worked upon Hegelian philosophy. These were: (1) granting the phantom-like shadow of Hegel, "prowling through the Nineteenth Century, and with whom men struggled in the dark," a *presence* via the translation of the *Phenomenology;* (2) by asking the questions: "Can any philosophy continue to exist that is no longer Hegelian? Is that which is anti-philosophical necessarily non-Hegelian?" (3) by relating Hegel as a schema to the experience of modernity and conversely by making modernity the "test of Hegelianism and, beyond that, of philosophy"; (4) by transforming the Hegelian theme of "the end of self-consciousness into one of repeated interrogation" of acquired generalizations to thereby "re-establish contact with the non-philosophical" from which arises the possibility of a philosophy which was "present, uncertain, mobile all along its line of contact with non-philosophy, existing on its own, however, and revealing the meaning this non-philosophy has for us." For Hyppolite the philosophy of totality represented by Hegel could be rejected "in the extreme irregularity of experience"; and (5) the final alteration: "if philosophy must begin as absolute discourse, then what of history, and what is this beginning which starts out with a singular individual, within a society and a social class, and in the midst of struggle?" (pp. 28–29).

11   Ibid., p. 28.

12   Poster observes that, like it or not, the French reception of Hegel gravitated toward the problematics of the *Phenomenology* even as the commentaries focused on other aspects of Hegel's *oeuvre;* for example, the philosophy of history or the science of logic. According to Poster, Hyppolite "taught the French to look at the magisterial unfolding of the historical shapes of human consciousness for the *secret of a new philosophical anthropology*" (Poster, *Existential Marxism in Postwar France*, p. 19, emphasis added). Jacques Derrida in the "Ends of Man," from his *Margins of Philosophy*, takes issue with the anthropologistic reading of the *Phenomenology,* claiming that the "science of the experience of consciousness . . . is rigorously distinguished from anthropology" and, moreover, that the critique of both empirical and transcendental anthropology in Husserl had been passed over in postwar France. Derrida is surprised that Heidegger, Husserl, and Hegel himself were not consulted for their critiques of humanism, but instead "amalgamated" with "the old metaphysical humanism" (pp. 117–23). Hyppolite himself was to deny that Hegel was putting forward a new anthropology in claiming that the subject of the *Phenomenology* was "*conscience de soi*" rather than man (Poster, *Existential Marxism in Postwar France*, p. 19). Kojève's readings unite this conscience de soi with man, thus uniting the humanist (Marxist and Feuerbachian) with the psychoanalytic interpretations. Kojève writes: "the profound basis of Hegelian anthropology is formed by the idea that Man is not a being that *is* in an eternal identity to itself in space, but a Nothingness that *nihilates* as Time in spatial Being, through the negation of this being, through the negation or transformation of the given, starting from an idea or an ideal that does not yet exist, that is still a nothingness (a

"project")—through negation that is called *Action* (*Tat*) of Fighting and Work (*Kampf und Arbeit*)" (Kojève, *Introduction to the Reading of Hegel*, p. 48).

13 As mentioned (n. 10 above), Wilden argues that Lacan's early theories of desire repeat Kojève's formulas found in the "influential first chapter" of Kojève's *Introduction to the Reading of Hegel*. This first chapter is both a translation and a close commentary of chapter 4 of the *Phenomenology*, devoted to the exploration of the dialectic of recognition, master/slave. In the "Propos sur la causalité Psychique" Lacan writes: "The very desire of man [Hegel] tells us is constituted under the sign of mediation; it is desire to make its desire recognized. It has for its object a desire, that of the other, in the sense that there is no object for man's desire which is constituted without some sort of mediation—which appears in his most primitive needs: for example, even his food has to be prepared—and which is found again throughout the development of satisfaction from the moment of the master-slave conflict throughout the dialectic of labor" (Lacan, *The Language of the Self*, p. 114, quoted in "translator's notes"). Lacan later in "The Subversion of the Subject and the Dialectic of Desire in the Freudian Unconscious," in *Ecrits: A Selection*, laments the impossibility of Hegel's *Selbstbewusstsein*, "the being conscious of self, the fully conscious self," leading him to forego the dialectic, since the history of science demonstrates that the progress of thought and theories does not fit together according to the thesis, antithesis, or synthesis dialectic. "It is elsewhere that the hour of truth must strike" (pp. 296–97).

14 Kojève, *Introduction to the Reading of Hegel*, p. 34.

15 Ibid., pp. 22–23.

16 Hegel's genealogy of philosophical consciousness sets out from the Parmenidean thesis "being is," transformed in the descriptive repetitions of philosophy until the ultimate synthetic statement "being is" completes the circular voyage of the dialectic. For Hegel, the movement of the philosophical consciousness corresponds to the process which the slave imagines before freedom is attained. The genealogy refers to the succession of philosophical ideologies. Stoicism can justify slavery by identifying the idea of freedom with freedom of thought. Stoicism ends in talk. Skepticism/ nihilism, on the other hand, culminates in solipsism, and the radical skeptic will commit suicide whilst the nihilist will recognize contradiction as the motor of the historical process. In either case there is no point to life if one denies the value of being and the human world. Out of this contradiction emerges Christian ideology. In this a point is granted in the beyond, and before the Christian God all are slaves, and there is no reason to struggle because in the beyond all are equal. But, "a liberation without a bloody fight . . . is metaphysically impossible" (ibid., p. 56). To be free of the eternal slavery of Christianity the slave must pay the price of death: atheism. Hegel's (or is it Kojève's?) pagan society is characterized as a society of masters who are obliged, due to prestige, to *subject* the others, the neighbors. The pagan state is the result of the victory of the city which becomes the capital of the empire. The citizens are those who are the masters of the city, but cease to be so because they cease to wage war. The bourgeoisie for Hegel are these masters without slaves who were themselves slaves without masters. "By becoming a private property owner . . . the Greek master, a *citizen* of the city, becomes a peaceful Roman Bourgeois, a *subject* of the Emperor, who himself is but a Bourgeois, a private property owner whose Empire is his patrimony" (ibid., p. 63). The empire is the *capital*. For the bourgeois the only means of a realization of the dialectic, mas-

ter/slave, is through the reinvention of the risk of death—in the form of revolutionary terror—and from this is born the modern state. For Hegel the universal cause is realized in the individual and a particular man, Napoleon, who lacks only self-consciousness, and this is Hegel. Here perhaps is the origin of the duality of Hegel's absolute ontology, between "man" and "consciousness of self," action/consciousness, Napoleon/Hegel.

17 Ibid., p. 139.
18 Ibid., p. 191.
19 Ibid., pp. 161–62.
20 Descombes, *Modern French Philosophy*, p. 31.
21 Michel Foucault in *Folie et déraison: histoire de la folie à l'âge classique*, quoted in Alan Sheridan, *Michel Foucault: The Will to Truth*, p. 15. The absence of work, a translation of "une absence d'oeuvre," appeared in the later discarded preface to the first edition. This book was translated by Richard Howard as *Madness and Civilisation*.
22 Descombes, *Modern French Philosophy*, p. 111.
23 Jean Baudrillard, in *L'Echange symbolique et la mort*, writes that "Foucault's analysis is a master-work of this veritable history of culture, this Genealogy of Discrimination in which work and production have taken, since the Nineteenth Century, a decisive place. However, there is an exclusion which precedes all the others, one more radical than that of the mad, children, 'inferior' races, an exclusion which precedes them all and which serves as their model and which is at the very basis of the 'rationality' of our culture: it is that of the dead and death," p. 195 (author's translation).
24 Ibid., pp. 195–96.
25 Baudrillard continues: "To be dead today is an unthinkable anomaly—all the others are inoffensive compared to this one. Death is a delinquence, an incurable deviance" (ibid., p. 196); and Paul Virilio in Paul Virilio and Sylvère Lotringer, *Pure War*, p. 140. In many ways Virilio seems to accept Baudrillard's general orientation regarding questions of the relationship of death and consciousness.
26 Kojève, *Introduction to the Reading of Hegel*, p. 254. According to Kojève, complete satisfaction for Hegel included "a perfect understanding of death." Cf. Virilio in *Pure War*, p. 123: "Death isn't sad, it's Being itself. Death is the founder of consciousness, and therefore of political awareness."
27 Kojève, *Introduction to the Reading of Hegel*, p. 254.
28 Gilles Deleuze and Félix Guattari, *Anti-Oedipus*.
29 See Jacques Derrida, *Dissemination*, "The Double Session."
30 Baudrillard, *L'Echange symbolique et la mort*, p. 12, writes that "all that remains for us is theoretical violence. Speculation to death, whose only method is the radicalization of all hypotheses."
31 See Jean-François Lyotard, *Driftworks*, in which he advocates the perspective of "active nihilism." This book is a translation of essays from his *Dérive à partir de Marx et Freud*.
32 It is unremarkable to make this claim, since the experience of reading Bataille is of a similar order to reading Kojève, Hyppolite, Foucault, or Sartre; this is to say that for successive generations of French intellectuals the question of positionality or situation in relation to the towering literary/theoretical figures has been virtually obligatory. Thus the figures cited are representative, rather than inclusive, of thinkers who

have placed themselves in relation to Bataille. At the same time the late reception of Bataille for English readers must occasion some reevaluation of the development and direction of critical theory in France in terms of preconceptions. For example, Foucault's shock of discovery that he had been listed in an encyclopedia of science as "a philosopher who founds his theory of history on discontinuity"—"that leaves me flabbergasted," suggests that we must look beyond Canguilhem and Bachelard in our efforts to understand and contextualize the work of Foucault. If we were to conceive Foucault's oeuvre as a unity we would be able to explain the late theme of the "history of sexuality" in terms of the early focus on sexuality in Foucault's meditation on "Transgression" in the essay on Bataille. Donald Bouchard does well to introduce Foucault's selected essays, *Language, Counter-Memory, Practice: Selected essays and interviews,* with the "Preface to Transgression." But can we speak, after the experience of Derrida and Foucault himself, of such unities?

33 Understandably these concepts refer us to Nietzsche. As in many other respects, the meditation and study of the work of Nietzsche was pioneered by Bataille; not in simple exegesis, but in an active intervention which attempted to wrest the philosopher from the grasp of the Fascists. It must be remembered that the period of Bataille's interest in Nietzsche, and his subsequent defense in "Réparation à Nietzsche," and "Nietzsche et les fascistes," in *Acéphale* 2, 1937, occurred after the betrayal of Nietzsche by Elizabeth Foerster's meeting with Hitler in 1933 and the recuperation of him to the "philosophy" of national-socialism by Alfred Rosenberg. Outside of Bataille, Michel Camus asks, what other figure in the French Left dared to restore (*réparer*) Nietzsche? "L'Acéphalité ou la réligion de la mort," in his introduction to the collection, *Acéphale 1–5, 1936–1939.*

34 Psychoanalysis demonstrates that these objects constitute a fundamental ensemble of signifiers at the level of the unconscious.

35 The proximity of this couplet to Emile Durkheim's work on the sociology of religion demonstrates a certain debt of Bataille to the French sociological school of Durkheim and Mauss. Bataille's use and understanding of the couplet must, however, be contrasted to the Durkheimian one. What is at issue in Bataille's text is the extent to which a sociological science à la Durkheim is capable of responding to the demand of the heterogeneous (see chapter 3), which says for Bataille that the principle governing the movement of society is outside of society; and the object of a social science can never be identical to this principle which puts an end to the thought of *Ratio.* (The mathematical ratio can well serve as a model for the philosophical, since it always implies a relationship of terms, of the part to the whole, origin to end, subject to object). Thus the science of economics, which since the time of Ricardo specified a relationship of the producing subject to the commodity through the agency of labor qua value, proves incapable, for Bataille, of being a rigorous predictive science because it fails to account for the uncountable and unaccountable behavior of subjects irreducible, ontologically as it were, to economic rationality. The implication is, of course, that Marxism too fails in the fashion of other sciences.

36 Jacques Derrida, *Writing and Difference,* "From Restricted to General Economy: A Hegelianism without Reserve," p. 253 (This essay first appeared in *L'Arc,* May 1967, and also appeared in *Semiotexte* 2:2, 1976, an issue devoted to Bataille.)

37 Derrida, *Writing and Difference,* p. 252. Bataille sleeps with reason whose slumber engenders monsters "then puts them to sleep. . . . The slumber of reason is not, perhaps, reason put to sleep, but slumber in the form of reason, the vigilance of the

Hegelian logos. Reason keeps watch over a deep slumber in which it has an interest." At dawn, or dusk, this sleep, in which has been contrived a discourse which has "completed itself" and anticipated "all the figures of its beyond"—is awakened by the only figure capable of escaping the grey extension of reason's twilight: laughter (pp. 251, 252).

38 The reception of Bataille in France constitutes a significant body of literature and research in its own right; this reception and its bibliography are discussed at greater length in chapter 3.

39 Michel Foucault, *The Order of Things: An Archaeology of the Human Sciences*, p. 330.

40 Ibid., p. 342. For Foucault it is anthropology which "constitutes perhaps the fundamental arrangement that has governed and controlled the path of philosophic thought from Kant to the present day."

41 Ibid., p. 343, quoting Kant's *Logik*, vol. 8. From this question sprouts a tree of "philosophical man," properly called the "human": homo sapiens for whom knowledge is sufficient, *homo faber* who redefines knowledge as savoir-faire, *homo oeconomicus* whose mode of existence takes precedence over specific knowledge or practice, whose being aims to correspond to a given *state* of society. In the Hegelian schema, since this is what we are describing, the flower of the genealogical process, solar in its circularity and enlightening in its force, is homo sapiens, now the man of absolute knowledge of action. In this schema, simplistic as it is, may be plotted the movement of the anthropological episteme. It is also possible to see how the French might come to regard a thinker such as Marx in terms of the enlarged Hegelian project, with no necessary contradiction implied. Marx completes the circular voyage of reuniting the alienated economic man with knowledge and rooting the anthropological analytic in the empirical and concrete science of human societies: historical materialism.

42 Ibid., p. 341.

43 Ibid., p. 342.

44 Bataille, "Réparation à Nietzsche," in Camus, *Acéphale* 2–3, p. 6.

45 Foucault, *The Order of Things*, p. 342.

46 Claude Lévi-Strauss in his introduction to Marcel Mauss, *Sociologie et Anthropologie*.

47 These forms of exchange are abstracted by Mauss from a vast store of ethnographic evidence in his key work: *The Gift: Forms and Functions of Exhange in Archaic Societies*. Among the sources which Mauss consulted were Franz Boas and Bronislav Malinowski. For their discussions on the forms, see Boas, *Race, Language and Culture*, "The Secret Societies of the Kwakiutl," and "Metaphor in Kwakiutl," and Malinowski, *Argonauts of the Western Pacific*.

48 Georges Bataille, *Oeuvres complètes*, 5:215–16, quoted in Michèle Richman, *Reading Georges Bataille: Beyond the Gift*, pp. 69–70.

49 This idea, which would appear as a central tenet of the situationists, was enunciated in the work of Roger Caillois, Bataille's co-founder of the Collège de Sociologie. See Caillois, *Man and the Sacred*, chapter 4.

50 See Georges Bataille, *La Part maudite, précedé par "La notion de dépense,"* part 5, section 1.

51 Richman, *Reading Georges Bataille*, p. 3.

52 Derrida, "From Restricted to General Economy," *Semiotexte* 2:42.

53 Derrida, *Writing and Difference*, p. 275.

54 Ibid., p. 274.

55 If Bataille claims to have surpassed Hegel, it is possible to demonstrate that he has not. Likewise, if he claims to have remained Hegelian, it is equally possible to point to his rejection of Hegelianism.

56 Jean Baudrillard, "Quand Bataille attaquait le principe métaphysique de l'économie," in *Le Quinzaine Littéraire*, June 1–15, 1976.

57 In addition to Mauss's *The Gift*, see also Henri Hubert and Marcel Mauss, *Sacrifice: Its Nature and Function*.

58 Mauss, *The Gift*, p. 1.

59 Ibid., p. 84.

60 "The millenium you have when you are not really having a millenium." According to Wilden in his introduction to Lacan, *The Language of the Self*, it was Kojève's assimilation of Hegel's theory of language, "attempting to integrate the Concept (the signifier in the wide sense) with time, the discourse, the consciousness-of-self, and consciousness-of-death, and equating the wisdom of the Hegelian sage with the authentic *Dasein* of Being-towards-death" (p. 195), which formed the basis of his notion of a "discursive truth" in Hegel, claiming that in the stage of the reciprocal recognition in the dialectic, as a "confrontation of two consciousnesses" (master and slave) in an imaginary conflict, "*language is the active mediator in this confrontation*" (p. 195). Further, this language and its meaning is both relational and temporal and "detached from reality" and "no longer subjected to the necessity which regulates essences bound to their respective natural supports." The significance of this for Kojève is that the possibility of truth and error emerge together in Hegel, "something which pre-Hegelian philosophies were never able to take into account" (p. 196). It is thus possible to infer, as does Wilden, that Lacan's linguistic foundations were as much Hegelian as Saussurian. The possibility of the error, whose falsity is revealed via determinate negation, connects us, in a vast and circuitous movement, to Lyotard's remarks on the paralogical character of postmodern science, "producing not the known, but the unknown." (It might be recalled in passing that Lyotard's first book was entitled *Phénomenologie*.)

Paralogics and History: On the Possibility of Error

A speculative extension of the potlatch suggests a strategy of challenge and defiance at a political level: could it be that the thinking of the antinuclear movement is all wrong? Should we rather organize large festivals in order to attract the bomb? *Bring it on!* Either it will not be dropped, in which case the strategy of terror will be revealed for what it is—the dissemination of its signs in order to produce the superstitution of its power; or else it will be dropped, and in that moment of incandescence we will assume grotesque mortuary positions in order to haunt the living who will creep out of their bunkers. In the reversal the dead will inherit the earth and the living will be confined to their tombs—bunkers and fallout shelters.

We all seem to suffer the ignominy of bankruptcy in the restricted economy of signification. In the famous Gold Standard of meaning the representational value of the signifier is fixed to a given quantum of the signified or referent meaning (gold). This is made possible by removing the gold from circulation in order to equilibrate the value of commodities in circulation (including money). When the total quantity of representational value exceeds the gold guarantee by too great a margin, the signifier is allowed to float. Mere anarchy is loosed upon the exchange system; signifiers establish value against each other and the economists of meaning scratch their heads and say that nothing means what it used to. Perhaps the truth of the disappearance of meaning in the gold economy is that a new system is at work: henceforth, it is the "Plutonium Standard" that governs the system of values, an economy whose inflation of its representational value makes the inflation of the gold economy look positively benign and precapitalist. Like gold that was formerly kept out of circulation, it is plutonium that is now strictly prohibited from circulation (enriched weapons-grade). Kept like a terrible deity in a sanctum, it can only be approached with extreme caution and due decorum. It is now a pure distilled mega-death that equilibrates the system of hyperproduction. Gold, now free to circulate and unmediated by taboo or the walls of a treasury, has a new role of perform: it is the thread that sutures the silicon chip to the networks and assemblages that lead the vanguard of the cybernetic revolution. In some primordial tale of gold, sand, and an alien intelligence there is a new dialectic put into play: the struggle between the organic body and its inorganic extension. If it is a question of intelligence measured as memory then the game is over, and the organic body is reduced to the state of the unemployed slave, as Deleuze and Guattari put it, a "residual subject off to the side, alongside the machine around the entire periphery, a parasite of machines, an accessory of vertebro-machinate desire" (Deleuze and Guattari, *Anti-Oedipus*, p. 285). Against this paralogy is opposed a model of the social composed of atoms in an excited state, and our question might be: should we welcome the particle that has escaped the chaos of Maxwell's chamber (by answering the riddle at the gate) in order to introduce new orders of disorder outside? Leaving only traces, the trajectory of this charmed particule is the one announced by Baudrillard in *Les stratégies fatales:* imminent reversibility; whatever is immanent is at the point of its disappearance.

Our present geopolitical predicament carries with it a certain irony. It is the revenge of the dinosaurs. Who knows what sealed the fate of the Saurian reptiles? Whatever it was is locked up in the sedimentary layers of the carboniferous era, a level that we suck and scrape to fuel our own species of technological dinosaurs: jetliners, killer submarines, and the entire range of domestic species. Like beached whales that are driven by some irresistible death-urge, the supertankers founder on the sands of the Gulf, discharging the residues and distillations that were the resting places of the once sovereign species. The dinosaurs aim to fuel our own destruction, incensed by the desecration of their world by our unquenchable thirst, disdainful of our pitiful mimicry of their forms, our simulation of their profligate mass. If the second era of dinosaurs is headed for extinction then the maxim is confirmed: their tragedy is our farce. "Usually reliable sources" have claimed that the greatest species of all, the brontosaurus, possessed not one, but two brains; one at the base of their spines controlling the servo-mechanisms of legs, tail, and other appendages, with a second brain lodged in their little heads—whence issued decisions of navigation, speed, etc. It is further claimed that due to their immense size and their unsophisticated nervous circuitry, messages travelling along their spines (from one brain to the other) took how long? Ten seconds? Ten minutes? At the moment of catastrophe the message might be sent: "It's all finished here, over and out!", even as the receiving brain hatched new stratagems of conquest and control, blithely ignorant of the imminent extinction. I tell this cautionary tale because it is possible that we are like the dinosaurs, that we also have two brains . . .

The last great work might involve the orderly evacuation of the earth, redoing history in reverse—bowing out gracefully by putting things back where we found them. The last man will be the guardian angel of the frozen embryo bank destined to thaw out in *n* million years, when nature has taken its course and civilization is but a trace in the sedimentary crust. The first people will be born into a garden of Eden; no true origin nor true end but eternal recurrence. As the anthropologist said (on the basis that if it is worth saying it is worth exaggerating) ours is the only culture that thinks it evolved from a primordial swamp. All the others think they descended from the gods.

2 The Gift of the Stars

1   Lacan refers to the "inviolable Debt" which ensures the cycle of gifts, of "wives and goods" which he identifies with the notions of *hau* and *mana* (in *The Language of the Self*, p. 42). Lacan makes further reference to Lévi-Strauss's interpretation of these notions, which appeared in Mauss's *The Gift*, as the basis of the former's concept of "zero symbolic" value, the overabundance of signifiers in relation to the available signifieds. Lacan, however, rejects Lévi-Strauss's algebraic reduction of symbolic efficacy.

2   Sigmund Freud, *Totem and Taboo*, chapter 4.

3   See Gilles Deleuze and Félix Guattari, *On the Line*, "Rhizome."

4   See Raoul Vaneigem, *The Revolution of Everyday Life*, chapter 8. Vaneigem writes "Sacrifice is the archaic form of exchange. . . . It dominated human relationships, including commercial relationships, until mercantile capitalism and its money as the measure-of-all-things had carved out such a large area in the world of slaves, serfs and, finally, burghers, that the economy came to appear as a particular zone, a domain separated from life" (p. 57). Vaneigem also recommends that "We will have to renew our acquaintance with feudal imperfection, not in order to perfect it, but in order to transcend it. We will have to rediscover the harmony of unitary society while freeing it from the phantom of divinity and from hierarchy sanctified . . . the inequality of blood is closer to the equality of free individuals, irreducible to one another, than bourgeois equality" (p. 59).

5   See Jacques Derrida, *Dissemination*, parts 1, 2, "Plato's Pharmacy," which traces the polysemy of the pharmakon (from the *Phaedrus*), linking the medicinal cure—drug, remedy, recipe, and poison—with the conceptual ambivalences of writing as a poisoned gift offered by Theuth to the king of the Egyptians, Thamus (later the god Ammon). Plato, like the king, is suspicious of the pharmakon and, hence, of writing, not only seeing it as harmful (there is no such thing as the harmless remedy) but as artificial; and not simply harmful to natural life, but to the life of disease as well. Thus the objection of the king to writing: "under the pretext of supplementing the memory, writing makes one even more forgetful; far from increasing knowledge, it diminishes it" (p. 100).

6   In addition to "Plato's Pharmacy," the *glissement* receives another treatment in relation to the question of style and women in Nietzsche, in Jacques Derrida, *Spurs—Nietzsche's Styles*. Derrida relates writing to the feminine in Nietzsche, attempting to reconcile apparently feminist propositions in *Beyond Good and Evil* and *Twilight of the Idols: The Anti-Christ* with his (Nietzsche's) "venemous anti-feminism." In "Le coup de don," Derrida links Nietzsche's analysis of sexual

difference based on modes of propriation—woman gives, man takes—with propositions of Rodolphe Gasché's "L'Echange heliocentrique," in *L'Arc* 48, 1972 (the first Bataille issue) and in Heidegger's *Zeit und Sein* where the question of being is submitted to the "enigmatic operation of the abyssal gift." According to Derrida, Heidegger denied that giving (*geben*) can be thought in terms of being: "Just as there is no such thing then as a Being or an essence of *the* woman or the sexual difference, there is no such thing as an essence of the *es gibt* in the *es gibt sein,* that is, of Being's giving and gift" (*Spurs,* "Le coup de don"); this of course throws into question any search for Foucault's "purified ontology of being" in the problematic of the gift. On the question of writing, this is feminine, because it plays at "dissimulation, at ornamentation, deceit, artifice, at an artist's philosophy" (p. 67). In Nietzsche "woman's great art is the lie, her supreme concern is appearance (*Schein*) and beauty." In a double relation of castration and circumcision, women and Jews are related, but not in a reference of condemnation, castration being "the simulacrum for which circumcision is the mark" (p. 69), but ambivalently—Jews are *littérateurs,* actors, and mountebanks; but before art "he (the philosopher of art) is a woman— and what is more he is a sterile woman . . . before art, the dogmatic philosopher, a maladroit courtesan, remains, just as did the second-rate scholar, impotent, a sort of old maid" (p. 77).

7   Lyotard, in *Economie libidinale,* asks, in reference to Baudrillard's use of the concept of symbolic exchange, "Why can't he [Baudrillard] see that the *whole problematic of the gift,* of symbolic exchange such as received from Mauss, with or without the addition or deflections of Bataille, Caillois and Lacan, belongs in full to Western imperialism and racism—for it is the good savage of ethnology (slightly libidinalized) who is inherited with the concept" (translation by author, emphasis added).

8   The meditation on otherness is a very ancient and modern phenomenon, pre- and postmodern perhaps. Thus Michel de Certeau in *Heterologies: Discourse on the Other,* chapter 5, writes that Montaigne's text is inscribed within a heterological tradition "in which the discourse about the other is a means of constructing a discourse authorized by the other . . ." arising "from the same problematic: the circularity between the production of the Other and the production of the text" (pp. 68–69). Montaigne credits the pious cannibal with an ethic whose "comparison must be sought among the most heroic examples Greek courage has to offer," and, in reference to the economy of gifts, compares the generosity implied by polygamy as comparable to the loftiest female figures of the Bible and antiquity. De Certeau: "The finest gold tradition has to offer is used to forge a halo for the cannibals" (p. 76).

9   Pierre Clastres, *Recherches d'anthropologie politique.*
10   Ibid., p. 56.
11   Ibid., p. 55.
12   Ibid.
13   Ibid.
14   Ibid., p. 56.
15   In this context Baudrillard provides a parodic reading of Hegel's genealogy of historical consciousness in an inversion which relies on the slightest inflection to subvert the latter's meaning. "Work," declares Baudrillard, "is slow death." Its origin is to be found in the warrior's refusal to put the captured prisoner to instant, sacrificial, and honorable death. The first political economist was the master who

realized the "economic" in the "deferred death" and the "different death" of the slave in servitude. Across the length of history the slaves are domesticated as a form until, in the democratic era they are freed. Free to do what? Free to work. And what is work? "Work is slow death." See Baudrillard, *L'Echange symbolique et la mort,* part 1, "Le travail et la mort." Marx's dialectical arrangement of capital and labor repeats Hegel's structure if, and when, one considers capital as dead labor. However, Baudrillard is critical of Marx for having underestimated the death in dead labor.

16 For Clastres, ethnocentrism is practically a formal characteristic of cultural formations: "The essence of culture is to be ethnocentric, precisely in the sense that all cultures consider themselves to be the culture *par excellence.*" Clastres, *Recherches d'anthropologie politique,* pp. 50–51. It is, therefore, not on the question of its ethnocentrism that Western culture must be interrogated, but on the consequences which stem from it.

17 Jean Baudrillard writes in "Modernité" (*Encyclopaedia Universalis,* vol. 11, 1972) that modernity is a characteristic mode of civilization "irradiating from the West." The meaning of modernity is something more than the old dualism ancient/modern. It describes a structure of change and crisis, "a canonic morality of change" which smashes traditional morality. The establishment of the administrative state, the secularization of the arts and philosophy of the everyday are characteristic of the mode of life in modernity. Ideologies are another expression of modernity, and this is revealed in the analysis of decolonization: the "field of anthropology shows more clearly than European history the truth of modernity—that it is really never a matter of change or revolution, but of entering into an implicit game with tradition, in a debate where the two are in a connected field, in a process of amalgamation and adaption. The *dialectic of rupture* largely gives way to a *dynamic of amalgamation*" (p. 141).

18 The work of Clastres is notable for its examination of those so-called primitive institutions which prevent divisions in the social body (which is in a sense a fundamental definition of the primitive society for Clastres: the undivided social body, the autarky). Division of the social body, which is to say the domination of the social totality by a group—warrior, caste, or class—is characteristic of all state formations. See Pierre Clastres, *La Société contre l'état.* The political domination by those who possess force is a split which precedes all the others, and it "founds the economic relation of exploitation."

19 See Michel Foucault, *The Order of Things,* chapter 9. He writes: "The unthought (whatever name we give it) is not lodged in man like a shrivelled-up nature or a stratified history; it is, in relation to man, the Other: the Other that is not only a brother but a twin, born not of man, nor in man, but beside him and at the same time, in an identical newness, in an unavoidable duality" (p. 326).

20 The high priest of simulation, Jean Baudrillard, writes in *L'Echange symbolique et la mort* that the carceral form of society has been diffused throughout the entire social space and is now invested "in all the moments of real life": "There have always been Churches to hide the death of God, or to hide the fact that God was everywhere—which is the same thing. There will always be reserves for animals and Indians to hide the fact that they are all dead, and that we are all Indians. There will always be factories to hide the fact that work is dead, that production is dead, or even that it is everywhere and nowhere. Nothing today will be served by combatting capital in its *determined forms.* On the contrary, if it became clear that it is no longer

determined by anything, and that its supreme weapon is to reproduce work as the imaginary, then it will be capital itself which will be on the point of its demise" (p. 36).

21 Mauss, *The Gift*.

22 Emile Durkheim was Mauss's uncle, and together they collaborated on several works; for example, *Essai sur la fonction du sacrifice, De quelques formes primitives de classification: contribution à l'étude des répresentations collectives*, etc.

23 Evans-Pritchard in Mauss, *The Gift*, p. vii.

24 With Durkheim, Mauss founded *L'Année Sociologique* in 1900. For commentary on Mauss see Henri Lévy-Bruhl, "In Memoriam: Marcel Mauss" in *L'Année Sociologique*, 1948–49, and Claude Lévi-Strauss, "Introduction à l'oeuvre de Marcel Mauss" in Mauss, *Sociologie et anthropologie*. In the latter Mauss is credited, with Durkheim, of introducing the "total social fact" which not only defines reality as the social, but also provides an insight that proves crucial for Lévi-Strauss's own method: "That the social fact be total does not only signify *that everything observed forms part of the observation*, but as well and above all in a science where the observer is of the same nature as his or her object, then *he or she is also part of the observation*." The observer is both subject and object, thing and representation.

25 It was Mauss's contribution to have added the "total" to Durkheim's notion of "social facts" in the essay on the gift. The important aspect of this notion is that there is a category of facts that is irreducible to individual psychology, and whose explanation in sociological terms relies on their referencing to other social facts. Further, social facts must be treated as things and can be observed according to the methods of a science and are external to the individual member of a society. See Emile Durkheim, *The Rules of Sociological Method*. Chicago, University of Chicago Press. See also Anthony Giddens, *Durkheim*.

26 According to Lévi-Strauss, Malinowski was burdened by the functionalist hypothesis which holds that universal truths are somehow immanent in the study of a single society. But what interests the anthropologist, writes Lévi-Strauss, "is not the universality of the function—which is far from definitely established . . . but, rather, the fact that [the] customs are so varied." In Lévi-Strauss, *Structural Anthropology*, p. 14.

27 Evans-Pritchard in Mauss, *The Gift*, pp. viii–ix.

28 Baudrillard, *L'Echange symbolique et la mort*, pp. 7–8.

29 It is interesting to reflect, in the light of Derrida's critique of logocentrism, this privilege which is accorded certain French thinkers of the twentieth century; neither de Saussure nor Kojève published their respective courses on semiology or Hegel.

30 See chapter 3.

31 Baudrillard, *L'Echange symbolique et la mort*, p. 8.

32 In Mauss, *Sociologie et anthropologie*, pp. xlix–1.

33 Discussion of reciprocity and obligations in the symbolic realm of the primitive are a clear index to the work of Mauss in Lévi-Strauss. For a discussion of the primal state of language see his introduction to Mauss's work in *Sociologie et anthropologie*, and for a general discussion of these matters see Lévi-Strauss, *Structural Anthropology*, chapters 3, 4, 5.

34 Baudrillard, *L'Echange symbolique et la mort*, p. 206. The imaginary here is to be understood in its Lacanian sense; that is, as the order of specular identifications and oppositions that is a reduction and solution to the basically insoluble oppositions of

the symbolic (Oedipal) order. For discussion of these orders see Anthony Wilden, *System and Structure: Essays in Communication and Exchange*, chapter 1. See also Lacan, *The Language of the Self*.

35 Mauss, *The Gift*. It is obligatory in this discussion to quote Lévi-Strauss describing his reaction to *The Gift* by quoting Malebranche on his first reading of Descartes: "le coeur battant, la tête bouillouiante, et l'esprit envahi d'une certitude encore indéfinisable, mais impérieuse, d'assister à un événement décisif de l'évolution scientifique." Lévi-Strauss in Mauss, *Sociologie et anthropologie*, p. xxxiii.

36 Lyotard, *Economie libidinale*, pp. 148–55.

37 Kojève, *Introduction to the Reading of Hegel*. Speaking of Hegel, Lacan wrote: "Before Darwin . . . Hegel had provided the ultimate theory of the proper function of aggressivity in human ontology, seeming to prophesy the iron law of our time. From the conflict of Master and Slave, he deduced the entire subjective and objective progress of our history, revealing in these crises the syntheses to be found in the highest forms in the status of the person in the West, from the Stoic to the Christian, and even to the future citizen of the Universal State." See Lacan, *Ecrits*, p. 26.

38 Emile Durkheim, quoted in Pierre Birnbaum, "Du Socialisme au don," in *L'Arc* 48, 1972. See also Marshall Sahlins, "Philosophie politique de l'essai sur le don," in *L'Homme* 8, no. 4, October/December 1968.

39 Mauss, *The Gift*, p. 3.

40 Finding it difficult to disengage the two orders (signs and symbols) Lévi-Strauss conflates the two. This confusion is apparent in the introduction to Mauss's *Sociologie et anthropologie*. Both Wilden, *System and Structure*, and Richman, *Reading Georges Bataille*, question Lévi-Strauss's use of semiological categories—the former preferring to restrict the use of the term symbol to analog signs, or icons in the Peircean sense, and, therefore, to treat the symbolic exchange of "cool" societies (Lévi-Straussian "coolness") as the exchange of signs (p. 32); the latter questioning the reduction of women to the status of signs (however privileged) in Lévi-Strauss's communication theories (p. 79). In the introduction to *Sociologie et anthropologie* one gets the impression that for Lévi-Strauss the symbol is but a special case of the sign.

41 Mauss, *The Gift*, p. 80.

42 On the law of the circulation of things and its relation to the communication of laughter, Serres writes: "Was it necessary to wander three centuries over the glaucous eye of the Pacific to learn slowly what we already knew ourselves, to attend overseas the same archaic spectacles we stage every day on the banks of the Seine, at the Théâtre Français, or at a brasserie across the street? But could we ever have read Molière without Mauss?" Michel Serres, *Hermes—Literature, Science, Philosophy*, p. 13.

43 Mauss, *The Gift*, pp. 66–67.

44 Emile Durkheim, *Elementary Forms of Religious Life*, p. 442, quoted in Marshall Sahlins, *Culture and Practical Reason*.

45 Denis Hollier, "Malaise dans la sociologie," *L'Arc* 48, 1972, p. 58.

46 Ibid.

47 Mauss, *The Gift*, pp. 78–79.

48 See Hollier, "Malaise dans la sociologie." The malaise is due to an irreconcilable difference between Marxism and Maussian sociology. Claiming to be independent of all metaphysics, materialist or otherwise, Mauss nonetheless invokes a meta-

physics of psychology and leaves himself open to the countercharges of the Marx-ists.

49   One of the remarkable aspects of Mauss's *The Gift* is its bibliographical depth and, therefore, this text should be consulted first for references concerning these primi-tive institutions.

50   Ibid., p. 30.

51   Maurice Merleau-Ponty, *Signs*, p. 118.

52   J. P. Terrail, in "Entre l'ethnocentisme et le Marxisme," *L'Arc* 48, 1972, claims that in breaking with ethnocentrism, Mauss was compelled to provide a new theory of exchange. This he failed to do—he defined a problematic without resolving it. Cf. Claude Meillassoux, "Essai d'interpretation du phénonème économique dans les sociétés traditionnelles d'auto-subsistence," *Cahiers d'Etudes Africaines* 4, 1960.

53   Hollier, "Malaise dans la sociologie," p. 60.

54   Ibid., p. 62.

55   This, of course, is precisely the conclusion that Bataille was led to in *La Part maudite*.

56   Mauss, *The Gift*, p. 33.

57   Ibid.

58   Ibid., p. 35.

59   Ibid.

60   Lyotard, *Economie libidinale*, p. 155. This is Lyotard's reply to Baudrillard's claim that there is no production, no unconscious, no economy in primitive society: "il *n'y a pas* du tout de sociétés primitives ou sauvages, nous sommes tous des sauvages, tous sauvages sont des capitalistes-capitalisés."

61   Richman, *Reading Georges Bataille*, p. 15.

62   Lyotard, *Economie libidinale*, p. 133. The great Zero is a figure borrowed from both Lévi-Strauss and Lacan, a signifying absence: "cette castration, ce négatif, ce qu'ici nous nommons le grand Zéro, bien loin d'y voir l'ordre du désir, qui est mouvements d'énergies, c'est pour nous d'y du capital au sens plus large, celui de la théologie qui capitalise les affects sur l'instance de l'Autre, *une* figure du désir" (p. 130).

63   The texts of Baudrillard are themselves haunted by the opening paragraph of *the Communist Manifesto*. In no less than four works can we observe its ghost stalking the scene: In *The Mirror of Production*, "A spectre haunts the revolutionary imagi-nation: the phantom of production"; in *L'Echange symbolique et la mort*, "There is no longer symbolic exchange at the level of modern social formations, it is no longer the organizational form. Of course, the symbolic haunts them as their true death. Precisely because it no longer rules the social form, they can only know its ghost"; in "La lutte enchantée ou la flute finale," in *Le P. C. ou les paradis artificiels du politique*, and *La Gauche divine*, "A spectre haunts the spheres of power: it's communism. But a spectre haunts the communists themselves: it's power."

64   Mauss, *The Gift*, p. 76.

65   Karl Polanyi, *Primitive, Archaic and Modern Economies*, quoted in Richman, *Reading Georges Bataille*, p. 25.

66   Foucault, *The Order of Things*, chapter 2, 3.

67   Ibid., p. 43.

68   Freud, *Totem and Taboo*, p. 56.

69   The symbol, for Julia Kristeva, is a universal abstract object, not as concrete as the object of a semiotic (as opposed to a symbolic) practice. The idea that there is a

136 Notes

practice, semiotic or otherwise, of the symbol is revealing, locking the discourse in a productive metaphor. What for Foucault is the third element of the sign—the conjuncture ("the similitudes that link the marks to the things designated by them")—is missing in Kristeva's account of the sign in the Renaissance which is characterized by a strict dyadic structure. For a comparison see Foucault, *The Order of Things*, chapters 2, 3, and Julia Kristeva, *Desire in Language: A Semiotic Approach to Literature and Art*, chapter 2.

70 Baudrillard, *L'Echange symbolique et la mort*, p. 80.

71 Jean Baudrillard, *Simulations*, p. 84.

72 Wilden, *System and Structure*, p. 32. Referring to the archaic sign Baudrillard muses, "If we are starting to dream again, today especially, of a world of sure signs, of a 'strong symbolic order,'" *Simulations*, p. 84.

73 Claude Lévi-Strauss, *The Savage Mind*.

74 Lévi-Strauss in Mauss, *Sociologie et anthropologie*, p. xlviii.

75 In communication theory, as expounded by Wilden, *System and Structure* (chapters 1, 7), a communication is said to be of a "higher logical type" if it is a "meta-communication." It is also said to be of a lower level of organization. Symbolic exchange would appear to satisfy the condition of a meta-communication as a message about a relationship.

76 Ibid., pp. 29–30. Wilden is sanguine about the possibilities of transcending the Imaginary: "in a socio-economic system like ours . . . all Symbolic values are reduced to Imaginary profits."

3 The Issue of Bataille

1 See *Critique* 195–96, August/September 1963, a special double issue devoted to Bataille who died in 1962.

2 See *Tel Quel*.

3 See, for example, *Semiotexte* 2, no. 2, 1976, or *October* 36, Spring 1986.

4 Georges Bataille, *Visions of Excess: Selected Writings 1927–1939*.

5 Francis Marmande, *Georges Bataille politique*, and Richman, *Reading Georges Bataille*.

6 Jürgen Habermas in "The French Path to Postmodernity: Bataille between Eroticism and General Economics," *New German Critique* 33, 1984.

7 For example, Baudrillard, "Quand Bataille attaquait le principe métaphysique de l'économie," and Habermas, "The French Path to Postmodernity."

8 See particularly Foucault, *The Order of Things*, chapter 9; and *Language, Counter-Memory, Practice*, "Preface to Transgression."

9 See Sigmund Freud, *Group Psychology and the Analysis of the Ego*, chapter 7.

10 In Denis Hollier, *Le Collège de sociologie, 1937–1939*. A collection of texts connected to the proceedings, including review articles until the 1950s. See particularly Georges Sadoul, "Sociologie sacrée," p. 569.

11 Jean-François Lyotard in *Instruction païennes*. He writes: "Some very good things have arrived in the name of commodities since the industrial revolution, why not ideas? Some are certainly feeble, but do you believe that those of Merleau-Ponty or Lévi-Strauss, which are certainly not, are exempt from all marketing?" (p. 13). "One may certainly judge our thinkers as lamentable, but let us not invoke from that the fact that they are famous" (p. 15). Great thoughts do not have to be produced in

obscurity, "The principle that the more it is obscure the more it is just, is false" (p. 16).

12 See *Bataille*, a publication of Tel Quel from a colloque at Cerisy-la-Salle in 1972 (Paris: 10/18, UGE, 1973).

13 *L'Arc* 32, 44.

14 This ethic at work is readable in the writings of Robert Jaulin, *La Paix blanche*, who argues that primitive societies are not "survivals," but diverse models of human society, some of which belong to the future. Likewise, Lyotard makes reference to Clastres's analysis of primitive society in terms of an ethic of the pagan in *Instructions païennes*, and *Rudiments païens*.

15 See Bataille, *Oeuvres complètes*. For excellent bibliographies refer to Richman, *Reading Georges Bataille*, or Marmande, *Georges Bataille politique;* to Alain Arnaud and Gisèle Excoffon-Lafarge in *Bataille*, or to *Semiotexte* 2, no. 2, 1976.

16 For Barthes, mutation rather than rupture characterizes the "relativization" of the relations between the writer, reader, and critic, in the wake of the demands of Marxism, Freudianism, and structuralism; relativity of the frames of reference of an Einsteinian rather than Newtonian order. There is also the requirement for a new object to oppose the disciplinary bound "work," and this is the Text. Barthes: "The Text is a methodological field." In Roland Barthes, "From Work to Text" in *Image, Music, Text,* essays selected and translated by Stephen Heath, pp. 153–64.

17 Ibid., p. 157. Barthes goes on to say: "If the Text poses problems of classification (which is furthermore one of its 'social' functions), this is because it always involves a certain experience of limits . . . the Text is that which goes to the limit of the rules of enunciation (rationality, readability, etc.). Nor is this a rhetorical idea, resorted to for some 'heroic' effect: the Text tries to place itself very exactly *behind* the limit of the *doxa* (is not general opinion—constitutive of our democratic societies and powerfully aided by mass communications—defined by its limits, the energy with which it excludes, its *censorship?*). Taking the word literally, it may be said that the Text is always *paradoxical*." pp. 157–58.

18 Of course, along with others: Mallarmé, Balzac, Lautréamont, Blanchot, etc.

19 The category of the heterogeneous is introduced in Bataille's essay, "La Structure psychologique du Fascisme," in *La critique sociale* 10, 11 (1933, 1934), the review coedited by Bataille and Boris Souvarine. The latter's split with the Communist party over the trial of Trotsky marked the start of a non-PCF Marxism in France. The essay is translated in Bataille, *Visions of Excess*.

20 See Freud, *Group Psychology and the Analysis of the Ego.* Freud, according to Franz Alexander, took a dim view on the viability of democracies and was "thoroughly impressed by the indestructibility of the profound emotional need of humanity for strong leadership, which is the cornerstone of all his sociological speculations" (p. ix).

21 Susan Sontag, "The Pornographic Imagination," in Georges Bataille, *Story of the Eye.* She writes, "Pornography that is serious literature aims to 'excite' in the same way that books which render an extreme form of religious experience aim to 'convert'" (p. 95). Pornography ultimately is more about death than it is sex; Thanatos surpasses Eros: an "erotics of agony."

22 Roland Barthes, "The Metaphor of the Eye," in Bataille, *Story of the Eye*, pp. 119–27.

23 For Bataille the taboo and the prohibition are essential preconditions for transgres-

sion. Taboos exist in the profane world, and it is only through limited acts of transgression that a sacred and ecstatic state can come about. In the case of the death of a sovereign the "door to unlimited transgression is opened." It was this mythic force and energy which exercised Bataille in his revolutionary writings of the 1930s, connected to the movement of *Contre-Attaque.*

24 There is a continent of thought just beyond the horizon; the matrix formed by Blanchot, Bataille, and Klossowski. This continent is the territory of an aesthetic of anti- or post-surrealism, its critique and its critical moment. The discourse on the relationship between death, sexuality, and writing is another means of describing the triad. In effect it is a Nietzschean aesthetic. See Pierre Klossowski, *Un si funeste désir,* and *Nietzsche et le cercle vicieux;* and Maurice Blanchot, *L'Espace littéraire,* and his *L'Entretien infini.*

25 Foucault, in *Language, Counter-Memory, Practice,* p. 32.

26 Georges Bataille, *L'Expérience intérieure.* Acephality or headlessness is the term Bataille coined to describe this lack of existential guarantee and loss of sovereignty produced by the death of God. *Acéphale* is the name of the review coproduced by Bataille, Klossowski, and Masson between 1936 and 1939.

27 Georges Bataille, "La Practique de la joie devant la mort," *Acéphale* 5, June 1939. The date of this last issue of *Acéphale* provides an unmistakable context for Bataille's meditations. In the sixth meditation Bataille declares, playing on the sense of his own name, "I AM MYSELF WAR. I represent a human movement and excitation whose possibilities are limitless: this movement and this excitation can only be *pacified* by *war.*" See "Méditation héraclitéenne," *Acéphale* 5, p. 22.

28 Klossowski, *Un si funeste désir,* p. 17.

29 Foucault, "Orders of Discourse," *Social Science Information* 10, 1971, p. 28.

30 Foucault, *Language, Counter-Memory, Practice,* p. 33.

31 *Critique* 195–96, August/September 1963. Klossowski writes in "A propos du simulacre dans la communication de Georges Bataille," that whoever says "atheology" (Bataille's concept) speaks of divine absence, of the place occupied by the name of God, the guarantee of the personal I. Klossowski refers to Bataille's concept of the simulacrum and its relationship to the *notion.* "The simulacrum constitutes the sign in an instantaneous moment and cannot establish an exchange between one mind and another, nor permit the passage of a thought to another. One can only exchange the waste or surplus of what one intends to communicate." Language is lacking for Bataille since it is made of these propositions which cause identities "to intervene" and since one "can no longer remain at the level of identities, *one is obliged to open notions beyond themselves.*" (Bataille quoted in *Critique* 195–96, p. 745.) Philippe Sollers in "L'Acte Bataille" claims that Bataille substitutes the instant of experience for Nietzsche's eternal return, and that these instants or moments of the unconscious, of eroticism, and of poetry, are what escape from "homogeneous production." In Tel Quel (ed.), *Bataille.*

32 In Marmande, *Georges Bataille politique,* p. 89.

33 See Richman, *Reading Georges Bataille,* p. 88.

34 Durkheim, *Elementary Forms of Religious Life,* pp. 53–54, quoted in Annette Michelson, "Heterology and the Critique of Instrumental Reason," *October* 36: 111–27. Michelson addresses many important themes concerned with the study of Bataille's heterology, including its relation to the critical model of the Frankfurt school.

35   Michelson, "Heterology and the Critique of Instrumental Reason," p. 115. Michelson refers to the "philological ambiguity" of the sacred, what for Freud was an example of the "antithetical meaning of primal words" by simultaneously referring to the "holy and the accursed."

36   Ibid., p. 116.

37   See Denis Hollier (ed.), *Le Collège de sociologie*.

38   A reproduction of the five issues of *Acéphale* has been published: Camus, *Acéphale*.

39   See Michelson, "Heterology and the Critique of Instrumental Reason," pp. 125–26. Michelson argues that the Odyssean myth in *Dialectic of Enlightenment* dates the birth of the bourgeois individual in the Homeric tale, giving rise to the reign of instrumentalism and to the domination of nature and men by rationality. Bataille, in common with other historians, identified the triumph of homogeneity later, with the demise of the feudal order. By paying tribute to the romantic critique of the bourgeoisie, he (Bataille) is likened, by Horkheimer and Adorno, to the "neo-Romantic reaction" which had identified world history with the enlightenment. See Theodor Adorno and Max Horkheimer, *Dialectic of Enlightenment*.

40   Ibid., pp. 38–41ff.

41   Marx and Engels in *The German Ideology* (in Karl Marx and Friedrich Engels, *Basic Writings on Politics and Philosophy*, ed. Lewis S. Feuer, p. 254). On the idea of a progression Marx and Engels write: "Empirically communism is possible only as the act of the dominant peoples 'all at once,' or simultaneously, which presupposes the universal development of productive forces and the world intercourse bound up with them" (p. 256).

42   Michelson reports that Horkheimer "was heard to observe toward the end of his life that even Marx appeared to envisage life as a vast workhouse." In "Heterology and the Critique of Instrumental Reason," p. 127.

43   See Baudrillard, *L'Echange symbolique et la mort*, chapter 2. Similarly, Georges Bataille in "Unknowing: Laughter and Tears," relates fishing to the concept of sovereignty: "Fishing is not quite work. It is, if we like, the work of primitive man, but it is work which does not create that alienation which characterizes the slave's work. In our time still, anyone who considers himself a master can fish. Fishing is the property of the master." *October* 36 (Spring 1986): 101.

44   Sahlins, *Stone Age Economics*, p. 1.

45   Marx and Engels, *Basic Writings on Politics and Philosophy*, p. 249.

46   See Clastres, *La Société contre l'état*.

47   Clastres, *Recherches d'anthropologie politique*, p. 184.

48   Bataille, *La Part maudite*.

49   See Guy Debord, *The Society of the Spectacle*.

50   *La Critique sociale* 7, January 1933. Translated in Bataille, *Visions of Excess*.

51   Jean Piel in the introduction to Bataille, *La Part maudite*, p. 17.

52   Ibid., parts 1, 2.

53   Baudrillard, "Quand Bataille attaquait le principe métaphysique de l'économie," p. 5.

54   Ibid., p. 6.

55   Ibid.

56   Ibid., p. 7.

57   Kojève, *Introduction to the Reading of Hegel*.

58   Raymond Queneau, in "Premières confrontations avec Hegel," wrote that he and

Bataille had hoped to come to the aid of a "sclerotic dialectical materialism" by enriching it with the best ideas of bourgeois thought, Freud, Durkheim, and Mauss. There is no dialectic of nature, but a dialectic rooted in the human condition and lived experience. This is the specific value of negativity in psychoanalysis and Marxism. Jean-Joseph Goux in *Freud, Marx, économie et symbolique,* claims that Marxism and Freudianism reveal a profound unity on the question of the constitution of the subject as an "ensemble" of relationships, either the subject of ideology or neurosis (pp. 31–39).

59 Jacques Derrida, "Of an Apocalyptic Tone Recently Adopted in Philosophy," *Oxford Literary Review* 6, no. 2, 1984.

60 Ibid., pp. 20–21.

61 Cf. Jean-François Lyotard and Jacob Rogozinski, "La Police de la pensée," *L'Autre Journal* 10, December 1985, and English translation "The Thought Police," in *Art and Text* 26, 1987.

62 Bataille, *Oeuvres complètes,* 6:350.

63 Foucault, *The Order of Things,* p. 328.

4 Theories of the Third Order

1 Plato, *The Republic,* pp. 370–86.

2 As identified for example by Jean-François Lyotard in *The Postmodern Condition,* and Hal Foster (ed.), *The Anti-Aesthetic.*

3 The use of such terms produces an effect heavy with connotation. The simulacrum is a term with an ambiguous paternity, having originally referred to Hellenistic and Roman priapic sculpture. It was subsequently employed by Pierre Klossowski and Georges Bataille; for them it is an avatar of the sign, an incommunicable moment of the sign that represents the totality of an experience which can neither be communicated nor determined. Notions, which are communicable, are the waste product (*déchet*) and residuum of the simulacrum. See Pierre Klossowski, "A propos du simulacre dans la communication de Georges Bataille," *Critique* 195–96, 1963. Simulation is best understood in terms of the "simulation model" in the form of the coded program of a computer. The hyperreal refers to the style of photographic realism. The wider connotation used here is in terms of an obscene saturation of an experience: quadraphonic sound in relation to music, hard pornography in relation to sex. See Jean Baudrillard, "Porno-stéréo," in *De la séduction.*

4 Baudrillard, *L'Echange symbolique et la mort.*

5 Without in any way wishing to infer from this either the definition or the existence of a "late" Baudrillard.

6 This theme is developed in relation to the media, about which Baudrillard writes in *For a Critique of the Political Economy of the Sign,* p. 170: "they speak, or something is spoken there, but in such a way as *to exclude any response anywhere.* This is why the only revolution in this domain—indeed the revolution everywhere: the revolution *tout court*—lies in restoring [this] possibility of response. But such a simple possibility presupposes an upheaval of the existing structure of the media."

7 Jean Claude Giradin, "Towards a Politics of Signs: Reading Baudrillard," *Telos* 20 (Summer 1974): 136.

8 A paradigm exemplified by Claude Lévi-Strauss's notions on structural anthropology, and by Roland Barthes's early writings on semiology.

9 Baudrillard, *Le Système des objets*, p. 29.
10 Mark Poster in two articles, "Technology and Culture in Habermas and Baudrillard," *Contemporary Literature* 22, no. 4, 1981, and "Semiology and Critical Theory: From Marx to Baudrillard," in *Boundary 2*, 8, 1979. Baudrillard might in fact decline this appellation and prefer to reserve it for the work of Derrida, Kristeva, and the *Tel Quel* group.
11 Levin in the introduction to Baudrillard, *For a Critique*, p. 11.
12 Levin opts to translate *l'ancien* as the "bygone" object, since no precise English equivalent exists. L'ancien implies no distinction between the authentic antique and the reproduction or pseudo-antique object.
13 So rescuing McLuhan—after a fashion—by affording his work a consideration often neglected, or eclipsed by his status as pop-philosopher. The "global village" is a spectacular image par excellence. On "hot" and "cool," Baudrillard writes: "Coolness . . . is the omnipotence of the operational simulation. So long as an affect and a reference remain, so long as there is a 'message,' one is in the 'hot' era. But when the medium becomes the message one enters the cool era. And this indeed concerns money: having arrived at a certain phase of disconnection it is no longer a medium or a means for the circulation of goods, it is *the circulation itself*, which is to say, the perfected form of the system in its abstract circularity." Baudrillard, *L'Echange symbolique et la mort*, p. 41.
14 Baudrillard, *Le Système des objets*, p. 119.
15 Ibid., p. 112.
16 Ibid., p. 113.
17 In Baudrillard, *For a Critique*, chapters 3, 7, and p. 137.
18 See Baudrillard, *La Société de consommation*, part 2.
19 Baudrillard, *For a Critique*, p. 185.
20 "The 'absence of style' is from the beginning an absence of space; maximum functionality is the solution for the unfortunate whose house without losing its boundaries, loses its internal organization." Baudrillard, *Le Système des objets*, p. 24.
21 In Baudrillard, *L'Echange symbolique et la mort*, "La Fin de la production." "The productive forces and the relations of production—otherwise called the sphere of material production—are perhaps only one of the possible conjunctures, and therefore historically relative, of the process of reproduction. Reproduction is a form which far surpasses economic exploitation. The play of productive forces is not therefore one of its necessary conditions" (p. 49).
22 Foucault, *The Order of Things*, chapter 10.
23 Alfred Jarry, "Veritable portrait of Monsieur Ubu," woodcut for the first edition of *Ubu Roi*, 1896. Reproduced in *Selected Works of Alfred Jarry*.

24 Diachronically, the movement from commodity to sign traces a progressive process of abstraction; synchronically, the process involves the framing of a message by a

meta-communication. The latter, according to Anthony Wilden, is said to be of a "higher logical type" but of a "lower level of organization." The theory of logical typing, as explained by Wilden, is useful for an understanding of the process of abstraction involved in the semiological reading of Marx's commodity performed by Baudrillard. Wilden writes that "logical typing . . . applies to certain abstract characteristics of the system (for example, the relationship between codes and the messages within it, or the relationship between various messages), and is not to be confused with the STATE of the system at any given time, to which the concrete description of organization more properly applies. *And every diachronic emergence of a new level of organization must necessarily require the reorganization of the logical typing of the system*" [emphasis added]. In Wilden, *System and Structure*, p. 172.

25 Baudrillard, *Le Système des objets*, p. 41.
26 Streamlining is the quintessential form of this aesthetic. See Jeffrey L. Meikle, *Twentieth Century Limited: Industrial Design in America, 1925–1939*, and Donald J. Bush, *The Streamlined Decade*.
27 The application of the theories of fluid dynamism became something of a metaphor for the productive system. It coincided (as a style) with a shift in the productive system away from production to productive consumption. Prior to the Depression, and throughout the entire history of capital, there had been a heavy preponderance of capital in fixed and infrastructural investment. This is not to say that there were no consumer objects or that the destiny of production was not consumption of some sort, just that in, and by itself, it was not the principle of the system; people consumed, and objects were produced. The Crash marked the movement of capital toward an investment in consumables, the objects of consumption, and the entire Western economy has come to depend upon the continual and ever-increasing movement of these objects through the system.
28 Bataille in *La Part maudite* writes: "In a fundamental way, the danger of war comes from the side of production: only war . . . can be the client of an industrial plethora" (p. 205). The distinction between "warrior" society and "military" society is drawn in relation to the Aztecs: "A truly *military* society is a business society [*société d'entreprise*] for which war has the meaning of the development of power, of a methodical progress of Empire" (p. 93). As we have already seen in relation to Clastres, such a perspective, reductive though it may be, constitutes the anthropological critique developed in relation to Hegelianism. See Clastres, "Archéologie de la violence: la guerre dans les sociétés primitives," and "Malheur du guerrier sauvage" in *Recherches d'anthropologie politique*, and *La Société contre l'état*.
29 Baudrillard, *Le Système des objets*, pp. 66–86.
30 Baudrillard, *La société de consommation*, p. 20.
31 Ibid., p. 29.
32 Ibid., pp. 27–29.
33 Baudrillard, *Le Système des objets*, pp. 232–34.
34 Ibid., pp. 212–13.
35 Baudrillard, *La Société de consommation*, p. 75.
36 Georg Lukács, *History and Class Consciousness*, p. 83. Baudrillard acknowledges Lukács as one of the few theorists, with his theory of reification, to have constituted the "only critical line of theoretical development between Marx and the Situationists" in *The Mirror of Production*, p. 121 (notes).

37 Levin in Baudrillard, *For a Critique*, p. 20.
38 Baudrillard, *Le Système des objets*, p. 167.
39 Lévi-Strauss, "Introduction à l'oeuvre de Marcel Mauss," in Mauss *Sociologie et anthropologie*, p. xix.
40 Baudrillard, *La Société de consommation*, p. 112.
41 Ibid., p. 225.
42 Ibid., pp. 315–16.
43 Adorno and Horkheimer, *Dialectic of Enlightenment*, and Theodor Adorno, *Prisms*, "Cultural Criticism and Society."
44 See Bataille, *Visions of Excess*.
45 Jaulin, *La Paix blanche*.
46 See Jean-François Lyotard, *La Condition postmoderne: rapport sur le savoir*.
47 Jean Baudrillard, *Simulacres et simulation*, "Sur le Nihilisme."
48 Paul Virilio, *Vitesse et politique*, and particularly, *Esthétique de la disparition*.
49 Baudrillard, *Simulacres et simulation*, p. 234.
50 Lyotard, *Economie libidinale*, p. 130.
51 Baudrillard, *For a Critique*, p. 45.
52 It is only within the framework of modernity that fashion exists—in the signifying alternation between the bygone and the modern. Baudrillard writes: "It seems that modernity simultaneously sets into motion a linear time which is that of technical progress of production and history, and a cyclical time, which is that of fashion." In Baudrillard, *L'Echange symbolique et la mort*, part 3, p. 136.
53 See, for example, Karl Marx, "A Critique of Political Economy," in Marx and Engels, *Basic Writings on Politics and Philosophy*, pp. 133–67.
54 From Karl Marx, *A Contribution to the Critique of Political Economy*, quoted in Lukács, *History and Class Consciousness*, p. 104.
55 Karl Marx, *Capital*, vol. 1, quoted in Baudrillard, *For a Critique*, p. 130.
56 Ibid., p. 130.
57 Ibid., p. 131.
58 Ibid., p. 132.
59 In the shadow of an Althusserian subject we meet Baudrillard's: "The individual is an ideological structure, a historical form correlative to the commodity form (exchange value), and the object form (use-value)." Ibid., p. 133.
60 Ibid., p. 144. The attempt to distinguish between the infra- and superstructure, Baudrillard asserts, produces the "desperate distortions," e.g., "dialectic," "structures in dominance," and so forth, which characterize Althusser's work on ideology, making it appear "as the overblown discourse of some great theme, content or value whose *allegorical* power insinuates itself into consciousness. . . . These become the *contents of thought* . . . a sort of cultural surf frothing on the beach-head of the economy." Ibid., p. 144.
61 Ibid., p. 148.
62 Ferdinand de Saussure, *Course in General Linguistics*.
63 Baudrillard, *For a Critique*, pp. 123–29. Baudrillard speaks of a "logic of symbolic exchange" as a "mode of *transgression* of the economic" and the "deconstruction" of the "commodity form" and the "sign form" which are the "*codes of value*." Properly speaking "there is no symbolic value, there is only symbolic exchange." The symbolic object, exemplified by the Maussian kula is exchanged without assuming any value of its own. "Once symbolic exchange is broken, this same

material is abstracted into utility value, commercial value, statutory value. The symbolic is transformed into the instrumental, either commodity or sign. Any one of the various codes may be specifically involved, but they are all joined in the single form of political economy which is opposed, as a whole, to symbolic exchange."

64 Ibid., p. 151.

65 Ibid.

66 Ibid., pp. 151–54.

67 Ibid., p. 160.

68 In the introduction Levin adds notes to the title *For a Critique of the Political Economy of the Sign* in order to bring out its parodic relationship to Marx's *Contribution* to the "Critique of Political Economy" in *Capital*.

69 In Baudrillard, *For a Critique*, pp. 123–29. The vertical slash is a bar of exclusion, and has its origin in Lacan's formulation using the linguistic sign:

$$\frac{S}{s}$$ ("Agency of the Letter in the Unconscious" in *Ecrits*)

"no longer that which articulates [as in the Saussurian model], but that which censors—and thus the locus of transgression" (p. 161).

70 Baudrillard, *The Mirror of Production*, p. 21.

71 Giradin, "Towards a Politics of Signs: Reading Baudrillard," p. 137.

72 The conjuncture of a level of development of the productive forces and the critical self-awareness of this development "is only the materialist variant of our culture's pretension to the privilege of being closer than any other culture to the universal, closer to the end of history or truth." Baudrillard, *The Mirror of Production*, p. 113.

73 It is the principle of symbolic exchange rather than primitive society which is privileged in Baudrillard's work. He might agree indeed with the decentering of the anthropological vision instituted by Mauss. According to Lévi-Strauss, Mauss denied the idea that objectivity, wisdom, or intellectual superiority resided with the observer over the observed, although he cautioned that logic and common sense should never be abandoned. Yet in *The Gift*, Mauss uses the Moari concept of *hau* to explain the process of obligation in the cycle of the gift-exchange. It is a theory explained by Tamati Ranaipiri in Elsdon Best's "Forest Lore," in *TNZI* 42:431. It is worth quoting: "I shall tell you about *hau*. *Hau* is not the wind, not at all. Suppose you have some object, *taonga*, and you give it to me; you give it to me without a price. We do not bargain for it. Now if I give this thing to a third person who after a time decides to give me something in repayment for it (*utu*), and he makes me a present of something *taonga*. Now this *taonga* I received from him is the spirit (*hau*) of the *taonga* I received from you and passed on to him. The *taonga* which I received on account of the *taonga* that came from you, I must return to you. It would not be right on my part to keep these *taonga* whether they were desirable or not. I must give them to you since they are the *hau* of the *taonga* you gave to me. If I were to keep this second *taonga* for myself I become ill or even die. Such is *hau*, the *hau* of personal property, the *hau* of the *taonga*, the *hau* of the forest. Enough on that subject." Quoted in Mauss, *The Gift*, p. 9. Hau is the spirit of the forest that returns to the forest, to the clan, tribe, or donor: "it seems to be the motivating force behind the obligatory circulation of wealth, tribute and gifts in Samoa and New Zealand" (Mauss, *The Gift*, p. 10). In spite of Lévi-Strauss's regard for Mauss, he felt that the latter allowed himself to be mystified by the indigene. Baudrillard sides here with

Lévi-Strauss against Mauss, but also against Lévi-Strauss: "Conceiving exchange as an operation between two separated terms, each existing in isolation prior to the exchange, one has to establish the existence of the exchange itself in a double obligation: that of giving and that of returning. Thus it is necessary to imagine (as Mauss and the native apparently do) an immanent power of the object, the hau whose force haunts the recipient and incites him to divest himself of it. The insurmountable opposition between the terms of the exchange is thus reduced at the price of a tautological, artificial, magical, supplementary concept, of which Lévi-Strauss, in his critique, has worked out the economics in positing exchange directly as structure." Baudrillard, *For a Critique*, p. 70. The point is, after this digression, that if ever Baudrillard were to idealize the primitive in symbolic exchange, then the concept of hau would be an ideal point of departure, either as magic or economic structure. Baudrillard eschews the terms of all economics.

74 Phase 1: only surplus is exchanged, the rest consumed by the producers, with vast sectors existing outside of commodity exchange. Phase 2: the entire volume of industrial material production is alienated in exchange (the birth of capital). Phase 3: even what is considered inalienable, knowledge, virtue, love, and consciousness—all elements of the superstructure—fall into the sphere of exchange. Baudrillard, *The Mirror of Production*, p. 119.

75 Ibid., p. 120.

76 Baudrillard, *L'Echange symbolique et la mort*, p. 18.

77 The operation finds its accomplices in the "new master disciplines of structural linguistics, semiology, information theory and cybernetics." Baudrillard, *The Mirror of Production*, pp. 121–22.

78 "Consumer engineering" is an expression coined in the 1930s to describe a technique that fuses advertising and marketing to habituate consumers to the cycles of fashion and planned obsolesence.

79 Baudrillard, *L'Echange symbolique et la mort*, p. 46.

80 Baudrillard, *The Mirror of Production*, p. 127.

81 Both economics and linguistics are systems "for equating things of different orders—labour and wages in one and a signified and signifier in the other" from Saussure's *Course in General Lingusitics*, quoted in Giradin, "Towards a Politics of Signs," p. 128.

82 Baudrillard, *L'Echange symbolique et la mort*, p. 18.

83 Ibid., p. 20.

84 Ibid., pp. 10–12. Pataphysics, in one definition, is "the science of laws governing exceptions"—creation itself is an event that is the exception to the laws of nature. In another, pataphysics defines God "as the shortest distance between zero and infinity." When asked if he was a Christian, Dr. Faustroll replied "I am God." (Definitions from Jarry, *Selected Works of Alfred Jarry*.) Baudrillard borrows Dr. Faustroll's remarks on identity: "Concerning some further and more evident meanings of the words 'HA HA,'" when A=A, "Toute système qui se rapproche d'une opérationalité parfaite est proche de sa perte. Quand le système dit 'A=A' ou 'deux et deux font quatre' *il approche à la fois du pouvoir absolu et du ridicule totale,* c'est à dire de la subversion immédiate et probable il suffit d'un coup de pouce pour se faire s'effondre. On sait la puissance de la tautologie lorsqu'elle redouble cette prétention du système à la sphericité parfaite (la gidouille d'Ubu)." Baudrillard, *L'Echange symbolique et la mort*, p. 11 (emphasis added).

5 Lyotard and the Jouissance of Practical Reason

1 See Lyotard and Rogozinski, "La police de la pensée."

2 See Jürgen Habermas "Modernity versus Postmodernity," in *New German Critique* 22, 1981. Lyotard's reply, such as it is, is in *The Postmodern Condition*, "Answering the Question: What is Postmodernism." See also Richard Rorty, "Habermas and Lyotard on Postmodernity," in Richard J. Bernstein (ed.), *Habermas and Modernity*.

3 Lyotard, *Le Postmoderne expliqué aux enfants*, p. 40. After the execution of Louis XVI, the people became the sovereign source of legitimation: "modern war between nations is always a civil war: me, the government of the people, contest the legitimacy of *your* government. With 'Auschwitz,' one has physically destroyed a modern sovereign: an entire people. One has tried to destroy it. It is the crime which opens postmodernity, the crime of lese-sovereignty, no longer regicide, but populocide (as distinct from ethnocide)" (pp. 39–40).

4 Ibid., p. 133. "Billet pour un nouveau décor."

5 Ibid., p. 150.

6 Therefore also a confirmation of the avant-gardes of history and a "politics by other means." It suffices to recall, lest we doubt the historical-political significance of the avant-gardes, "the fate meted out to the so-called historical 'avant-gardes' by political totalitarianisms. Or to observe in the alleged 'surpassing' [*dépassement*] by today's avant-gardism, armed with the pretext of returning to a communication with the public, a scorn towards the responsibility of resisting and bearing witness, a responsibility the avant-gardes assumed for over a century." Ibid., p. 150.

7 Lyotard, *La Condition postmoderne*, p. 7ff.

8 Specifically, in Jean-François Lyotard, *Le Différend. Le différend*, which translates as the "disagreement" or the difference of opinion, also means a conflict of irreconcilable frames of reference or discourses. It is a trait of the aesthetic judgment in Kant. Matters of taste "cannot be demonstrated by the means of 'determinate concepts'; it is necessary to make the rules on the basis of a given singularity."

9 In addition to the piece by Guattari, "The Postmodern Dead End," Lyotard's thought and writing has attracted considerable attention in the global sphere of contemporary theory. At random, consider the French *L'Arc* issue devoted to his reception in France, primarily concerned with the "aesthetic of desire" set into play by Lyotard in *Economie libidinale*. Hubert Damisch, "Dynamique libidinale," remarks that Lyotard's enterprise is one of "theoretical licentiousness" which has started to "bear some fruits," in terms of the analysis of the economic functioning of a psychic apparatus, giving it precedence over its *topical* (Freud) and *structural* levels (*L'Arc* 64, 1976). From England one might refer to the publication in 1986 of *Postmodernism* in the ICA Documents series, based on a two-day conference held in 1985 devoted, largely, to questions raised in the reception of Lyotard's *The Postmodern Condition*. In addition, one might refer to articles in the *New Left Review:* Peter Dews, "Adorno, Post-Structuralism and the Critique of Identity" (*New Left Review* 157, May/June 1986), which involves an examination of the figure of Adorno in the post-structuralists' encounter with Nietzsche, and the critique of identity as expounded by Lyotard; and on a more polemical note refer to Terry Eagleton's "Capitalism, Modernism and Postmodernism" (*New Left Review* 152, July/August 1985), lamenting the wrong turn which postmodernism took by crossing its avant-gardism (as though this was not a modernism) "with the *unpolitical*

impulses of modernism." This is going to forestall the development of "an authentically political art." (Reproduced in Terry Eagleton, *Against the Grain: Selected Essays.*) In particular, these two articles, along with Fredric Jameson, "Postmodernism, or the Cultural Logic of Late Capitalism" (*New Left Review* 146, July/August 1984), indicate the contours of a political response to post-structuralism emerging in Anglo-American criticism. The post-structuralist reception in Germany has likewise produced a dialogue with the post-Frankfurt school theorists—for example, Albrecht Wellmer refers to Lyotard's philosophy as the most "pregnant expression" of the "search" for postmodernist thought, in which "*aesthetic*" postmodernism appears as radical aesthetic *modernism,* "as the self-consciousness as it were of modernism." (In Albrecht Wellmer, "On the Dialectic of Modernism and Postmodernism," *Praxis International* 4, no. 4, January 1985.) However, in my opinion Wellmer mistakenly reads the "pluralism" of language games (cf. Lyotard, *The Postmodern Condition*) as the "horizon" of Lyotard's political thought and reduces it too quickly to a "limp ideology of consensus," in Lyotard's terms, inherent in the Habermasian theory of communicative action, in order to rethink, in Wellmer's words, "the moral-political universalism of the Enlightenment, the ideas of individual and collective self-determination, reason and history in a new fashion" (Wellmer, "On the Dialectic of Modernism and Postmodernism," p. 360).

10   Cf. Lyotard, "La police de la pensée," accusing the neo-Kantians of waging a bitter and vengeful campaign against the most radical advances of modernism, which include the work of Lacan, Foucault, and Derrida. The thought of Kant, however, is too important to leave to the neo-Kantians, among whom Lyotard numbers L. Ferry and A. Renaut (*La Pensée '68*), and J. Bouveresse (*La Philosophie chez les autophages,* and *Rationalité et cynicisme*). This last writer is one of the rare French philosophers to specifically place himself in relation to the British analytic tradition of philosophy. There are many interesting parallels between the work of the neo-Kantians, in their calls for "a return of the subject," "ordinary language," and "common (linguistic) sense," and the recent work of Anthony Giddens in his Wittgensteinian turn (Giddens in a public lecture, "Recent Social Theory," Melbourne, 1986.)

11   Georges Bataille quoted in Arnaud and Excoffon-Lafarge, *Bataille,* p. 67.

12   Translator Allan Stoekl writes in the introduction to Bataille's *Visions of Excess* (p. xi), that *heterogeneous* matter was "matter so repulsive that it resisted not only the idealism of Christians, Hegelians and surrealists, but even the conceptual edifice-building of traditional materialists. It was indeed an all-out assault on dignity."

13   Guattari, "The Postmodern Dead End." The impulse toward inclusivity in the construction of a discursive totality is one which post-structuralism both disavows and implicitly engages in. It is the paradox of making general statements about discontinuous phenomena. Fredric Jameson does something similar in *The Political Unconscious: Narrative as a Socially Symbolic Act,* when he suggests that post-structuralism—in the forms of Deleuze and Guattari's schizo-analysis, Foucault's archeology and political-technology of the body, Derrida's grammatology and deconstruction, Lyotard's libidinal economy, Baudrillard's symbolic exchange, and Kristeva's *sémanalyse*—can be grasped as a "new hermeneutic in its own right." These practices amount to "an *anti*-interpretive method" and "a demand for the construction of a new and more adequate, immanent or anti-transcendent hermeneutic model" (p. 23).

14 In Raymond Bellour and Catherine Clement (eds.), *Claude Lévi-Strauss.*
15 In Descombes, *Modern French Philosophy,* p. 180.
16 In particular, Gilles Deleuze, *Nietzsche et la philosophie.*
17 Descombes, *Modern French Philosophy,* p. 181.
18 Ibid.
19 The prime movers of this group were Cornelius Castoriadis and Claude Lefort. Arthur Hirsh, in his historical analysis of the review *Socialisme ou barbarie,* argues that at the end of a long engagement with the theoretico-practice, Castoriadis came to reject the moves to existentilize or revise and no doubt to structuralize Marx in the light of what is at least inconsistent in the theoretical system of Marxism. Questioning the nature of theory per se, Castoriadis viewed the return to Marx "as inconsistent with Marx's own contention that a theory should be judged by what it has become in practice." (In Hirsh, *The French New Left: An Intellectual History from Sartre to Gorz,* "The Gauchist Rejection." To judge from Lyotard's own evidence in *Economie libidinale,* the split in 1964 was a bitter experience. Lyotard's split from the group—and the splinter review, *Pouvoir ouvrier*—occasioned some rancour, which Lyotard expresses in both *Dérive à partir de Marx et Freud,* and *Economie libidinale.*
20 Developed in the pages of *Socialisme ou barbarie* between 1949–1965, and brought together in Cornelius Castoriadis, *La Société bureaucratique: les rapports de production en Russie.*
21 Several of the essays in this work are included in the collection by Lyotard, *Driftworks.* On a vaguely textual note about the translations: be warned. For unacknowledged reasons, sections of the opening essay, "Adrift," as well as other essays in the collection, have been excised. These sections include a discussion of the events surrounding the split with *Socialisme ou barbarie,* and thus address the political significance of drifting. One gains the impression that the editors wished to present, cut and pasted, an aestheticized Lyotard. In any event, to edit the text is one thing . . .
22 Ibid., p. 11.
23 Lyotard, *La Condition postmoderne.* In an interview Lyotard has spoken about this work: "I told stories in the book, I referred to a quantity of books I'd never read, apparently it impressed people, it's all a bit of a parody. . . . I remember an Italian architect who bawled me out because he said it was a pointlessly sophisticated, complicated book, and the whole thing could have been done much more simply. . . . I wanted to say first that it's simply the worst of my books, they're almost all bad, but that one's the worst . . . really that book is related to a specific circumstance, it belongs to the satirical genre." Interviewed and translated by Arias-Mission for *Lotta Poetica,* republished in *Eyeline,* November 1987, p. 17.
24 The idea of such a community is a major figure in Lyotard's meditations on Kant, particularly in relation to the ethics pursued in *Le différend* ("Le Signe d'histoire"). Lyotard writes, in "Notice Kant 4, 5," that "The *sensus communis* forms . . . part of aesthetics as the total of all reasonable practices in ethics. It is an appeal to the community which is made a priori, and which judges without a rule of direct presentation; simply, the community is necessary as a moral obligation for the mediation of a concept of reason, the Idea of liberty, whereas the community of senders and receivers of statements about the beautiful are invoked immediately, without mediation of any concept, by feeling alone for whatever can be shared *a*

priori. It already exists as taste, but does not yet exist as rational consensus" (p. 243). In the aesthetic antinomy, continues Lyotard, the antinomy of the *sublime* is the most extreme because it involves both a finality and an anti-finality, "a pleasure for pain," whereas in the beautiful there is a finality without end, based on the free accord of the faculties. "With the sublime Kant advanced a long way into a sort of heterogeneity in which the solution to the aesthetic antinomy appears more difficult for the sublime than for the beautiful" (p. 243).

25 Lyotard and Rogozinski, "La police de la pensée," p. 34.

26 Lyotard, *Driftworks*, endnotes.

27 Vaneigem, *The Revolution of Everyday Life*, p. 136. The passive nihilist "compromises with his own lucidity" about the collapse of values: "He makes one final nihilistic gesture: throws [the] dice to decide his 'cause,' and becomes a devoted slave, for Art's sake, and for the sake of a little bread. . . . Nothing is true, so a few gestures become hip. Joe Soap intellectuals, pataphysicians, crypto-fascists, aesthetes of the *acte gratuit*, mercenaries, Kim Philbys, pop-artists, psychedelic impresarios—bandwagon after bandwagon works out its own version of the *credo quia absurdum est:* you don't believe in it, but you do it anyway; you get used to it and you even get to like it in the end" (p. 136).

28 Jean-François Lyotard and Jean-Loup Thébaud, *Au juste: conversations*, pp. 11–17.

29 Nonnegotiable in the sense that the poet does not concern him or herself with whether the reader or listener has understood the poem.

30 In Lyotard, *Economie libidinale*, part 1, "La grande pellicule éphémère."

31 Allen Weiss, in "A Logic of the Simulacrum or the Anti-Roberte" (*Art and Text* 18 July 1985) writes that: "Phantasms may be considered to represent the solution of an enigma. According to psychoanalytic theory, phantasmic fabulations reveal the origins of subjectivity: the phantasm of a primal seduction is at the origin of sexuality; the phantasm of castration is at the origin of sexual differentiation; the phantasm of the primal scene is at the origin of individuality" (p. 115). Weiss points to the fundamental opposition in the thought of Klossowski's *Roberte Ce Soir and the Revocation of the Edict of Nantes*, and *Sade mon prochain*, between the simulacrum of the unique sign—"monstrous, perverse, transgressive" and the system of exchangeable signs—it is "always recuperated within the general system of exchange by means of the simulacra which expresses it. Such a misappropriation may well explain the confusion of the stereotype with reality and the rational with the real, a confusion which is at the very center of Western metaphysics" (p. 119). Such a conception may be compared with Lyotard's distinction, in *Economie libidinale*, between the intense sign and the intelligible sign, proposed in relation to Klossowski's *Monnaie vivante*.

32 In addition to Lyotard, *Discours, figure*, see his "Par delà la représentation," in the introduction to Anton Ehrenzweig, *L'Ordre caché de l'art*, and Lyotard's "Contribution des tableaux de Jacques Monory à l'intelligence de l'économie politique libidinale du capital dans son rapport avec le dispositif pictural," in Collectif, *Figurations*.

33 Sigmund Freud, *Group Psychology and the Analysis of the Ego*, chapter 7.

34 Ibid., p. 56.

35 Sigmund Freud, *On Metapsychology: The Theory of Psychoanalysis*, in particular, "The Economic Problem of Masochism."

36 Lyotard, *Economie libidinale*, p. 27. Freud in *On Metapsychology*, "The Economic Problem of Masochism," writes that the pleasure principle can no longer be considered solely as the lowering of tension due to stimulus, since pleasure may be obtained in the heightening of excitation. The Nirvana principle, which Freud calls a case of Fechner's tendency toward stability, would represent the pleasure principle in the service of the death instincts which seek to return "the restlessness of life into the stability of the inorganic state." (This latter theme is developed in his *Beyond the Pleasure Principle*.) Freud further writes, in a passage critical to the concept of the libidinal economy: "The *Nirvana* principle expresses the trend of the death instinct; the *pleasure* principle represents the demands of the libido; and the modification of the latter principle, the *reality* principle, represents the influence of the external world. . . . None of these three principles is actually put out of action by one another. As a rule they are able to tolerate one another, although conflicts are bound to arise occasionally from the fact of the differing aims that are set for each—in one case a quantitative reduction of the load of the stimulus, in another a qualitative characteristic of the stimulus, and, lastly [in the third case], a postponement of the discharge of the stimulus and a temporary acquiescence in the unpleasure due to tension" (pp. 413–15).

37 Lyotard, *Economie libidinale*, pp. 58–59.

38 In Jean-François Lyotard, "Psychanalyse et la peinture," *Encyclopaedia universalis*.

39 Ibid., pp. 745–49.

40 Lacan, *Ecrits*, p. 25.

41 Lyotard, *Economie libidinale*, p. 119.

42 Also known as *le surmâle* (the supermale), the title of Jarry's novel of 1902 about a future (1920s) man, super in every way. In "The Tears of the Supermale," Nigey Lennon writes that "Marcueil, although he is far superior to everyone else, feels that he must disguise his superiority from the prying eyes of the world by pretending to be thoroughly average and mundane, a man who 'embodied so absolutely the average man that his very ordinariness became extraordinary,' " in Lennon, *Alfred Jarry: The Man with the Axe*. Lyotard uses *super-mâle* to describe Castoriadis's concept of "generalized creativity" in a "parenthesis of hate" in the *Economie libidinale*, pp. 142–46.

43 Ibid., p. 122.

44 Ibid.

45 Ibid., p. 127.

46 Ibid.

47 A related theme is addressed, among other things, in *Instructions païennes*. Lyotard argues, in the form of a dialogue, for the justice of impiety. This manifests itself as disrespect for political institutions of the left and right, and a generalized short-circuiting of the meta-narratives by the impious, heterogeneous (i.e., unassimilable) genre of the *petit récit*.

48 Lyotard, *Economie libidinale*, p. 136.

49 Ibid., p. 137.

50 Ibid., p. 144.

51 Ibid., pp. 144–45.

52 One might recall, to recall something which does not exist, the absence of the sought-after response from Foucault solicited by Baudrillard's "Oublier Foucault," in Peter Botsman (ed), *Theoretical Strategies*.

53   Lyotard, *Economie libidinale,* p. 132.
54   Ibid., p. 133.
55   Jean-François Lyotard and Jean-Loup Thébaud, *Just Gaming,* p. 5. (Originally published as *Au juste: conversations.*)
56   "America," continues Baudrillard, "is hell, after a fashion; I loathe it, but there is something infernal in its seduction over me. So I don't criticize, but expel at the same time as intensely absorb. In all of this there is hardly room for the critical subject, it's banal to say it." Baudrillard in an interview with Jacques Henric and Guy Scarpetta, "L'amérique comme fiction," *Art press* 103 (May 1986): 40–42.

6   Revenge of the Mirror People

1   Jorge Luis Borges, *The Book of Imaginary Beings,* pp. 67–68. The story appears in Lyotard's "Contribution des tableaux de Jacques Monory" Collectif, *Figurations,* and in Dews, "Adorno, Post-Structuralism and the Critique of Identity."
2   Borges, *The Book of Imaginary Beings,* p. 14.
3   See particularly Michel Foucault, *Discipline and Punish.* The "normalizing gaze" both punishes and rewards through the process of examination. Deviation from the norm constitutes a type of sickness which necessitates the examination of the social body. "The judges of normality are present everywhere," writes Foucault. See also Alan Sheridan, *Michel Foucault: The Will to Truth,* part 2, "Society, Power, and Knowledge."
4   In Clastres, *Recherches d'anthropologie politique,* "De l'ethnocide."
5   Theodor Adorno in *Prisms,* p. 34, remarks that "To write poetry after Auschwitz is barbaric. And this corrodes even the knowledge of why it has become impossible to write poetry today. Absolute reification, which presupposes intellectual progress as one of its elements, is now preparing to absorb the mind entirely. Critical intelligence cannot be equal to this challenge as long as it confines itself to self-satisfied contemplation." Adorno later writes that "Literature must resist this verdict, in other words, be such that its mere existence after Auschwitz is not a surrender to cynicism." "Commitment," *New Left Review* 87–88 (September/December 1974): 84. Adorno puts the question in a different way, asking: "Whether after Auschwitz you can go on living—especially whether one who escaped by accident, one who by rights should have been killed, may go on living. . . . His mere survival calls for coldness, the basic principle of bourgeois subjectivity, without which there could have been no Auschwitz; this is the drastic guilt of him who was spared." Quoted by Martin Jay, *Marxism and Totality,* p. 243, from Adorno, *Negative Politics.*
6   Lyotard, *Le Postmoderne expliqué aux enfants,* p. 40.
7   Jacques Lacan, *Ecrits,* p. 16.
8   Ibid., p. 8.
9   Freud, *Beyond the Pleasure Principle.*
10 Both these works are found in Freud, *On Metapsychology,* dated 1923 and 1924.
11 Sigmund Freud, *Civilization and Its Discontents,* chapter 6.
12 Ibid., p. 93.
13 Ibid., p. 104.
14 Ibid.
15 Lacan, *Ecrits,* p. 26.

16 Ibid., "The mirror stage as formative of the function of the I as revealed in psychoanalytic experience," p. 7.
17 Ibid., pp. 26–27.
18 Ibid., p. 143.
19 Thus argues Jane Gallop in *Reading Lacan*, chapter 3.
20 Lacan, *Ecrits*, p. 4.
21 Freud, *On Metapsychology*, p. 425.
22 Gallop, *Reading Lacan*, p. 81.
23 Lyotard makes considerable use of this inorganic body in his concept of the libidinal Marx and indeed his libidinal Baudrillard. Lyotard's Freudian reading of Marx concerns the biological impulse of the death drive to return to an anterior, inorganic state. In Marx this is to return to an order in which land appears as part of man's inorganic nature, and in which the individual is part of this inorganic nature insofar as he/she is a subject. "A paradise remains as the place for a support for the critical view and a revolutionary project." Lyotard, *Economie libidinale*, p. 159.
24 Lacan, *Ecrits*, "Function and field of speech and language," part 2.
25 See, for example, Robert Hefner, "Baudrillard's Noble Anthropology: The Image of Symbolic Exchange in Political Economy," *Sub-Stance* 17, 1977, or Karlis Racevskis, "The Theoretical Violence of a Catastrophical Strategy," *Diacritics*, September 1979.
26 Baudrillard, *L'Echange symbolique et la mort*, p. 228.
27 Baudrillard, "Beyond the Unconscious: The Symbolic," *Discourse* 3 (Spring 1981): 86. This essay is a translation of the final chapter of *L'Echange symbolique et la mort*, "Le Witz, ou le phantasme de l'économie chez Freud," with an added footnote, specifying the nature of the resolution: "The unconscious and the symbolic are not to be confused with each other. The unconscious is as yet only the *symptom* of the symbolic—the fantasized form . . . of the symbolic within the (psychoanalytic) framework of an autonomization of the psyche. The concept of the unconscious is in a way itself only a fantasy, in the same way that the concept of ideology is itself an ideological concept. The symbolic is the resolution of that fantasy" (p. 86). (Translation by Lee Hildreth.)
28 Baudrillard, *L'Echange symbolique et la mort*, p. 242 (emphasis added).
29 And Baudrillard retorts: "The difference between the symbolic and the libidinal unconscious, at present obscured by the privilege afforded psychoanalysis, should be reinstalled—to prevent psychoanalysis from meddling where it has no business: on the poetic (the work of art), on the symbolic, on (primitive) anthropology, neither Marx nor Freud had anything to say that was not reductive, either to the mode of production or to repression and castration." Baudrillard, *L'Echange symbolique et la mort*, p. 342.
30 Baudrillard, *Simulations*, pp. 8–9.
31 Jonathan Arac (ed.), *Postmodernism and Politics*, p. xiii, mischievously translates *grands récits* as "tall tales," and *petits récits* as "white lies." The latter he associates with language games which "operate over smaller units both conceptually and demographically" than the stories of speculation or emancipation. He writes that Lyotard "looks to situations where power and language intersect to victimize minorities wrongly treated as if they were members of a community from which they actually differ in ways that are 'not presentable under the rules of knowledge.' "

32 See Stuart Sim, "Lyotard and the Politics of Anti-Foundationalism," *Radical Philosophy* 44, Autumn 1986.

33 Habermas writes, "In the unmediated confrontation between the two," an opposition between relativism and absolutism, or between "pure historicism and pure transcendentalism," that there are failures of both positions: "the burden of self-referential, pragmatic contradictions and contradictions that violate our need for consistency," and the burden of a "foundationalism that conflicts with our consciousness of the fallibility of human knowledge." In Bernstein, *Habermas and Modernity,* p. 193.

34 Habermas, "Modernity versus Postmodernity," *New German Critique* 22 (Winter 1981): 13. Speaking of the young conservatives he writes, "On the basis of modernistic attitudes, they justify an irreconcilable anti-modernism. They remove into the sphere of the far away and the archaic the spontaneous powers of imagination, of self-experience and of emotionality. To instrumental reason, they juxtapose in manichean fashion a principle only accessible through evocation, be it the will to power or sovereignty, Being or the dionysiac force of the poetical. *In France this line leads from Bataille via Foucault to Derrida*" (emphasis added).

35 Lyotard, *The Postmodern Condition,* "Answering the Question: What is Postmodernism?" and Lyotard in "The Sublime and the Avant-Garde," *Artforum,* April 1984.

36 Meaghan Morris, "Postmodernity and Lyotard's Sublime," *Art and Text* 16, Summer, 1984–85.

37 Ibid. Morris writes, "It is banal because it restores us to the paradox of a history driven by the sole, and *traditional,* imperative to break with tradition. . . . It is adroit because in appropriating for *post*-modernism the gestures classically associated with the avant-garde, it decrees that we cannot escape from the problematic of the latter—least of all at a time of '*post,*' i.e., ruptural rhetoric pronouncing the escape to be a *fait accompli.* At the same time, it conserves the possibility of rejecting the academicization of art—henceforth called 'modernism.' One way of describing Lyotard's move here is to say that it imposes a double bind" (pp. 63–64).

38 Ibid., p. 64.

39 Friedrich Nietzsche, in the *On the Genealogy of Morals,* "What is the Meaning of Aesthetic Ideals?" and *A Nietzsche Reader,* pp. 134–36.

40 *A Nietzsche Reader,* p. 136.

41 See Sigmund Freud, *Leonardo da Vinci and a Memory of His Childhood,* pp. 29–30.

42 Lyotard, *The Postmodern Condition,* p. 79. He writes: "the avant-gardes are perpetually flushing out artifices of presentation which make it possible to subordinate thought to the gaze and to turn it away from the unpresentable. If Habermas, like Marcuse, understands this task of derealization as an aspect of the (repressive) 'desublimation' which characterizes the avant-garde, it is because he confuses the Kantian sublime with Freudian sublimation, and because aesthetics has remained for him that of the beautiful."

43 Jean-François Lyotard and Jacob Rogozinski, "The Thought Police," *Art and Text* 26 (September/November 1987): 30.

44 Ibid.

45 Lacan, *Ecrits,* p. 27.

BIBLIOGRAPHY

Books in English

Theodor Adorno, *Prisms*, translated by Samuel and Shierry Weber. Cambridge, Mass.: MIT Press, 1981.

Theodor Adorno and Max Horkheimer, *Dialectic of Enlightenment*, translated by John Cummins. London: Allen Lane, 1973 (1947).

Louis Althusser, *Lenin and Philosophy and Other Essays*, translated by Ben Brewster. New York: Monthly Review, 1971.

Jonathan Arac (ed.), *Postmodernism and Politics*. Manchester: Manchester University Press, 1986.

Georges Balandier, *Political Anthropology*, translated by Sheridan Smith. London: Penguin, 1970 (1967).

Roland Barthes, *Image, Music, Text*, essays selected and translated by Stephen Heath. Glasgow: Collins, 1977.

Georges Bataille, *Death and Sensuality: A Study of Eroticism and Taboo*. New York: Walker, 1962.

———, *Literature and Evil*, translated by Alastair Hamilton. London: Calder and Boyars, 1973 (1957).

———, *Story of the Eye*, with essays by Susan Sontag and Roland Barthes, translated by Joachim Neugroschal. Harmondsworth, England: Penguin, 1982 (1928).

———, *Visions of Excess: Selected Writings, 1927–1939*, translated by Allan Stoekl, Carl Lovett, and Donald Leslie, Jr. Manchester: Manchester University Press, 1985.

Jean Baudrillard, *The Mirror of Production*, translated by Mark Poster. St. Louis, Mo.: Telos, 1975 (1973).

———, *For a Critique of the Political Economy of the Sign*, introduction and translation by Charles Levin. St. Louis, Mo.: Telos, 1981 (1972).

———, *Simulations*, translated by Paul Foss, Paul Patton, and Philip Beitchman. New York: Semiotexte, 1983.

Marshall Berman, *All That Is Solid Melts into Air: The Experience of Modernity*. London: Verso, 1983.

Richard J. Bernstein (ed.), *Habermas and Modernity*. London: Polity, 1985.

Franz Boas, *Race, Language and Culture*. New York: Free Press, 1966 (1940).

Jorge Luis Borges, *The Book of Imaginary Beings*, translated by Norman Thomas di Giovanni. Harmondsworth, England: Penguin, 1980 (1967).

Paul Buck (ed.), *Violent Silence: Celebrating Georges Bataille*. London: Georges Bataille Event, 1984.

Donald J. Bush, *The Streamlined Decade*. New York: Braziller, 1975.

Rober Caillois, *Man and the Sacred*, translated by Meyer Barash. Glencoe, Ill.: Free Press of Glencoe, 1959 (1939).

Michel de Certeau, *Heterologies: Discourse on the Other*. Minneapolis: University of Minnesota Press, 1986.

Guy Debord, *Society of the Spectacle*, translated and revised 1977. Detroit: Black and Red, 1983 (1967).

Gilles Deleuze, *Kant's Critical Philosophy*, translated by H. Tomlinson and Barbara Habberjam. London: Althone, 1984 (1963).

Gilles Deleuze and Félix Guattari, *Anti-Oedipus*. New York: Viking, 1977.

———, *Nomadology: The War Machine*. New York: Semiotexte, 1980.

———, *On the Line*, translated by John Johnston. New York: Semiotexte, 1983.

Jacques Derrida, *Of Grammatology*, translated, with introduction, by Gayatri Chakravorty Spivak. Baltimore: Johns Hopkins University Press, 1976.

———, *Writing and Difference*. London: Routledge and Kegan Paul, 1978.

———, *Spurs—Nietzsche's Styles*, translated by Barbara Hanlon. Chicago: University of Chicago Press, 1979 (1978).

———, *Dissemination*. Chicago: University of Chicago Press, 1981 (1972).

———, *Positions*. Chicago: University of Chicago Press, 1981 (1972).

———, *Margins of Philosophy*, translated by Alan Bass. Brighton, England: Harvester, 1982 (1972).

Vincent Descombes, *Modern French Philosophy*, translated by L. Scott-Fox and J. M. Harding. Cambridge: Cambridge University Press, 1980 (*Le Même et l'autre*. Paris: Minuit, 1979).

Marguerite Duras, *Outside: Selected Writings*, translated by Arthur Goldhammer. Boston: Beacon, 1986.

Emile Durkheim, *The Rules of Sociological Method*, translated by S. A. Solovay and J. Mueller. Chicago: University of Chicago Press, 1938.

———, *Elementary Forms of Religious Life*, translated by Joseph Ward Swain. New York: Free Press, 1965.

Terry Eagleton, *Against the Grain: Selected Essays*. London, Verso, 1986.

Hal Foster (ed.), *The Anti-Aesthetic: Essays on Postmodern Culture*. Port Townsend, Wash.: Bay, 1983.

Michel Foucault, *Madness and Civilisation*, translated by Richard Howard. London: Tavistock, 1967 (1961).

———, *The Order of Things: An Archeology of the Human Sciences*. New York: Vintage, 1973 (1966).

———, *The Archeology of Knowledge and the Discourse on Language*. New York: Harper Colophon, 1976.

———, *Discipline and Punish*, translated by Alan Sheridan. New York: Pantheon, 1977 (1975).

———, *Power/Knowledge: Selected Interviews and Other Writings, 1972–1977*. New York: Pantheon, 1980.

———, *Language, Counter-Memory, Practice: Selected Essays and Interviews*, translated by Donald Bouchard and Sherry Simon. Ithaca, N.Y.: Cornell University Press, 1981.

André Frankovits (ed.), *Seduced and Abandoned: The Baudrillard Scene*. Glebe, N.S.W.: Stonemoss, 1984.

Sigmund Freud, *Totem and Taboo*. London: Ark, Routledge and Kegan Paul, 1950 (1913).

——, *Beyond the Pleasure Principle*, translated by James Strachey. New York: W. W. Norton, 1961 (1920).

——, *Civilization and Its Discontents*, translated and edited by James Strachey. New York: W. W. Norton, 1961 (1930).

——, *Leonardo da Vinci and a Memory of His Childhood*, translated by Alan Tyson. New York: W. W. Norton, 1964 (1910).

——, *Group Psychology and the Analysis of the Ego*, translated by James Strachey, introduction by Franz Alexander. New York: Bantam, 1965 (1921).

——, *On Metapsychology: The Theory of Psychoanalysis*, vol. 11. Harmondsworth, England: Pelican, 1984.

Jane Gallop, *Reading Lacan*. Ithaca, N.Y.: Cornell University Press, 1985.

Anthony Giddens, *Durkheim*. Glasgow: Fontana, 1978.

André Gorz, *Farewell to the Working Class*. London: Pluto, 1982 (1980).

Félix Guattari, *Molecular Revolution*, Harmondsworth, England: Penguin, 1984.

Jürgen Habermas, *Toward a Rational Society*. London: Heinemann, 1971 (1968).

Friedrich Hegel, *The Phenomenology of Mind*, translated by J. B. Baillie. London: Swan Sounenschein, 1910 (1807).

Arthur Hirsh, *The French New Left: An Intellectual History from Sartre to Gorz*. Boston: South End, 1981.

Henri Hubert and Marcel Mauss, *Sacrifice: Its Nature and Function*, translated by W. D. Hulls. Chicago: University of Chicago Press, 1964.

Jean Hyppolite, *Studies on Marx and Hegel*, translated by John O'Neill. London: Heinemann, 1969 (1955).

I.C.A. (ed.), *Postmodernism*, I.C.A. Document Series, London, 1986.

Fredric Jameson, *The Prison House of Language*. Princeton, N.J.: Princeton University Press, 1974.

——, *The Political Unconscious: Narrative as a Socially Symbolic Act*. Ithaca, N.Y.: Cornell University Press, 1981.

Alfred Jarry, *Selected Works of Alfred Jarry*, Roger Shattuck and Simon Watson Taylor (eds.). New York: Grove, 1980.

Martin Jay, *Marxism and Totality*. Berkeley: University of California Press, 1984.

Joel S. Kahn and Josep R. Llobera, *The Anthropology of Pre-Capitalist Societies*. London: Macmillan, 1981.

Pierre Klossowski, *Roberte Ce Soir and the Revocation of the Edict of Nantes*. New York: Grove, 1969.

Alexandre Kojève. *Introduction to the Reading of Hegel's Phenomenology of Mind*, assembled by Raymond Queneau, edited by Allan Bloom, translated by James Nichols, Jr. New York: Basic Books, 1969.

Julia Kristeva, *Desire in Language: A Semiotic Approach to Literature and Art*, translated by Tom Gora and Alice Jardine. Oxford: Blackwell, 1980 (1977, 1979).

——, *The Powers of Horror*. New York: Columbia University Press, 1982.

Jacques Lacan, *The Language of the Self: The Function of Language in Psychoanalysis*, translated by Anthony Wilden. New York: Delta, 1968.

——, *Ecrits: A Selection*, translated by Alan Sheridan. London: Tavistock, 1977 (1966).

——, *The Four Fundamental Concepts of Psycho-Analysis.* New York: W. W. Norton, 1978 (1973).

Charles Lemert and Garth Gillan, *Michel Foucault: Social Theory and Transgression.* New York: Columbia University Press, 1982.

Nigey Lennon, *Alfred Jarry: The Man with the Axe,* illustrations by Bill Griffith. Los Angeles: Panjandrum, 1984.

Claude Lévi-Strauss, *The Raw and the Cooked.* New York: Harper and Row, 1969 (1964).

——, *The Savage Mind.* London: Weidenfeld and Nicolson, 1972 (1962).

——, *Structural Anthropology,* translated by Claire Jacobson and Brooke Grundfest Schoepf. Harmondsworth, England: Penguin, 1972 (1958).

Georg Lukács, *History and Class Consciousness,* translated by Rodney Livingstone. Cambridge, Mass.: MIT Press, 1971.

Jean-François Lyotard, *Driftworks,* edited by Roger McKeon. New York: Semiotexte, 1984.

——, *The Postmodern Condition: A Report on Knowledge,* translated by Geoff Bennington and Brian Massumi, foreword by Fredric Jameson. Manchester: Manchester University Press, 1984 (1979).

——, and Jean-Loup Thébaud, *Just Gaming,* translated by Wlad Godzich. Manchester: Manchester University Press, 1985.

Bronislav Malinowski, *Argonauts of the Western Pacific.* London: G. Rutledge, 1922.

Karl Marx and Friedrich Engels, *Basic Writings on Politics and Philosophy,* edited by Lewis S. Feuer. Garden City, N.Y.: Anchor, 1959.

——, *The Holy Family, or Critique of Critical Criticism.* Moscow: Progress, 1980 (1844).

Marcel Mauss, *The Gift: Forms and Functions of Exchange in Archaic Societies,* translated by Ian Cunnison, introduction by E. E. Evans-Pritchard. London: Routledge and Kegan Paul, 1974 (1925).

Jeffrey L. Meikle, *Twentieth Century Limited: Industrial Design in America, 1925–1939.* Philadelphia: Temple University Press, 1979.

Maurice Merleau-Ponty, *Signs,* translated by Richard C. McCleary. Evanston, Ill.: Northwestern University Press, 1982 (1960).

Michel de Montaigne, *The Essays of Montaigne,* translated by E. J. Trechmann, vol. 1. London: Oxford University Press, 1927.

Alan Montefiore (ed.), *Philosophy in France Today.* Cambridge: Cambridge University Press, 1983.

Friedrich Nietzsche, *On the Genealogy of Morals,* and *Ecce Homo,* commentary by Walter Kaufmann. New York: Vintage, 1969.

——, *Twilight of the Idols: The Anti-Christ.* Harmondsworth, England: Penguin, 1971.

——, *A Nietzsche Reader,* selected and translated by R. J. Hollingdale. Harmondsworth, England: Penguin, 1977.

Plato, *The Republic,* translated by H. D. Lee, Harmondsworth, England: Penguin, 1955.

Mark Poster, *Existential Marxism in Postwar France from Sartre to Althusser.* Princeton, N.J.: Princeton University Press, 1975.

Wilhelm Reich, *The Mass Psychology of Fascism,* Harmondsworth, England: Penguin, 1978 (1946).

Michèle Richman, *Reading Georges Bataille: Beyond the Gift.* Baltimore: Johns Hopkins University Press, 1982.

Marshall Sahlins, *Stone Age Economics*. Chicago: Aldine and Atherton, 1972.
———, *Culture and Practical Reason*. Chicago: University of Chicago Press, 1976.
Ferdinand de Saussure, *Course in General Linguistics*, with introduction by Jonathan Culler. London: Fontana/Collins, 1974.
Michel Serres, *Hermes—Literature, Science, Philosophy*. Baltimore: Johns Hopkins University Press 1982.
Alan Sheridan, *Michel Foucault: The Will to Truth*. London: Tavistock, 1980.
Raoul Vaneigem, *The Revolution of Everyday Life*, translated by Donald Nicholson-Smith. London: Left Bank and Rebel, 1983.
Thorsten Veblen, *The Theory of the Leisure Class: An Economic Study of Institutions*, introduction by C. Wright Mills. London: George Allen and Unwin, 1970.
Paul Virilio and Sylvère Lotringer, *Pure War*. New York: Semiotexte, 1983.
Anthony Wilden, *System and Structure: Essays in Communication and Exchange*. London: Tavistock, 1972.

Articles in English

Theodor Adorno "Commitment," *New Left Review* 87–88, September/December 1974.
Georges Bataille, "Unknowing: Laughter and Tears," *October* 36, Spring 1986.
Jean Baudrillard, "Beyond the Unconscious: The Symbolic," *Discourse* 3, Spring 1981.
———, "The Beaubourg Effect: Implosion and Deterrence," translated by Rosalind Krauss and Annette Michelson, *October* 20, Spring 1982.
———, "Oublier Foucault," in *Theoretical Strategies*, Sydney: Local Consumption, 1982.
———, "Please Follow Me," translated by Paul Foss, *Art and Text* 23/24, March–May 1987.
David Bloor, "Durkheim and Mauss Revisited: Classification and the Sociology of Knowledge," *Studies in the History and Philosophy of Science* 13, no. 4, 1982.
Peter Dews, "Adorno, Post-Structuralism and the Critique of Identity," *New Left Review* 157, May/June 1986.
Jacques Derrida, "From Restricted to General Economy: A Hegelianism without Reserve," *Semiotexte* 2, no. 2, 1976.
———, "Of an Apocalyptic Tone Recently Adopted in Philosophy," *Oxford Literary Review* 6, no. 2, 1984.
John P. Diggins, "Reification and Cultural Hegemony of Capitalism: The Perspective of Marx and Veblen," *Social Research* 45, 1978.
Terry Eagleton, "Capitalism, Modernism and Postmodernism," *New Left Review* 152, July/August 1985.
Paul Foss, "Entr'Acte: A Slim Note," in Peter Botsman (ed.), *Theoretical Strategies*, Sydney: Local Consumption, 1982.
Michel Foucault, "Orders of Discourse," *Social Science Information* 10, 1971.
Jean Claude Giradin, "Towards a Politics of Signs: Reading Baudrillard," *Telos* 20, Summer 1974.
Félix Guattari, "The Postmodern Dead End," *Flash Art* 128, May/June 1986.
Jürgen Habermas, "Modernity versus Postmodernity," *New German Critique* 22, 1981.
———, "The French Path to Postmodernity: Bataille Between Eroticism and General Economics," *New German Critique* 33, 1984.
Robert Hefner, "Baudrillard's Noble Anthropology: The Image of Symbolic Exchange in Political Economy," *Sub-Stance* 17, 1977.

Peter Hohendahl, "The Dialectic of Enlightenment Revisited: Habermas' Critique of the Frankfurt School," *New German Critique* 35, 1984.

Denis Hollier, "Bataille's Tomb: A Halloween Story," *October* 33, Summer 1985.

Fredric Jameson, "Postmodernism, or the Cultural Logic of Late Capitalism," *New Left Review* 146, July/August 1984.

Charles Larmore, "Bataille's Heterology," *Semiotexte* 2, no. 2, 1976.

Sylvère Lotringer, "Defunkt Sex," *Semiotexte, Polysexuality*, 1981.

Jean-François Lyotard, "One of the Things at Stake in Women's Struggle," *Sub-Stance* 20, 1978.

———, "The Dream-Work Does Not Think," translated by Mary Lydon, *The Oxford Literary Review* 6, no. 1, 1983.

———, "The Sublime and the Avant-Garde," translated by Lisa Liebmann, *Artforum*, April 1984.

———. Interview with Arias-Mission, *Eyeline*, November 1987.

Jean-François Lyotard and Jacob Rogozinski, "The Thought Police," translated by Julian Pefanis, *Art and Text* 26, September/November 1987.

Annette Michelson, "Heterology and the Critique of Instrumental Reason," *October* 36, Spring 1986.

Meaghan Morris, "Postmodernity and Lyotard's Sublime," *Art and Text* 16, Summer 1984/5.

Mark Poster, "Semiology and Critical Theory: From Marx to Baudrillard," *Boundary 2*, 8, 1979.

———, "Technology and Culture in Habermas and Baudrillard," *Contemporary Literature* 22, no. 4, 1981.

Karlis Racevskis, "The Theoretical Violence of a Catastrophical Strategy," *Diacritics*, September 1979.

———, "The Discourse of Michel Foucault: A Case of an Absent and Forgettable Subject," *Humanities in Society* 3, 1980.

John Rajchman, "Foucault: Or the Ends of Modernism," *October* 24, Spring 1983.

Klaus R. Sherpe, "Dramatization and De-dramatization of the 'End': The Apocalyptic Consciousness of Modernity and Postmodernity," *Cultural Critique* 5, Winter 1986–87.

Stuart Sim, "Lyotard and the Politics of Anti-Foundationalism," *Radical Philosophy* 44, Autumn 1986.

Allen Weiss, "A Logic of the Simulacrum or the Anti-Roberte," *Art and Text* 18, July 1985.

Albrect Wellmar, "On the Dialectic of Modernism and Postmodernism," *Praxis International* 4, no. 4, January 1985.

John Adams Wettergreen, Jr., "Is Snobbery a Formal Value?" *Western Political Quarterly* 26, 1973.

Hayden White, "Getting Out of History," *Diacritics* 12, 1982.

Books in French

Alain Arnaud and Gisèle Excoffon-Lafarge, *Bataille*. Paris: Seuil, 1978.

Georges Bataille, *Oeuvres complètes*, introduction by Michel Foucault. Paris: Gallimard, 1970–79.

———, *La Part maudite précédé par "La notion de dépense*," introduction by Jean Piel. Paris: Les Éditions de Minuit, 1980 (1967).

————, *L'Expérience intérieure*. Paris: Gallimard, 1983 (1954).

Jean Baudrillard, *La Société de consommation, ses mythes, ses structures*, introduction by J. P. Mayer. Paris: Gallimard, 1970.

————, *Le Système des objets*. Paris: Donoël/Gonthier, 1975 (Gallimard, 1968).

————, *L'Echange symbolique et la mort*. Paris: Gallimard, 1976.

————, *Le P. C. ou les paradis artificiels du politique*. Paris: Utopie, 1979.

————, *De la séduction*. Paris: Donoël/Gonthier, 1979.

————, *Simulacres et simulation*. Paris: Galilée, 1981.

————, *Les Stratégies fatales*. Paris: Grasset, 1983.

————, *La Gauche divine*. Paris: Grasset, 1985.

————, *Amérique*. Paris: Grasset et Fasquelle, 1986.

Raymond Bellour and Catherine Clement (eds.), *Claude Lévi-Strauss*. Paris: Gallimard, 1979.

Maurice Blanchot, *L'Espace littéraire*. Paris: Gallimard, 1955.

————, *L'Entretien infini*. Paris: Gallimard, 1969.

Cornelius Castoriadis, *La Société bureaucratique: les rapports de production en Russie*, in 2 vols. Paris: 10/18, UGE, 1973.

Michel de Certeau, *La Culture au pluriel*, Paris: Christian Bourgois, 1980 (1974).

Pierre Clastres, *La Société contre l'état*. Paris: Minuit, 1974.

————, *Recherches d'anthropologie politique*. Paris: Seuil, 1980.

Collectif, *Les Dieux dans la cuisine: Vignt ans de philosophie en France*. Paris: Aubier, 1978.

Gilles Deleuze, *Nietzsche et la philosophie*. Paris: Presses Universitaires de France, 1962.

Anton Ehrenzweig, *L'Ordre caché de l'art*. Paris: Gallimard, 1974.

Michel Foucault, *Folie et déraison: histoire de la folie à l'âge classique*. Paris: Plon, 1961.

Réne Girard, *La Violence et le sacré*. Paris: Pluriel, 1972.

Jean-Joseph Goux, *Freud, Marx, économie et symbolique*. Paris: Minuit, 1973.

Denis Hollier (ed.), *Le Collège de sociologie, 1937–1939*. Paris: Gallimard, 1979.

L'Internationale Situationniste, *La Véritable scission dans l'Internationale*. Paris: Champ Libre, 1972.

Robert Jaulin, *La Paix blanche*. Paris: Seuil, 1970.

Pierre Klossowski, *Sade mon prochain*. Paris: Seuil, 1947, 1967.

————, *Un si funeste désir*. Paris: Gallimard, 1963.

————, *Nietzsche et le cercle vicieux*. Paris: Mercure de France, 1969.

————, *Monnaie vivante*. Paris: Losfeld, 1970.

Ruy Launoir, *Clefs pour la 'pataphysique*. Paris: Seghers, 1969.

Henri Lefebvre, *La Vie quotidienne dans la monde moderne*. Paris: Gallimard, 1968.

Michel Leiris, *Cinq études d'éthnologie: le racisme et le tiers monde*. Paris: Donoël/Gonthier, 1969 (1951).

Jean-François Lyotard, *Phénoménologie*. Paris: Presses Universitaires de France, 1954.

————, *Discours, figure*. Paris: Klincksieck, 1971.

————, *Dérive à partir de Marx et Freud*. Paris: 10/18, UGE, 1973.

————, *Economie libidinale*. Paris: Minuit, 1974.

————, *Instructions païennes*. Paris: Galilée, 1977.

————, *Rudiments païens*. Paris: 10/18, UGE, 1977.

————, *La Condition postmoderne: rapport sur le savoir*. Paris: Minuit, 1979.

————, *Le Différend*. Paris: Minuit, 1983.

162 Bibliography

—, *Le Postmoderne expliqué aux enfants*. Paris: Galilée, 1986.
Jean-François Lyotard and Jean-Loup Thébaud, *Au Juste: conversations*. Paris: Christian Bourgois Editeur, 1979.
Raoul and Laura Makarius, *Structuralisme ou ethnologie, pour une critique radicale de l'anthropologie de Lévi-Strauss*. Paris: Anthropos, 1973.
Francis Marmande, *Georges Bataille politique*. Lyon: Presses Universitaires de Lyon, 1985.
Marcel Mauss, *Sociologie et anthropologie*, introduction by Claude Lévi-Strauss. Paris: Presses Universitaires de France, 1973.
Octavio Paz, *Conjonctions et disjonctions*. Paris: Gallimard, 1969.
Jean Pouillon, *Fétiches sans fétichisme*. Paris: Maspero, 1975.
Jean-Paul Sartre, *Critiques littéraires (Situations, 1)*. Paris: Gallimard, 1975 (1948).
Tel Quel (ed.) *Bataille*, Paris: 10/18 UGE, 1973.
Paul Virilio, *Vitesse et politique*. Paris: Galilée, 1977.
—, *Esthétique de la disparition*. Paris: Balland, 1980.

Articles in French

Catherine Backès-Clement, "Le Mauvais Sujet," *L'Arc* 48, 1972.
Georges Bataille, "La Structure psychologique du Fascisme," *La Critique Sociale* 10, 1933 (part 1), 11, 1934 (part 2).
—, "Nietzsche et les fascistes," *Acéphale* 2, 1937.
—, "Réparation à Nietzsche," *Acéphale* 2, 1937.
—, "La Practique de joie devant la mort," *Acéphale* 5, June 1939.
—, "Méditation héraclitéenne," *Acéphale* 5, June 1939.
Georges Bataille and Raymond Queneau, "La Critique de la Dialectique Hegelienne," *La Critique Sociale* 5, 1932.
Jean Baudrillard, "Modernite," *Encyclopaedia Universalis*, vol. 11, 1971.
—, "Quand Bataille attaquait le principe métaphysique de l'économie," *Le Quinzaine Littéraire*, June 1–15, 1976.
—, "L'Amérique comme fiction," an interview with Jacques Henric and Guy Scarpetta, *Art press* 103, May 1986.
Jean-Marie Benoist, "Le Retour du symbolique," *le Quinzaine Littéraire* 144, July 1972.
Pierre Birnbaum, "Du Socialisme au don," *L'Arc* 48, 1972.
Jean Bruno, "Les Techniques d'illumination chez Georges Bataille," *Critique* 195–96, 1963.
Michel Camus, "L'Acéphalité ou la réligion de la mort." Introduction to the Collection of *Acéphale* 1–5, June 1936–1939, reimpression 1980, Paris: Jean-Michel Place, 1980.
Hubert Damisch, "Dynamique libidinale," *L'Arc* 64, 1976.
Claude Debar, "Retour aux textes," *L'Arc* 48, 1972.
Christian Descamps, "La Perte du réel derrière jeux de signes et simulacres," *Le Quinzaine Littéraire* 230, April 1976.
Louis Dumont, "Une science en devenir," *L'Arc* 48, 1972.
Rodolphe Gasché, "L'Echange heliocentrique," *L'Arc* 48, 1972.
Denis Hollier. "Malaise dans la sociologie," *L'Arc* 48, 1972.
Asger Jorn, "La Pataphysique, une religion en formation," *Intérnationale Situationniste* 6, 1961.

Pierre Klossowski, "A propos du simulacre dans la communication de Georges Bataille," *Critique* 195–96, 1963.

Alexandre Kojève, "Preface à l'oeuvre de Georges Bataille," *L'Arc* 44, 1971.

Michel Leiris, "De Bataille l'impossible à l'impossible 'Documents,'" *Critique* 195–96, 1963.

Henri Lévy-Bruhl, "In Memoriam," *L'Année Sociologique*, 1948–49.

Jean-François Lyotard, "Psychanalyse et peinture," *Encyclopaedia Universalis*. 1972.

————, "Contribution des tableaux de Jacques Monory à l'intelligence de l'économie politique libidinale du capital dans son rapport avec le dispositif pictural," in Collectif, *Figurations*. Paris: 10/18, UGE, 1973.

Jean-François Lyotard and Jacob Rogozinski, "La Police de la pensée," *L'Autre Journal* 10, December 1985.

André Masson, "Le Soc et la Charrue," *Critique* 195–96, 1963.

Claude Meillassoux, "Essai d'interpretation du phénomène économique dans les sociétés traditionnelles d'auto-subsistence," *Cahiers d'Etudes Africaines* 4, 1960.

Alfred Metraux, "Rencontre avec les ethnologues," *Critique* 195–96, 1963.

Serve Moscovici, "Le Marxisme et la question naturelle," *L'Homme et la Société* 13, July 1969.

Raymond Queneau, "Premières Confrontations avec Hegel," *Critique* 195–96, 1963.

Marshall Sahlins, "Philosophie politique de l'essai sur le don," *L'Homme* 8, no. 4, October/December, 1968.

Boris Souvarine, "Prologue," *La Critique Sociale, Revue des Idées et des Livres*, 1931–1934, reimpression 1983. Paris: Editions de la Différance, 1983.

J. P. Terrail, "Entre l'ethnocentrisme et le Marxisme," *L'Arc* 48, 1972.

Index

Abundance, 67; and production, 51
Acéphale, 49
Acephality, 5, 16, 46, 61, 138 n.26
Adorno, Theodor, 49–50, 139 n.39;
    Auschwitz and poetry, 107, 151 n.5;
    critique of culture industry, 71; on se-
    rialism, 93
Advertising. *See* Publicity
Aesthetics, 105; and the death drive,
    108–9, 106–8; of the spectacle, 112,
    114; of the sublime, 116–17
Aggressivity, 108, 110
Alterity, 26, 35
Althusser, Louis, 9, 31–32; Baudrillard's
    critique, 143 n.60; ideology, 64, 88
Althusserianism, 4
Ambivalence, 75
Anthropology, 15; Baudrillard's revolu-
    tionary anthropology, 77–80; critique
    of totality, 2; dialectical, 50; evolution-
    ary, 52; Foucault's critique, 16–17;
    French, 26; Marxist, 77; Maussian, 3;
    Nietzscheanism and, 16; and Western
    colonialism, 15
Aufhebung, 18–19, 86
Auschwitz, 90, 107, 146 n.3, 151 n.5
Avant-garde, 118, 153 n.42

Barthes, Roland, 39, 43, 137 n.16
Bataille, Georges, 5, 9, 16–20, 30, 71,
    100–101; anthropology, 3; Baudrillard
    and, 61; context of his work, 40; crit-
    ical theory and, 50; death and, 14–15,

44, 113; dépense, 28; dialectical
    thought, 3; and excretion, 41; and
    French thought, 125 n.32; general
    economy, 4, 77; gift economy, 3; He-
    gelianism, 16; heterology, 43–44, 119;
    influence of de Sade, 86; influence of
    Durkheim, 126 n.35; influence of Ko-
    jève, 55; master/slave dialectic, 55;
    Mauss and, 54; Maussian concepts,
    19–21, 35, 126 n.35; military and in-
    dustrial society, 66; mysticism, 46;
    Nietzschean thought, 42, 86, 126 n.33;
    pornographic works, 44, 57, 137 n.21;
    postmodernists, 3; potlatch, 112; psy-
    choanalytic model, 41; role of excess,
    14; sacred and the profane, 48–49;
    sacrifice, 44; signifying chain, 14; sim-
    ulacrum, 60, 138 n.31; 140 n.3; sov-
    ereignty, 18–19, 47–48; taboos, 137
    n.23; transgression, 4, 19, 47, 85–86;
    warrior and military society, 142 n.28
Baudrillard, Jean, 9, 11, 17–18, 50, 71;
    aesthetics, 5; on Althusser, 143 n.60;
    anti-productivism, 77–81, 86, 89;
    Bataille's influence, 54, 61; consump-
    tion, 62; counter-gift, 27–29; counter-
    feit, 63; on criticism, 89; critique of
    anthropology, 77–80; critique of labor
    theory of value, 73–74; critique of
    Lévi-Strauss, 4, 29–30, 69–70, 77–80,
    133 n.34; on death, 13, 112–13, 125
    n.25; desire, 60; epistemologies, 65; on
    Foucault, 125 n.23; the gift, 3;

Baudrillard, Jean (*cont.*)
Lyotard's critique of, 99–100, 114,
142 n.23; and Marxism, 4, 23, 68;
Maussian/Bataillean problematic, 35;
on modernism, 132 n.17; the object,
60, 63–65; potlatch and kula, 29; and
psychoanalysis, 113; sacrifice, 55;
signs, 37, 62, 76–77, 119; on simulation, 132 n.20; on the symbolic, 152
n.27; symbolic exchange, 30, 38, 143
n.63; theorist of the third order, 60;
transgression, 22, 143 n.63; on work,
131 n.15
Benjamin, Walter, 49, 71
Benveniste, Emile, 75–76
Blanchot, Maurice, 45
Borges, Jorge Luis, 103–5, 109

Caillois, Roger, 49
Capitalism: and ethnocide, 23–25; the li-
bidinal economy, 98
Castoriadis, Cornelius, 88, 99, 148 n.19
Certeau, Michel de, 131 n.8
Clastres, Pierre, 50, 53, 107, 119, 132
n.18; on ethnocide, 23–25
College of Pataphysics, 121 n.4 (chap. 1)
College of Sociology, 49
Colonialism: and ethnocide, 23–25
Commodities, 38; Lyotard on, 136 n.11;
and the sign, 68–69, 77–80, 141 n.24;
and value, 72–74, 78–80
Commodity fetishism, 74
Consumer society, 18
Consumption, 65–66, 68, 69–70, 76;
conspicuous, 68
Counter-gift, 61; in Baudrillard, 27–29.
See also Gift; Gift-economy
Critical theory, 49–50; homogeneity and
production, 50. *See also* Adorno, The-
odor
Criticism, critique of, 86; Baudrillard on,
89; Lyotard on, 89

Death: Baudrillard on, 125 n.25; and joy,
46; and knowledge, 55; of the other,
14; philosophy of, 46; and ritual, 55;
and sexuality, 45; sovereignty, 14–15,
48; taboos, 44; transgression, 48

Death drive, Freudian, 5, 93; and post-
modernism, 109
Deleuze, Gilles, 9, 91
Dépense, 3–4, 15, 17, 28, 54–55; con-
sumption and, 18
Derrida, Jacques, 4, 18, 123 n.12;
Aufhebung, 19; and Bataille, 19, 126
n.37; difference, 115; end of history,
56–57; on Heidegger, 130 n.6; on
Kant and mystagogues, 56–57; on
Nietzsche, 130–31; "pharmakon," 22,
130 n.5
Descombes, Vincent, 122 n.9; on
Lyotard, 87
Desire: analytic of, 86, 92; in
Baudrillard, 60; dialectic of, 111; and
Marx, 93–99; philosophical concept
of, 1
Dialectic of Enlightenment (Adorno and
Horkheimer), 50
Don. *See* Gift
Duras, Marguerite, 39
Durkheim, Emile, 48–49, 126 n.35; ideal
society, 31; influence on Mauss, 26;
"total social fact," 133 n.24

L'Echange symbolique et la mort
(Baudrillard), 13, 27, 61–62, 80
Economic rationalism: gift opposed to,
22–23; Marxist and Maussian cri-
tiques, 23
Economie libidinale (Lyotard), 91–92;
on Marx, 94–99
Economy: and language, 38
Écriture, 5, 43. *See also* Writing
Epistemology, Western, 60
Equivalence, 4, 75, 79. *See also* General
economy
Ethnocentrism, 51, 132 n.16
Ethnocide: and capitalism, 23–24; and
the state, 24–25
Evans-Pritchard, E. E., 26
Exchange value, 73, 79
Experience: in Bataille's work, 47

"Fauna of the Mirror" (Borges), 103–5;
as allegory, 105–6
Fictive criticism, 4–5
Fluid dynamism, 66, 142 n.27

For a Critique of the Political Economy of the Sign (Baudrillard), 68–69

Foucault, Michel, 5, 9, 65, 85, 125 n.32; on alterity, 26, 132 n.19; critique of anthropology, 15–17, 127 n.40; debt to Hyppolite, 123 n.10; difference, 115; epistemology, 119; and Hegelianism, 46–47; influence of Bataille, 3; influence of Nietzsche, 16, 87; and madness, 13; normality, 151 n.3; the sign, 36; transgression, 45–46; unthought, 40; on work, 125 n.21

Frankfurt school, 71. *See also* Adorno, Theodor; Critical theory

Freud, Sigmund: aggression, 111; and Bataille, 41; on death, 36–37, 93, 108–10; leadership, 137 n.20; theory of the libido, 92–94

Galbraith, John Kenneth, 67

General economy, 17, 54, 71; and Baudrillard, 62, 77; of Bataille, 4; dépense, 28; versus restricted economy, 4

The German Ideology (Marx), 50–51

Gift, 144 n.73; as phenomenological, 30; and structuralism, 52–53. *See also* Counter-gift; Gift-economy

The Gift (Mauss): critique of political economy, 33

Gift-economy, 19–20, 26; economy of prestations, 30–31, 33; of excess, 22; as the general form, 27; Lyotard and, 100; obligations within, 31; versus political economy, 33; and reciprocity, 3; significance, 22; structuralist interpretation, 21–22; transgression, 22. *See also* Counter-gift; Gift

Guattari, Felix, 6–8, 86, 146 n.9

Habermas, Jürgen, 40, 83, 115; critique of Lyotard, 116, 152 n.33, 153 n.34; on modernism, 116

Hau, 31, 144 n.73

Hegel, G. W. F.: and fascism, 16; French appropriation of, 1–2, 124 n.13; Kojève's reading of, 1–3, 11–14, 30; master/slave relation, 134 n.37; theory of language, 128 n.60; and work, 98

Heidegger, Martin, 2–3

Heterogeneity, 115, 118. *See also* Heterology

Heterology, 3, 5, 15, 43, 58, 71, 89, 119, 138 n.34; defining method, 44; and the sacred and the profane, 49; and scientific analysis, 45. *See also* Heterogeneity; Post-structuralism

Hirsh, Arthur, 148 n.19

Hollier, Denis, 32

Horkheimer, Max, 49–50, 139 n.42

Hyppolite, Jean: reading of Hegel, 122 n.9; influence on Foucault, 123 n.10

Immanent reversibility, 71

Industrial society, capitalist and socialist, 18; and consumption, 54

Jameson, Fredric, 6–8, 147 n.13

Jarry, Alfred, 9–10, 81, 121 n.4, 150 n.42

Jaulin, Robert, 71

Jorn, Asger, 121 n.4

Jouissance, 95–96

Juarès, Jean, 30

Kant, Immanuel: aesthetics, 117–18; Lyotard on, 148 n.24; on mystagogues, 56–57

Klossowski, Pierre, 45, 47; influence of Nietzsche, 86; simulacrum, 138 n.31, 140 n.3

Kojève, Alexandre, 5; desire for recognition, 12; "end of history," 2, 12–13; post-history, 13; reading of Hegel, 1–3, 11–14, 30, 55, 122 n.9, 123 n.12, 124 n.13

Kristeva, Julia, 37, 39, 43; the symbol, 135 n.69

Kula, 17, 28–33; as exchange, 53

Labor theory of value, 73

Lacan, Jacques, 1, 119, 122 n.9, 124 n.13; aggressivity, 108, 110; death drive, 108, 110; desire, 111; kula, 28–29; reciprocating relations, 21–22; symbolic order, 21

Lefort, Claude, 148 n.19

Leiris, Michel, 49

Levin, Charles, 63, 69, 77

Lévi-Strauss, Claude, 17, 52; don, 21; epistemological model, 69; the gift, 3, 28, 61–62; the kula, 53; on Malinowski, 133 n.26; origin of language, 29; reading of Mauss, 29, 31, 33, 133 n.33, 144 n.73; on reason, 37–38; reciprocating relations, 21

Libidinal economy, 5, 86, 152 n.23; and capital, 98; and death drive, 111–12; and political economy, 97; and symbolic exchange, 97

Libido, Freud's theory of, 92–94

Lukács, Georg, 68

Lyotard, Jean-François, 4, 9, 11, 30, 42; aesthetics of the sublime, 5, 116–18; analytic of desire, 86, 92–99; commodities, 136 n.11; context of his writing, 84–86; critique of Baudrillard, 99–100, 114, 152 n.23; critique of Lévi-Strauss, 87; critique of political faith, 86, 96–97; death drive, 111–12; development of his thought, 86–91; difference, 115; end of modernism, 83; English critiques of, 146 n.9; "Great Narrative," 5; Habermas's critique of, 116, 152 n.33; incredulity, 71, 87, 90; influence of Bataille, 86; influence of Frankfurt School, 71; libidinal economy, 91–99, 111–12, 152 n.23; on Kant, 148 n.24; on Marx, 94–99, 152 n.23; Nietzschean style, 84, 90–91; populocide, 107; productivism, 86, 101; symbolic exchange, 131 n.7; universalism, 89, 115, 117

McLuhan, Marshall, 63, 141 n.13

Marmande, Francis, 40

Marx, Karl, 68–69, 71, 76, 139 n.41; commodities, 72–73; and Hegel, 127 n.41; labor theory of value, 73; in Lyotard's study, 95–99; role of production, 50–51

Marxism: and capitalism, 26; Lyotard's rejection of, 87–88; reevaluation in the West, 1

Marxist epistemology, 77–78

Marxist theory: and Lacanian theory, 38

Mauss, Marcel, 19–20, 61–62, 100; and anthropology, 27–28; collective subject, 32; ethnology, 21–22; the gift, 3, 112, 144 n.73 (see also Gift; Gift-economy); and Hegelian thought, 30; ideal society, 31; influence of Durkheim, 26–27; and Malinowski's research, 27–28; and primitive thought, 17; and production, 52; reciprocity, 33; "total social fact," 3, 133 n.24

Merleau-Ponty, Maurice, 33

Meta-narratives, 10–11, 15, 84

Method of obstinancy, 86

Metonymy, 93, 95, 112

Mirror of Production (Baudrillard), 77–78

Modern French Philosophy (Descombes), 87

Modernism: end of, 2, 83, 107; Baudrillard on, 132 n.17; Habermas on, 116

Monopoly capital, 79

Morris, Meaghan: study of Lyotard, 116, 153 n.37

Nazism: populocide, 106–7

Needs, 65, 76, 79; and abundance, 67

Nietzsche, Friedrich, 3, 10, 117, 86–87, 126 n.33, 130 n.6; and bourgeois thought, 46; style, 22

Nietzschean concepts, 2; and Bataille, 42; and Baudrillard, 60–61; and death of God, 45

Nihilism, 91, 114, 124 n.16, 149 n.27

Nirvana principle, 93, 109, 149 n.36

Object, 60, 63–64, 68; analysis of, 71–72, 80; as commodity, 65; discourse of, 70; and publicity, 66–67; utility of, 74

Oedipus complex, 63, 111

The Order of Things (Foucault), 65

Paralogics, 128

La Part maudite (Bataille), 3, 53–54

Pataphysics, 9, 60, 81, 115, 121 n.4 (chap. 1), 145 n.84

Partie communiste français (PCF), 4

Plato: "pharmakon," 22, 130 n.5; third
order representations, 59
Polanyi, Karl, 36
Political economy, 61; Baudrillard's critique, 77–81; and gift-economy, 26; as
libidinal economy, 97; and semiology,
75–76; and the sign, 75; and structuralism, 62
Populocide, 83, 106–7; and postmodern-
ism, 107
Pornography, Bataille's, 57, 137 n.21
Poster, Mark, 122 n.9
Post-history, 2, 90
The Postmodern Condition (Lyotard),
11, 87, 89–90, 148 n.23
"The Postmodern Dead End" (Guattari),
6–8, 86, 146 n.9
Postmodernism: aesthetics, 5, 116–18;
and the death drive, 109; Habermas's
critique, 152 n.33; and Hegelian
thought, 2; and modernism, 84; and
multinational capitalism, 6–8
"Postmodernism and Consumer Society"
(Jameson), 6–8
Postmodern science, 11
Post-structuralism, 3, 147 n.13; and
Bataille, 50; French, 85; and Hegelian
thought, 2. *See also* Heterology
Potlatch, 17, 28–35, 100, 112, 128 n.60;
against accumulation, 53; transgres-
sion, 22; as war, 53
Power, 67, 89, 100, 105
Production, 60; and accumulation, 53–
54; Baudrillard's critique, 77–81, 86;
critique of central role, 50–51;
Lyotard on, 86
Productivity: and ethnocide, 25
Publicity, 66–67
Psychoanalysis, 105, 108–14

Queneau, Raymond, 2

Reason: critique of, 15–16; and degradation of the sign, 35–36; Lévi-Strauss
on, 37–38; Lyotard on, 89–90; and
the poetic and prophetic, 57
Reciprocity, 33, 37, 69, 112
Referent, 75–76

Reification, 63
Representations, 59, 78–80
Restricted economy, 18
Richman, Michèle, 34, 40

Sacred and profane, 48–49
Sacrifice, 48; absence of, 49; as social ex-
clusion, 44
Sade, Marquis de, 42, 44, 86
Sahlins, Marshall, 51
Saussure, Ferdinand de, 75–76, 80; ana-
grams, 27–29
Scarcity: and production, 51
Science, 90; postmodern, 11
Semio-linguistics, 61–62, 69, 76
Semiology: and political economy, 75–76
Semiurgic society, 64
Serres, Michel, 31
Sexuality: and death, 45
Sign: arbitrariness of, 75–76; and com-
modities, 78–79, 141 n.24; competi-
tion, 37, 79–80; critique of, 62; as
form, 76–77; and political economy,
75; and reason, 35–36; reciprocity, 37
Signification, modes of, 79–80
Sign-object, 72; and obligation, 72–73
Simulacrum, 60, 138 n.31, 140 n.3, 149
n.31
Situationists, 22
Socialisme ou barbarie, 4, 87, 89
La Société de consommation
(Baudrillard), 70
Sollers, Philippe, 39, 43
Sontag, Susan, 137 n.21
Sovereignty, 14–15, 18; in Bataille, 47–
48; writing of, 19
Stalinism, 98
Stein, Gertrude, 2
Structuralism, 3, 69; and anthropology,
52; the gift and, 21. *See also* Lévi-
Strauss, Claude
Structural law of value, 80
Surplus value, 73
Symbolic exchange, 3, 5, 27, 30, 72–78,
86, 131 n.7, 136 n.75; as critique, 61;
and death drive, 112; and the eco-
nomic, 35–36; versus exchange of
equivalences, 38; genealogy of, 61–62;

Symbolic exchange (*cont.*)
as libidinal economy, 97; and Marxism, 99; model of critique, 77; and
transgression, 143 n.63

Taonga, 144 n.73
Tel Quel, 42–43
Totalitarianism, 83
Totality, critique of, 2, 5
Totalization of cultures, 71
Totem and Taboo (Freud), 36–37
Transgression, 3–5, 45, 61, 75; as
method of obstinacy, 47; and pot-
latch, 22; and replacement of dialec-
tics, 85–86; of sovereignty, 46–48;
and symbolic exchange, 143 n.63; and
taboos, 137 n.23

United States: as final stage of Marxist
communism, 2, 13
Use value, 65, 72–74, 77

Value. *See* Exchange value; Labor theory
of value; Surplus value; Use value
Vaneigem, Raoul, 91, 130 n.4, 149 n.27
Veblen, Thorstein, 67–68
Virilio, Paul, 14
Visions of Excess (Bataille), 39

Wilden, Anthony, 37–38, 122 n.9
Work, 48, 98
Writing: Baudrillard and Lyotard on,
101; and death, 45; philosophy of, 5,
19, 39, 57–58, 84

About the Author

Julian Pefanis is a lecturer in Visual Cultures of the Twentieth Century at the Power Institute of Fine Arts, University of Sydney, Australia. He has published articles, essays, and translations in journals and collections. He has recently co-translated a selection of essays by Jean Baudrillard, *Revenge of the Crystal,* and is currently editing a translation of Jean-François Lyotard's *The Postmodern Explained for Children.*

Library of Congress Cataloging-in-Publication Data
Pefanis, Julian.
Heterology and the postmodern : Bataille,
Baudrillard, and Lyotard / by Julian Pefanis.
— (Post-contemporary interventions)
Includes bibliographical references.
ISBN 0-8223-1075-9. — ISBN 0-8223-1093-7 (pbk.)
1. Postmodernism. 2. Structuralism. 3. Bataille,
Georges, 1897–1962. 4. Baudrillard, Jean.
5. Lyotard, Jean François. I. Title. II. Series.
B831.2.P44 1991
194—dc20   90-3381 CIP